Cultural, Training and Educational Spaces

Cet ouvrage est dédié à la mémoire de notre ami
le Professeur Maurice Tardif

This book is dedicated to the memory of our friend
Professor Maurice Tardif

Education Set

coordinated by
Angela Barthes and Anne-Laure Le Guern

Volume 15

Cultural, Training and Educational Spaces

A Renewal of Relationships with Knowledge

Edited by

Theodora Balmon
Bruno Garnier

WILEY

First published 2023 in Great Britain and the United States by ISTE Ltd and John Wiley & Sons, Inc.

ISTE Ltd
27-37 St George's Road
London SW19 4EU
UK

www.iste.co.uk

John Wiley & Sons, Inc.
111 River Street
Hoboken, NJ 07030
USA

www.wiley.com

Any opinions, findings, and conclusions or recommendations expressed in this material are those of the author(s), contributor(s) or editor(s) and do not necessarily reflect the views of ISTE Group.

Library of Congress Control Number: 2023942097

British Library Cataloguing-in-Publication Data
A CIP record for this book is available from the British Library
ISBN 978-1-78630-902-0

Contents

Chapter 6. Institutionalization of Passion Instead of Competence
Nathanaël WADBLED

Chapter 7. The Contribution of Museums in Non-formal Education
and Cultural Transmission
Anik MEUNIER and Camille ROELENS

Chapter 8. Cultural Space, Digitization and Training in the Museum
Corinne BAUJARD

Presentation of the Authors

Theodora Balmon is a researcher in educational sciences at the Université du Québec à Montréal (UQAM) and the Université de Corse Pasquale Paoli and a library curator. She is interested in adult education, learning, emancipation, lifelong and life-wide capacitation, inclusive education and educational public policies that are, in particular, beyond the school form.

Géraldine Barron is a curator of libraries and has a doctorate in history. She is assistant director of the library of the Université du Littoral Côte d'Opale (France) and a researcher associated with the ICT (Identités-Cultures-Territoires) (Identities-Cultures-Territories) laboratory at the Université de Paris. Her research focuses on maritime history, the history of techniques and museum collections of the 18th–20th centuries.

Corinne Baujard is a university professor in education and training sciences, director of the Proféor research team of the Centre interuniversitaire de recherche en éducation de Lille – CIREL (Interdisciplinary Center for Research in Education) laboratory and pedagogical director of the master's degree (equivalent to master's degree of the Quebec system) in educational work research (Université de Lille). She conducts scientific work on the transmission of cultural knowledge and educational learning in the digital environments of public and private organizations. Her recent research on museums, visitors' access to exhibition spaces and professional identities in the cultural professions has been published in numerous scientific journals and in her own personal work and regularly presents at international conferences. She is regularly invited to foreign universities as a lecturer (Russia, Ukraine, Belgium, Morocco, Tunisia, Senegal).

Nathalie Bertrand is a certified teacher of literature and a field trainer in French for primary and secondary schools. Nathalie Bertrand has been teaching since 2009 at the Institut national supérieur du professorat et de l'éducation of the Université de Strasbourg, providing the initial training for students of the master's degree in teaching, education and training. She is particularly interested in the links between schools and cultural partners in order to develop strong acculturative practices and to promote a new and engaging approach to reading and writing.

Rana Challah is a doctor in educational sciences. She is a postdoctoral researcher specialized in higher education pedagogy at the Université Gustave Eiffel in Paris and is also a professor in the Department of Education Sciences at Université Rennes 2. She is an associate member of CREAD (Centre de recherches sur l'éducation, les apprentissages et la didactique) (Center for Research on Education, Learning, and Didactics).

Sylvie Condette is a teacher-researcher in educational sciences at the Université de Lille (France), a member of the CIREL laboratory (EA 4354) and a researcher associated with LACES (EA 7437) (Laboratoire cultures, éducation, sociétés) (Culture, Education, and Societies Laboratory) at the Université de Bordeaux. Her work focuses on the ways in which the various actors of the educational community are involved in the life of the institution and the life of the city, in the French context and, more broadly, in a comparative approach. She is interested in school democracy and media education issues, mediation and non-violent conflict management, forms of collaboration and relational quality between educational actors and the development of human resources in the educational environment.

Denise Gisele de Britto Damasco teaches French as a foreign language at the Institute of Letters at the University de Brasilia (UnB) (Central Institute of Sciences – University of Brasilia). She holds a PhD in Education and is currently carrying out her post-doctoral research at the Pontifícia Universidade Católica de São Paulo – PUC-SP (Pontifical Catholic University of São Paulo). Denise Gisele de Britto Damasco served as president of the Fédération brésilienne des professeurs de français – FBPF (Brazilian Federation of French Teachers) between 2018 and 2022. Currently, she is vice president of the FBPF.

Martine Derivry-Plard is a university professor of English studies and language sciences at the Université de Bordeaux. She is deputy director of the ECOr (Évaluation, comportements et organisations) (Evaluation, Behavior, and Organizations) Research Department, to which the LACES is attached. She is president of the association Transit-lingua (a network of researchers on plurilingualism and pluriculturalism) and co-ordinates the first bilingual network on intercultural mediation in language didactics of the Association internationale de linguistique appliquée – AILA (International Association of Applied Linguistics).

Her areas of research and teaching include plurilingualism and pluriculturalism, language ideologies (native and non-native), the intercultural dimension of language teaching/learning and intercultural (tele)collaborations.

Mary Grace Flaherty is professor emeritus in the School of Information and Library Science at the University of North Carolina at Chapel Hill. She holds a PhD. in Information Science from Syracuse University, for which she was awarded an Institute of Museum and Library Services (IMLS) Fellowship. She holds a Master of Library and Information Science (MLS) from the University of Maryland and a Master of Science (MS) in Behavioral Science from Johns Hopkins University. She was also a Fulbright Scholar in Malawi. Mary Grace Flaherty has extensive experience in a variety of information science fields and has published widely on the topic of libraries and health.

Bruno Garnier is a professor of education and training sciences, a researcher at the Unité Mixte de Recherche – UMR (Joint Research Unit) Centre national de recherche scientifique – CNRS (National Center for Scientific Research) Lieux, Identités, eSpaces et Activités – LISA (Places, Identities, eSpaces and Activities) 6240 at the Université de Corse Pasquale Paoli and an international researcher at Centre de recherche interuniversitaire sur la formation et la profession enseignante – CRIFPE (Interuniversity Research Center for Training and the Teaching Profession) in Montreal. He first studied literary translation before taking an interest in the history of political rhetoric in education at the UMR éducation et politiques (Louis Lumière Lyon 2), and then in the democratization of education and the relationship between diversity and equality in education.

Pascale Gossin is a lecturer in information and communication sciences. Pascale Gossin is assigned to a national teacher training institute. Her research interests include reception theory, children's literature, reading didactics and librarianship.

Salma Itsmaïl is currently the director of a school in Marrakech, and has a PhD in education sciences from the Université de Corse Pasquale Paoli and the Université Cadi Ayyad in Marrakesh.

Alain Jaillet is a university professor at the Université de Cergy-Pontoise. His research focuses on educational technologies. He has developed several software programs for distance learning and digital environments in the school and university system (Liberscol, Audio-videocours, Acolad, E-Space, etc.).

Pierre Kahn is a professor emeritus at the Université de Caen Normandie. His research focuses on the cultural, social, epistemological and pedagogical issues of the history of education, and on secularism in and out of school.

Geneviève Lameul, a university professor, is co-director of the CREAD research laboratory at the Université of Rennes 2. A teacher-researcher in education and training, she is responsible for the Master 2 SIFA (Strategies and training engineering) and co-ordinates the Living Lab (research division) project Développement d'un enseignement supérieur à Rennes – DESIR (Development of higher education in Rennes).

Isabelle Lebrat is an associate professor of literature, with a doctorate in French literature, Institut national supérieur du professorat et de l'éducation – Inspé (National Institute for Higher Professorship and Education), Université de Strasbourg. Her research focuses on the didactics of poetry, on the use of voices and on reading aloud.

Régis Malet is a university professor in education and training sciences at the Université de Bordeaux. After having co-administered and then directed the LACES for more than six years, he was appointed in 2018 as a senior member of the Institut universitaire de France. Régis Malet is also president of the AFEC (Association francophone d'éducation comparée) (Francophone Association of Comparative Education) and editor-in-chief of the international research journal *Éducation comparée* since 2006. His areas of research and teaching include comparative and international education, educational policy analysis, teacher training, social inclusion and citizenship education, identity dynamics and educational and social management in intercultural settings.

Anik Meunier is a full professor in museology and education at UQAM, where she directs the GREM (Groupe de recherche sur l'éducation et les musées) (Education and Museum Research Group). She is interested in the field of cultural mediation, that is, in the analysis of the professional practices of the actors, the methods they use and their effects on the different categories of public. She is particularly concerned with mediation in heritage and museums, known as museum education. She leads numerous research projects funded by Canadian, Quebec and international research granting agencies, among others. She is also involved in various activities in the educational and museum fields, including the design and evaluation of museum education programs for teachers and students. The expertise she has developed over the years is reflected in her extensive list of scientific papers and publications.

Camille Roelens is a researcher at the Centre interdisciplinaire de recherche en éthique (Interdisciplinary Center for Research in Ethics) at the Université de Lausanne, an associate researcher at the CIREL Laboratory (Proféor team) at the Université de Lille, at ECP laboratory (Éducation, Cultures, Politiques/Education, Cultures, Policies) at the University of Lyon, at LIRFE laboratory (Laboratoire Interdisciplinaire de Recherche sur les Questions Vives en Formation et en

Éducation/Interdisciplinary Research Laboratory on Live Issues in Training and Education) at the University of Angers, and a scientific collaborator of the CREN (Centre de Recherche en Éducation/Educational Research Center) in Nantes. Secretary of the French-speaking Société francophone de la philosophie de l'éducation. Co-secretary of the Association des enseignants et chercheurs en sciences de l'éducation, Membre du Rhodes (Francophone Network of Philosophy of Education in Praxis) and of the Ethical Research Group in Education and Training (Montreal). Recent publications are *Manuel de l'autorité. La comprendre et s'en saisir,* Chronique Sociale, Lyon, 2021; *L'Autorité bienveillante dans la modernité démocratique,* Presses universitaires de Rouen et du Havre, Mont-Saint-Aignan, 2022.

Maurice Tardif† was a full professor in the Faculty of Education at the Université de Montréal. Maurice Tardif was at the origin of the creation of the Centre de recherche interuniversitaire sur la formation et la profession enseignante (CRIFPE) (Interuniversity Research Center for Training and the Teaching Profession) in 1993 and he directed it until 2005, then again from 2021 to 2022. For many years, he was interested in the evolution and working conditions of school personnel and teachers, as well as their training, interactions and professional knowledge. He published 30 books on these subjects. His work has been disseminated in 30 countries in French, English, Portuguese, Spanish, German, Arabic and Farsi. He was a visiting professor at several universities in Europe and Latin America. He was vice president of the CSSE (Canadian Society for the Study of Education), rector of the La Haute Ecole Pédagogique-BEJUNE, president of the research sector of the Commission des recteurs et directeurs des hautes écoles pédagogiques et des universités en Suisse romande (Commission of Rectors and Directors of Pedagogical Higher Education Institutions and Universities in French-speaking Switzerland), and a member for 10 years of the Canadian Commission on Education of the United Nations Educational, Scientific and Cultural Organization (UNESCO). He regularly intervened as an expert in educational organizations. He received several scientific awards, including the 2016 Whitworth Award from the Canadian Education Association and the 2008 Association francophone pour le savoir – ACFAS (Francophone Association for Knowledge) Marcel-Vincent Award. He was a fellow of the Academy of Social Sciences of the Royal Society of Canada from 2010. Recently on March 29, 2023, Professor Maurice Tardif was named member emeritus of the Ordre de l'excellence en éducation du Québec (Quebec Order of Excellence in Education).

Marion Trannoy Voisin is the head of mission for the requalification of the site of the citadel of Corte (Corsica). After having been responsible for the Americas and Polar Circle collections at the Muséum de Lyon, which became the Musée des Confluences from 2003 to 2009, she joined the Guiana Amazonian Park, one of the 10 French national parks, for three years as head of mission for human sciences and cultural development, before being appointed director of the Musée de la Corse until December 2020. Trained in anthropology and geography at the universities of Lyon (France), Fortaleza (Brazil) and Bordeaux (France), her work focuses on the processes and issues of heritage, as well as the modes of collaboration between institutions and local actors. She is also interested in questions of intercultural mediation, mechanisms of recognition of intangible heritage, Indigenous claims, forms of territorialization and museography.

Nathanaël Wadbled is a researcher associated with the Université de Lorraine, holds a doctorate in information and communication sciences, a master's degree in history and philosophy and a professional license as a guide-lecturer.

Introduction

The Cultural Spaces of Training, Danger or Opportunity for the School Form?

General problem

"When the frontier is well drawn, and there is no disputed ground between the two domains, no one is tempted to cross it," said Jules Ferry in 1881 at the pedagogical congress, speaking of the necessity for the public school institution, to define its own space in distinction to the space occupied by Catholic education[1]. But as Jacqueline Gautherin commented, the frontier of which Jules Ferry spoke was to separate other geographical and symbolic territories, in accordance with the principle of secularism conceived "as a great division: on the one hand, the Republic, public institutions, the school, teachers, students, learned knowledge, and universal culture; on the other, the Churches, communities, families, children, vernacular knowledge, and particular cultures" (Gautherin 2005: 137, authors' translation). Between these various bodies, Jules Ferry intended to draw a bitterly disputed border, economically and politically, supported by a State charged with emancipating the citizen from "particular and local groups that tended to absorb them, family, city, corporation" (Durkheim 1975, p. 177). Later, this boundary and these competing worlds in the vast terrain of education were fortified by sociology and the sciences of education, which from their inception reduced them to the categories of common sense (Elias 1991, p. 9), erecting their objects of study into

Introduction written by Bruno GARNIER and Theodora BALMON.

1 See the lines preceding these: "When we have done this, gentlemen, and I have the firm hope that we will succeed, we will have created between the ministers of religion and the teachers a regime of life, a *modus vivendi*, as they say, much more solid and more secure than today. To establish peace and good understanding between two neighboring and rival powers, I know of no more effective means than to give them good borders!" (Ferry 1881, p. 585, authors' translation).

essentially distinct categories: sociology of religions, of the family, of the school and political sociology.

The aim of this book, like the *symposium* from which it stems[2], is to rethink these categories in a critical and comparative way on an international scale, in relation to the spaces of education and training, with a resolute emphasis on the cultural spaces of training outside the school institution as a whole, but not without interactions with it. This introduction is intended to present the key concepts and to recall the cross-cutting issues in a dialogical approach highlighting the links between the chapters that deal with different objects, methods, actors and audiences in a desire for thematic networking. Indeed, this book brings together, in various configurations, the problematic of the relationships to knowledge that the "cultural spaces of training" (Le Marec 2006, authors' translation) authorize for the publics concerned and measures their effects in terms of emancipation and development of the people's power to act. The international opening is intended to submit to comparison the French framework that is known to be particularly impregnated with the separation between the public school institution and other educational bodies, in the wake of the aforementioned frontier promoted by Jules Ferry at the end of the 19th century.

The temptation of a school-centered approach

The choice to escape the prism of a focus on the school can be based on the recent work of certain historians and sociologists of education who have resisted the still dominant tendency to systematically confuse the history of education with the history of the school, as, in fact, has long been the case in French historical publications on education[3]. There are two reasons for the prevalence of the school-centered approach in socio-historical studies. The first reason is the political importance of the school in France, which, since the French Revolution, has become a matter of State and a matter of school (Nique 1990). In addition, the construction throughout the 19th century of the educating State, which Jules Ferry completed in the 1880s, led to the undermining of the autonomy of non-school forms of education. The importance of school in education has since emerged as a historical reality (Garnier and Kahn 2016, p. 7).

---

2 *Symposium* entitled "Les espaces culturels de formation: quels nouveaux rapports aux savoirs ?", chaired by Bruno Garnier and Theodora Balmon, as part of the 8th International *Centre de recherche interuniversitaire sur laformation et la profession enseignante* (CRIFPE) (Center for Interuniversity Research on Training and the Teaching Profession) Conference, Montreal, April 29–30, 2021.

3 A look at the issues of the journal *Histoire de l'éducation* would suffice to attest to this: If we take the 21 thematic issues (i.e. excluding "varia") from 2002 to 2014, we see that 19 of them focus on one aspect of school life and only one does not concern it at all, issue 132, 2014/4, devoted to the education of Louis XV.

A second reason can be given to account for the prominence of the school institution in historical, and also sociological studies of education, which helps to give this book its raison d'être, in reaction against this distorting prism: it is the construction of the concepts of school form and school culture.

It was Guy Vincent who first defined the school form in a landmark work (1980), based on the search for what is common in the school's relationship with all students, at different times and in different countries, not only in France, but also throughout the modern West, from Europe to America, and even in China (Vincent 2009), drawing on the Weberian typology of the three forms of domination (legal-rational, traditional and charismatic) (Vincent 2000). In doing so, Guy Vincent noted the invariant characteristics of the school form since its origin in the classes of the Christian schools of the 16th century, theorized by Jean-Baptiste de La Salle in the following century. These invariant characteristics are of various kinds and reside in particular in a whole series of tools appropriate to the profession of schoolgirl and schoolboy, such as textbooks, notebooks, pens, chalk, slates, blackboards, desks, etc. Other characteristics are related to the methods used. Jean-Baptiste de La Salle enjoined us to proceed in our studies with a calculated slowness, to say only what was necessary and to avoid "haste and promptitude" in all things (La Salle 1951). However, much later, the organization of the three successive courses (elementary course, middle course, higher course) of the French public school, which are age classes, did not have as its meaning the deepening and extension of knowledge, but to come back again and again to the same questions, letting the principle of the Lassallian pedagogy persist: repetition and slowness (Vincent 1980, p. 41).

Cut off from the commercial world, in the school form, writing is no longer a merchant's technique or a copyist's art, but a means of learning to behave according to written rules, in contrast to the more ancient methods of learning by seeing and by hearsay, which are still dominant in societies that are not mainly concerned by the scriptural forms of socialization and by the centralization of political power. Through the school form, according to Guy Vincent, the child, by reading and writing, learns obedience, through rules that apply to all, to the teacher themself, for the teachers of Christian schools must speak as little as possible (Ariès 1973). The school form separates school times and spaces from those of personal, family and economic life. In its pure form, it sanctuaries the school space and transmits teaching content that is removed from the socioeconomic context of its environment and blind to the territories of life or origin of children and young people. Tending to conquer new domains, the school form spreads in higher education and even in learning linked to leisure activities, such as riding or skiing schools, which borrow its degrees, its qualifications and its planning according to age groups. Later, Guy Vincent observes that in several European countries, in the 19th century, with the elimination of the forms of education born with industrialization, notably mutual teaching, a school developed whose main function was political, and he concludes that the school form reinforced the norms of social life advocated by the political power in place (1995). This scrutiny allows us to define the school form as "the set and configuration of the constituent elements of what we call the school and, on the assumption that it is neither eternal nor universal, to investigate when and how this form was constituted" (Vincent 1980, p. 10, authors' translation).

This temporal continuity of the school form is not, however, unanimously accepted by historians, some of whom have seen against it a series of radical breaks, in France, with the period of the Ancien Régime, in the reform projects of the Age of Enlightenment (Lelièvre 1990), in the French Revolution (Julia 1981), in the establishment of a State school (Chapoulie 2010), and, more recently, in the opening of the school to its environment, against the backdrop of the globalization of the economy. In order to reconcile the points of view, it must be admitted that the school form is rich in variations, over the centuries, but that it has remained a specific form of socialization, linked to a dedicated place and time, during a period that corresponds to the modern era of education and whose structure has not changed functionally, from Jean-Baptiste de La Salle to Jules Ferry, even in spite of the secularization of the public school that took place in the last quarter of the 19th century in France[4], and perhaps even in part to the present day. It also remains true that the school form has become a normative model, despite its internal mutations under the impulse of the social and economic transformations of the 19th and 20th centuries, as well as the beginning of the 21st century. The notion of the school form has thus greatly contributed to reinforcing the tropism exercised by the school on educational issues.

Developed by André Chervel (1988), the concept of school culture also contributes to reinforcing the normative model of the school institution in terms of education, in two respects: first, the self-production by the school of the knowledge it teaches, and second, the social importance of this knowledge, which defines the very idea that we may have at a given moment of what general culture should be. In other words, "school culture" should be understood to mean not only access to the knowledge produced by the school, but knowledge produced by the school, and, more profoundly, its capacity to define, according to Octave Gréard's famous formula (1882, pp. 63–64) what it is not permitted to ignore[5].

---

4 This point will be discussed by Pierre Kahn in Chapter 3 of this book.

5 "The object of primary education is not to cover, on the various subjects it touches, all that it is possible to know, but to learn well, in each of them, what it is not permitted to ignore. Fourteen years before Jules Ferry, it was the author of these lines, Octave Gréard, Director General of Public Instruction, who in 1868 drew up the new organization of French elementary school into three cycles of two years each (elementary course, middle course, and higher course), leading to the certificate of studies."

Diversity issues at the risk of the school form

However, there are several indications and reasons that lead us today to move away from the tropism of the school form in order to study the policies and places of education. The first reason has to do with the differences that exist in the countries of the Western world in the relationship between the school form and other modalities of education and training outside or on the periphery of the school, such as families, religious, professional and associative communities, museums, libraries, places of leisure and the virtual spaces offered by the Internet and social networks, to which the coronavirus pandemic has given a considerable boost since 2020. It is certainly accepted, in most countries of the world, that school has two missions, and that these two missions are placed under the imperative need for justice: to provide everyone with the knowledge indispensable for life in our societies and to prepare individuals to assume specialized functions or, to put it more succinctly, functions of integration and differentiation (Touraine 1997; Sen 2000; Rosanvallon 2008; Maulini and Mugnier 2012). But the differences in the fulfillment of the school's missions between countries are considerable and are based on different conceptions of the school's relationship with training spaces outside it.

Many of the most significant differences are revealed by the way in which educational systems treat cultural minorities in the territories where they are located, and more specifically the place they give, in the students' relationship to knowledge, to ethnic, cultural, linguistic, social and religious identities acquired outside the school. The importance given by the school institution to the teaching of children's mother tongues or languages of origin in relation to that of the majority language or language of instruction is one of the markers of the degree of openness of the school to cultural knowledge acquired outside the school, within the family, in daily and social life, or in associations and religions. In this respect, the degree of porosity between the school form and other forms of learning by impregnation, osmosis and immersion of the person in their life setting describes great differences according to the regions of the world and their cultural, philosophical and political traditions. As a result of the harm caused by certain extreme positions of this cursor, sociolinguists have called "linguistic insecurity" the result produced on children by the lesser consideration given by the school to the language spoken in their family, in the street or in places of worship and collective life when it differs from the language of instruction, for example, for Maghrebian children living on both shores of the Mediterranean (Garnier 2014).

However, before school can form a social being in the individual (Durkheim 2006, p. 102), the individual's territory of origin or residence has already forged cultural references that structure their identity and that require recognition and development through education in all its forms. In the French tradition of indifference to differences stemming from a holistic conception of citizenship, which has strongly colored the notion of school form in France, schools have long taken into account the different identities of students only within the framework of a patrimonial conception of the nation, which sees in the diversity of the territories of the Republic (including the colonies in the past) so many "small homelands" that favor the formal integration of the subject into the unitary national whole (Chanet 1996). But in the United States and Canada, and more generally, in the English-speaking world, the communities that make up the national fabric have become aware of the specificity of the identities they represent and are demanding "recognition" of them, particularly in terms of the right to an education in diversity, in and out of school. In these regions of the world, citizenship is much less formal and much more experiential, the citizen being a person capable of social action, of freely affiliating with collectives and of enjoying all the individual and collective freedoms related to their affiliations. This spread of personal and citizen identity, which goes back at least to the Anglo-Saxon philosophers Hobbes[6] and Locke[7], has reappeared noisily on the occasion of the fights led in the United States in the years 1950–1960 by the Black minorities or minority cultural groups. The common issue is the recognition of the identity of disadvantaged cultural minorities. Charles Taylor has attempted to theorize this claim to identity, beginning with the argument that "our identity is partly formed by recognition, or by the lack of it, or by the misperception of it by others" (Taylor 1994, p. 41, authors' translation).

Expanding the education market in times of crisis

From then on, the school will have to reckon with this process undertaken outside it. Several authors have studied it, showing the diversity of territorial scales to which individuals can refer to find invariant characteristics, founders of their own identity (Soundjock 1981; Tiemele 2011). There are subnational territories, such as the neighborhood, the village, the region, or foreign national territories (especially for populations of immigrant origin), or supranational territories (e.g. religious territories, such as Islam, which is, however, a religion with a universalist vocation), not to mention identities that are not necessarily territorialized.

---

6 "By the people in this place we understand, not one civil Person, namely, the City itself which governs, but the multitude of subjects which are governed; for the City was not instituted for its own, but for the subjects sake" (Hobbes 1983, XIII, 3).

7 Locke defined the natural right of man as that of an individual "absolute Lord of his own Person and Possessions" (Locke 1994, IX, 123, authors' translation).

All identities attached to real or symbolic territories have their own dimension, the nature of which can be described as "cultural" (Průcha 2004, p. 121). All the places and environments of education outside the school form constitute the educational ecosystem of a person from birth, and they induce modalities of apprehension of the world and of relationship to knowledge – as to savoir-être – which structure their individual and collective identity and their capacity to act in the society where they live.

Once they have freed themselves from the tentacular grip of the school form in order to understand the facts and policies of education, the researcher concerned with the cultural spaces of training cannot, however, evacuate the question of the relationships between education in and out of school. Now, if the school form, according to Guy Vincent, is synonymous with uniformity throughout the territory of a nation and with formal equality of education for all school-going publics, this equation is, historically, quite recent. Compared to other educational spaces, it is not impossible that the school form finally constitutes a parenthesis of only a few centuries, so to speak. Since the economic crisis due to the oil shocks of 1973 and 1980, followed by a whole series of economic and social crises up to the time of writing, for different reasons, it could well be that the school form has begun to lose its luster. The governments of the Western democracies have had to change the relationship between schooling, labor market integration and territorial scales. The *Rapport sur l'insertion professionnelle et sociale des jeunes* (report on the professional and social integration of young people), drawn up in France by Bertrand Schwartz in 1981, was already based on the observation that the unemployment rate of young people exceeded that of adults, that the jobs they held were of short duration, that the number of young people having to deal with the law was increasing, as was the number of suicides. The report recommended restoring the pedagogical function of the training-production alternation, through a process of validation of school achievements for those who did not obtain a diploma and through the implementation of the individualized training project which should lead to a "professional and social qualification contract" (Schwartz 1981, authors' translation). Bertrand Schwartz denounced the fact that the school form had conferred a central point on the school, on the periphery of which other educational actors gravitated without any real cohesion (local authorities, the world of work and the associative sector), and he considered that this configuration was about to mutate into "a complex set-up showing numerous contradictions, but also very forward-looking innovations". The associative and local bodies that previously operated horizontally had to be fully integrated into the vertical culture of the school system through the establishment of territorial partnerships.

This was the initial point of a process of change in the school form, which gradually brought together, through the search for complementarity and partnerships, schools and public educational establishments, on the one hand, and sociocultural and economic actors, on the other hand (Van Zanten 2004). This was only the beginning of a process that brought into interaction the actors of the school and the sociocultural and economic actors of its environment. Breaking with a centuries-old tradition, teachers found themselves required to interact at the interface between several worlds (Derouet 2000).

The logic of the educating city is a new step. It is the city itself and the cultural, social and professional training bodies that it houses, subsidizes or supervises that become the framework of experience, being henceforth the place, and also the instance of socialization. According to the observations made in the United States in the 1980s, the leeway acquired by the various actors in defining cooperation and communication strategies responds to an "order of interaction", which is a normative order. Since the early 2000s, the logic of the territorial educational project has been deployed, of which the city of education is a further step. Under these conditions, education is not only carried out in the city, it is carried out through the city and its cultural spaces, in particular museums and libraries (Vilarrasa et al. 2007), but also through virtual spaces, such as media libraries and multimedia supports: working on education means working on the city, with those in charge of urban and social policies, urban planners and the cultural, associative and economic fabric in all its diversity.

All of these training spaces, now multiplied by digital resources, are enough to make one dizzy and give the observer the impression of being placed in front of a nebula whose training objectives and democratic dimension are difficult to discern, in view of the extent of the educational market and the magnitude of the financial stakes that are hidden behind its innumerable actors. This proliferation leads, by feedback, to the reinvigoration, in the eyes of leading political forces, of the sanctuary of the school form preserved from the incursions of mercantile and ideological pressure groups of all kinds. A little clarity is needed as to the criteria of educational and democratic validity of cultural training spaces, which could give rise to criteria for labeling, and this is not the least of the objectives of this book. This objective requires an effort to clarify some key concepts, or rather families of systemic concepts that are closely linked to one another. Here are two of them, among, no doubt, a few others to be discovered in the body of the book.

Challenges of hypermodernity: literacy and empowerment

First, the requirements for "literacy" are multiple and constantly increasing. It should be specified here that, among the fundamental components of any capacity to act (or empowerment), the ability to understand and use information in everyday life, at home, at work, in the community, is in first place. It is information that is most often written, perhaps even more often than in the past through the mediation of the Internet, that we must apprehend and interpret, assimilate, that is, make one's own in order to appropriate it and make a controlled and constructive use of it. This ability is called "literacy", because it goes beyond the ability to read and write that is usually called "literacy" and can also be applied to the omnipresent audiovisual languages. However, the territories of life or origin, as well as the temporal axis – life paths, school paths, professional paths, paths in society – are producers of inequalities in the learning acquired, particularly in the level of "literacy" of the person. It is not just a question of differences, but of inequalities in access to audiovisual information and scriptural knowledge. Since Pierre Bourdieu's and Jean-Claude Passeron's justly famous work on the reproduction of social inequalities by the school (1970), whose continuators now fill entire libraries, very little has been written about the resilience, or even the reparation, that non-formal educational spaces are likely to offer to those defeated by meritocratic selection, in order to restore a relationship with knowledge that is useful for the development of their "social and professional action". This democratic imperative seems all the more imperative as lifelong learning modalities, outside the time of initial training, and the validation of acquired experience are now advocated throughout the world.

These other modalities of learning concern individuals of various statuses, as much pupils and students as teachers, professionals and, in reality, any citizen, and they are crossed by *hypermodern mediations*. This expression, used in this book by Anik Meunier and Camille Roelens (section 7.1), designates a set of complex resources, ruptures, and also perhaps autonomy, creativity and solidarity, which itself is part of hypermodernity:

> The hypermodern world is thus characterized by the exponential multiplication both of the type of mediations necessary to construct oneself as a human subject in a world of culture, and of the diversity of the proposals of mediations that an individual can be led to meet and to seize. In other words, when individual autonomy becomes the keystone of the functioning of societies, it affects both the *matter* and the *way* of mediation understood as an essential activity of the human being as a cultural being. It affects *in fine* the way in which authority [...] can be exercised, certainly in the professions of cultural mediation, in the school or in the museum, in particular, but also more widely across the whole broad spectrum of formal and non-formal education today (Roelens 2021, authors' translation).

Let us specify here that the *postmodern* current conveyed tendencies towards disenchantment, pessimism, and skepticism with regard to the values inherited from the Enlightenment. Habermas spoke of "entering the anarchist clearing of postmodernity, where everything is unraveled and where the refusal of univocal representations of the world, of totalizing visions, of dogmas, of imputations of meaning is affirmed" (Habermas 1988, authors' translation). On the contrary, the current that can be called *hypermodern* represents, if not an overcoming, at least a new impulse towards a modernity more liberated from ideological, psychological, aesthetic inhibitions; this is true both in individuals and in the global society (Tapia 2012, p. 7).

In this conceptual framework, the present times are characterized by ways of feeling and thinking here and at a distance, which reflect a state of the conditions of the individual's relationship to the world within a sociocultural collective. Linked to the mode of existence of the objects and the men and of their relations, the forms of sensory perception and intellectual apprehension reveal the processes of subjectivation: they are shaped by the economic, technological and cultural transformations of an era now marked by the globalization of connections, and also by the threat that this globalization poses to humanity in its diversity (Haroche 2012, p. 6) and to the possibility of a social bond between citizens who increasingly think of themselves as individuals with special needs. Can the school form remain indifferent to such changes, and should it not incorporate the ways of relating to knowledge that non-formal training spaces offer to their users?

Thus, education, in all its forms, is supposed to put each person, at their level, with their resources, networks, and also constraints, in a position to face this new configuration. Now, according to the democratic requirement, each person must be able to interact with it, to contribute to it. Faced with this observation, how can we think of a system that is sufficiently inclusive, that favors knowledge and capacitation, that effectively contributes to socialization? The school and university form, an undisputed success that has conquered many fields of society, is struggling to respond to these new dynamics, not because of reluctance or disapproval, but because of its very structure. Could cultural institutions, museums, libraries, historical and environmental sites, long-time partners of the school, have a role to play in initiating and assisting substantial transitions?

Knowledge and methods: educational concepts to be clarified

Second, the study of cultural spaces of training outside the school form requires a clarification of the methods of acquiring knowledge and of the status of this knowledge itself, insofar as this book envisages new paradigms of education and learning, theoretical and experiential; empirical and reflexive.

A series of definitions have been proposed for at least the last 50 years. Informal education has been described as "the process by which a person acquires and accumulates knowledge, skills, attitudes, and concepts during their lifetime, through daily experience and relationships with the environment"; while in contrast, formal education is an "institutionalized, chronologically graded, and hierarchically structured system of education that extends from elementary school to university". In between, non-formal education is presented as "all educational and systematic activity conducted outside the formal system to provide different types of learning to particular groups of the population, both adults and children" (ACCT 1985, authors' translation).

There are a multitude of problems with these definitions. The texts of UNESCO and other international bodies provide such definitions according to the programs that member countries intend to fund, not according to research of scientific truth. From these fluctuating economic orientations, it follows that formal and non-formal education are sometimes processes, sometimes programs or institutions, while the adjective "informal" sometimes qualifies a modality of access to knowledge, sometimes the knowledge itself. However, if we define the first two terms as programs or institutions, it is clear that they are mutually exclusive concepts. On the contrary, if we consider formal, non-formal and informal education as modes of learning, it becomes possible to see them functioning simultaneously or alternatively rather than as separate entities. This is what has made it possible, for example, to associate formal learning with informal learning in a search for complementarity in lifelong learning programs (La Belle Thomes 1982). One of the semantic difficulties in using the word informal is that it cannot be applied equally to the process and to the products (knowledge or learning as outcome). It is questionable to assimilate these two meanings by considering that informal learning can only produce informal knowledge (Maulini and Montandon 2005). Considered as a result of learning, knowledge resulting from informal processes can thus claim a cognitive status equivalent to knowledge resulting from formal learning. Is knowledge only self-aware, in other words, inscribed in a metadiscourse (Bier et al. 2010, p. 201)?

This is also what has made it possible to think that in school, there is the formal teaching of the teacher, and also non-formal education through organized cultural activities or "education for" which aim at knowing how to be as much as knowing how to do (Barthes and Alpe 2012, authors' translation) and an informal education through interpersonal contacts. The porosity between this new modality of the school form (but is it still the "school form"?) and the cultural spaces of non-school training is perhaps one of the criteria for the validity of such spaces to nourish, enrich and repair certain dysfunctions that appeared in the last quarter of the 20th century, during the transformations of the school form. First, successive education policies have led to the juxtaposition of two organizational systems, one bureaucratic (with steering by a hierarchical center), and the other post-bureaucratic (where professionals are incited to take responsible initiatives at the local level) with the concern to modernize the relationship with "users", parents and students, by considering their individual characteristics and their personal claims Second, developments linked to certain problems of students (absenteeism, indiscipline, school failure, dropping out of school). Finally, the school form has become more porous to the injunctions of society (Derouet and Dutercq 2004, p. 1).

Ultimately, it appears that inclusion and *capacitation* are key drivers of these different paradigms that call for inter-institutional (school/cultural), inter-professional (teacher/mediator) and sometimes hybridization collaboration. These orientations are taking shape through research and educational experiments conducted in places and environments with a high community and epistemic value: museums, libraries, and also primordial actors today, even more than yesterday, such as historical and environmental sites. There is also a change of perspective where the school is no longer systematically at the center of the educational dynamic. Thus, the center–periphery distribution is not fixed and follows the path of the educational project of each and everyone.

Structure of the book

The primary purpose of this book is to study the relationships to knowledge induced by the articulations between the school form and the cultural spaces of training, as well as their effects on the professional identity of the actors concerned, through a historical, pedagogical and philosophical perspective. The book has received critical contributions opened by Jürgen Habermas' definition of the library as a space of inter-comprehension for political dialogue (1987), here applied to other cultural spaces of training. Other questions are raised here: if Daniel Urrutiaguer was able to apply the concept of "third place" to libraries (2018), under what conditions can such a criterion be applied to other informal or non-formal training places and settings? How can we verify and evaluate that the ease of access to knowledge supports in such spaces implements different relationships to knowledge than those practiced in school?

The second purpose of the book is the critical study of pedagogical practices, in a comparative approach between different cultural training spaces, such as libraries, media libraries, museums and historical sites, places of heritage, history and entertainment and even virtual spaces, such as social networks and multimedia supports. What new pedagogical practices are made possible by the school's contact with cultural training spaces? For what purposes and in what ways can these spaces be places of teacher training?

In order to deal with the multiple aspects of the problem, this book is made up of four parts, in which researchers from France, Canada, the United States, Brazil,

Morocco and Switzerland have worked. Each part is briefly introduced by the coordinator who has accepted the responsibility for it.

The first part, entitled "The Cultural Spaces of Knowledge", coordinated and introduced by Régis Malet, deals with the new ways of sharing knowledge between different training spaces and groups of actors from an educational community perspective. These considerations allow for a critical review of the very notion of the school form and its capacity to describe the new issues at stake in the relationship between the school and its educational environments.

The second part, coordinated by Anik Meunier and entitled "Museums and the School Form: What are the Interactions?" This part also takes into consideration the sometimes biased relationships between actors of non-school training spaces and teachers of school disciplines.

The third part, coordinated by Denise Damasco, under the title "Reading and Cultural Mediation", focuses on the status of reading and the acquisition of literacy skills through book mediators in schools.

Finally, Sylvie Condette coordinates the fourth part of the book entitled "Informal Learning, Formal Learning, Hybrid Training". This part emphasizes the combination, and even the intertwining, of learning modalities, from elementary school to higher education, in particular.

In addition to these four main parts, the critical points of view and counterpoints by Maurice Tardif and Alain Jaillet are appended, offering some perspectives to be explored in greater depth, as well as a conclusion summarizing the results. Finally, the authors' notes complete this book.

References

ACCT (1985). Le formel et le non formel dans l'éducation de masse. *Conférence :* Session d'étude sur les interactions du formel et du non formel dans le contexte d'une politique d'éducation de masse, Agence de coopération culturelle et technique, Paris.

Ariès, P. (1973). *L'Enfant et la vie familiale sous l'Ancien Régime.* Le Seuil, Paris.

Barthes, A. and Alpe, Y. (2012). Les éducations à, un changement de logique éducative ? L'exemple de l'éducation au développement durable à l'université. *Spirale*, 50, 197–209.

Bier, B., Chambon, A., De Queiroz, J.-M. (2010). *Mutations territoriales et éducation. De la forme scolaire vers la forme éducative ?* ESF, Issy-les-Moulineaux.

Bourdieu, P. and Passeron, J.-C. (1970). *La Reproduction, éléments pour une théorie du système d'enseignement.* Les Éditions de Minuit, Paris.

Chanet, J.-F. (1996). *L'École républicaine et ses petites patries.* Aubier, Paris.

Chervel, A. (1988). L'histoire des disciplines scolaires : réflexions sur un domaine de recherche. *Histoire de l'éducation,* 38, 59–119.

Derouet, J.-L. (ed.) (2000). *L'école dans plusieurs mondes.* De Boeck, Louvain-la-Neuve.

Derouet, J.-L. and Dutercq, Y. (eds) (2004). Un "bougé de la forme scolaire" ? In *Le collège en chantier.* Institut national de recherche pédagogique, Lyon.

Durkheim, É. (1975). De l'État. Une révision de l'idée socialiste. In *Textes, Volume III,* Karady, K. (ed.). Les Éditions de Minuit.

Durkheim, É. (2006). *Éducation et sociologie,* 1st edition. Quadrige/Presses universitaires de France, Paris, Alcan, Paris.

Elias, N. (1991). *Qu'est-ce que la sociologie ?* Éditions de l'Aube, Paris.

Ferry, J. (1881). Discours de M. le Ministre de l'Instruction publique au congrès pédagogique de 1881. *Revue pédagogique,* 7(1), 572–590.

Garnier, B. (ed.) (2014). Insécurité linguistique en éducation : approche sociologique comparée des élèves issus du Maghreb. *Études de linguistique appliquée,* July–September, 175.

Garnier, B. and Kahn, P. (eds) (2016). *Éduquer dans et hors l'école. Lieux et milieux de formation. XVIIe – XXe siècle.* Presses universitaires de Rennes, Rennes.

Gautherin, J. (2005). Quand la frontière est bien tracée.... *Éducation et Sociétés,* 2(16), 137–154.

Gréard, O. (1882). Instructions et directions pédagogiques relatives à la nouvelle organisation pédagogique de 1868. *Règlement d'organisation pédagogique des écoles primaires publiques.* Bibliothèque du Musée pédagogique, Paris.

Habermas, J. (1987). *Théorie de l'agir communicationnel.* Fayard, Paris.

Habermas, J. (1988). *Le discours philosophique de la modernité : douze conférences.* Gallimard, Paris.

Haroche, C. (2012). Généalogie des processus hypermodernes (de la condition de l'homme moderne à la condition de sujet visible). *Connexions,* 97, 27–40.

Hobbes, T. (1983). In *De Cive, The English Version,* Warrender, H. (eds). The Clarendon Press, Oxford.

La Belle Thomes, S. (1982). Formal, non-formal and informal education: A holistic perspective on lifelong learning. *International Review of Education,* 28(2), 159–176.

de La Salle J.-B. and Anselme, F. (1951). *Conduite des écoles chrétiennes. Introduction et notes comparatives avec l'édition princeps de 1720.* FSC/Éditions du manuscrit français, Paris.

Le Marec, J. (2006). Les musées et bibliothèques comme espaces culturels de formation. *Savoirs,* 11(2), 9–38.

Lelièvre, C. (1990). *Histoire des institutions scolaires*. Nathan, Paris.

Locke, J. (1994). *Le second Traité du gouvernement*. Presses universitaires de France, Paris.

Maulini, O. and Montandon, C. (eds) (2005). *Les formes de l'éducation : variété et variation*. De Boeck, Louvain-la-Neuve.

Maulini, O. and Mugnier, C. (eds) (2012). Entre éthique de l'intégration et pratiques de la différenciation : (re)penser l'organisation du travail scolaire ? *Revue française de pédagogie. Recherches en éducation*, Special issue.

Nique, C. (1990). *Comment l'école devint une affaire d'État (1815–1840)*. Nathan, Paris.

Průcha, I. (2004). *Interkulturní psychologie. Sociopsychologické zkoumání kultur, etnik, ras a národů*. Portál, Prague.

Roelens, C. (2021). Penser l'éducation avec Gilles Lipovetsky. *Penser l'éducation*, 49, 77–104.

Roelens, C. (2023). *Quelle autorité dans une société des individus ?* Presses universitaires de Rouen et du Havre, Mont-Saint-Aignan.

Rosanvallon, P. (2008). *La légitimité démocratique. Impartialité, réflexivité, proximité*. Le Seuil, Paris.

Schwartz, B. (1981). L'insertion professionnelle et sociale des jeunes. Report, La Documentation française, Paris.

Sen, A. (2000). *Repenser l'inégalité*. Le Seuil, Paris.

Soundjock, E. (1981). Affirmation de l'identité culturelle. In *L'affirmation de l'identité culturelle et la formation de la conscience nationale dans l'Afrique contemporaine*. UNESCO, Paris.

Tapia, C. (2012). Modernité, postmodernité, hypermodernité. *Connexions*, 97, 15–25.

Taylor, C. (1994). *Multiculturalisme : différence et démocratie*. Flammarion, Paris.

Tiemele, B. (2011). Que faire de nos identités multiples ? In *Identités individuelles, identités collectives*, Tanon-Lora, M. (ed.). L'Harmattan, Paris.

Touraine, A. (1997). *Pourrons-nous vivre ensemble, égaux et différents ?* Fayard, Paris.

Urrutiaguer, D. (2018). Le modèle du troisième lieu appliqué aux Bibliothèques municipales : quels déplacements de frontières ? In *Bibliothèques en mouvement. Innover, fonder, pratiquer de nouveaux espaces de savoir*, Maury, Y., Kovacs, S., Condette, S. (eds). Presses universitaires du Septentrion, Lille.

Van Zanten, A. (2004). Les politiques de l'action éducative. In *Mutations territoriales et éducation : de la forme scolaire vers la forme éducative ?*, Vol. 2010, Bier, B. Chambon, A., de Queiroz, J.-M. (eds). ESF editions, Issy-les-Moulineaux.

Vilarrasa, A., Bier, B., Richez, J.-C. (2007). Villes éducatrices. L'expérience du projet de Barcelone. *Cahiers de l'action*, 17.

Vincent, G. (1980). *L'école primaire française. Étude sociologique*. Presses universitaires de Lyon, Lyon.

Vincent, G. (ed.) (1995). *L'éducation prisonnière de la forme scolaire? Scolarisation et socialisation dans les sociétés industrielles*. Presses universitaires de France, Lyon.

Vincent, G. (2009). Les types sociologiques d'éducation selon Max Weber. *Revue française de pédagogie*, 168, 75–82.

Weber, M. (2000). *Confucianisme et taoïsme*. Gallimard, Paris.

The Cultural Spaces of Knowledge

Introduction to Part 1

This first part of this book brings together contributions that question, on an empirical basis and from a critical point of view, the contemporary forms of renewal of the spaces and times of knowledge construction, inside and outside the classroom and mobilizing a diversity of actors involved in educational action. Part 1 simultaneously outlines these new cultural spaces of training in terms of ideas, practices and devices, in different places and geographical areas.

In her contribution, Sylvie Condette reports on a research project conducted in the north of France. The project's objective was to set up an experimental coeducation system in kindergarten over two school years, with the aim of fostering the relationship between school and family, which has been for too long and still is very often distant. Together, the school's educational staff, the social center and the local media library have created over time alternative spaces for coeducation, contributing to the emergence of new cohesive links for the educational community and spaces for the construction of knowledge, inter-knowledge and recognition between the educational staff and the parents. The long-term follow-up of the project reveals a territorial dynamic that contributes to reappropriation and knowledge sharing by the different actors of the educational community, linking different spaces of life and education in and around the school.

Mary Grace Flaherty then examines, in light of numerous experiments and observations in the United States, the central function of public libraries in education, that of accessibility to culture and knowledge sharing, by focusing her study on a lesser-known dimension of the role of American public libraries – that of health promotion. Articulating awareness-raising, education and training mechanisms at different ages of life, these institutions reveal an essential role in maintaining or building educational, social and intergenerational links.

Introduction written by Régis MALET.

While the first two chapters of this first part resolutely question the in situ forms and the modalities of construction and knowledge sharing between different training spaces and groups of actors in an educational community perspective, Pierre Kahn's contribution proposes a critical return to the very notion of school form and questions its capacity to describe the new stakes of the relations between the school and its educational environments. The notion of the school form, which is often used whenever changes affect the school in a programmatic or real way, has lost in analytical virtue what it has gained in popularity. By restoring its consistency by linking it conceptually, socially and historically, this last chapter also invites us to point out its limits in order to account for the contemporary transformations of the cultural forms of knowledge construction, in a school inhabited and transformed by social practices that take place outside its walls.

Local Educational Community and New Knowledge Sharing

For many years in France, the relationship between schools and families has given rise to mutual distrust (Plaisance 1986; Meirieu 2000), with teachers refusing any form of interference in their professional practices, and parents feeling judged and despised by a school system that accords them only a minor role (Lahire 1995). In an attempt to counter this persistent misunderstanding (Dubet 2003), the legacy of a long history in which the French Republic relied on schools to assert itself against the influence of the clergy and families (Luc et al. 2020), French public policies have been mobilizing for the past 30 years to strengthen the link between schools and families, by multiplying coeducation actions (Leclercq 1995; Rayna et al. 2010) or by initiating programs that promote early schooling for children (from the age of 2), especially for those from disadvantaged families (Pétreault and Buissart 2014). The idea is to consider all parents as full partners by inviting them to take a real place within the school. This translates into various proposals aimed at parents who are already in close contact with the school environment (by inviting them to regular information meetings, by soliciting their participation in classroom activities, etc.). This also translates into targeted actions, dedicated to the most absent parents, those who remain distant from the school culture. For these parents, the objective is twofold: to fight against the inequalities rooted in society thanks to the beneficial contributions of the school and to offer each child equitable conditions to lead them towards academic success. It is known that students who, from a very early age, evolve in a family environment in which culture is an integral part of their daily lives, are more successful in their studies, because they develop mental and behavioral patterns adapted to school learning situations (Lahire 1995). This scheme, which develops through contact with the school, enables them to better understand school codes and to meet teachers' expectations. Yet, children's

Chapter written by Sylvie CONDETTE.

academic success cannot be fully achieved without the active participation of parents in this educational process (Condette 2018). In other words, children can only develop positively and progress serenely if there is a minimum of educational convergence between school and family (Condette et al. 2016). However, some parents are so distant from the school that they are reluctant to accept the idea of a possible collaboration, despite incentives.

What levers can then be activated to overcome these fears and misunderstandings?

For two years (2018 and 2019), we accompanied the implementation of an experimental extended coeducation device, aimed at fostering relationships between school and families. This device relied on structures outside the school that functioned as real places of reassurance. The staff of a kindergarten worked closely with the social center and the media library, both in close proximity, to create alternative spaces and facilitate parents' access to knowledge, thus linking non-academic and academic knowledge. The three structures used their complementarity and implemented different types of mediation. This new organization has gradually produced convincing results, succeeding in changing the way people look at school and, more broadly, at school culture. In a way, and this is what seemed particularly original to us, informal education (Garnier 2018) has come to the rescue of the school form (Vincent 1994).

Our contribution aims to examine this mechanism and to show how a new territorial dynamic centered on the reappropriation and knowledge sharing has gradually taken hold. In this mode of collaboration, we first observe the process undertaken and then study the quality of the interactions that lead to a new diffusion of knowledge where each participant, whatever their status, contributes their knowledge and shares their questions and concerns, contributing to the birth and growth of a local educational community.

1.1. Working together: local resources to mobilize

The system under study follows research commissioned in 2015 by the Nord prefecture (Northern region of France) on the obstacles to preschooling (Condette et al. 2016). The results highlighted the need to involve families more and differently in the schooling process; they also insisted on the need to organize professional collaborations to avoid dispersion or juxtaposition of educational offers. The recommendations made at the end of the research were applied, particularly in a nursery school where the teachers and the district inspector initiated other working methods. It is these methods that we had the opportunity to examine, within the framework of a new research contract.

1.1.1. *General context of the action*

This new project, supported by the École supérieure du professorat et de l'éducation of Lille[1], relied on a qualitative field methodology that involves personal contact with the research subjects (Paillé and Mucchielli 2021). We conducted three sets of one-week observations, one in late September (after the students returned to school), one in February to March, and one at the end of the school year (between June and early July). These observations of a variety of educational situations in the classroom and outside (at the media library and the social center), over a period of two years, coupled with semi-directive interviews (with professionals and parents) and progress reports from the teams involved, enabled us to gather rich material that revealed changes, recurrences, obstacles, divergent assessments and new proposals.

The educational project dedicated to this collaborative work, in the sense of Desgagné (1997), originated in a district of a city in the north of France, classified as a city policy. This classification means that the neighborhood meets the criteria of the 2014-173 programming law for the city and urban cohesion of February 21, 2014[2]. The law effectively introduces a new geography that corresponds to urban concentrations of poverty. In the neighborhood of our study, there is a kindergarten, which serves children aged 2–5, and an elementary school, which serves children aged 6–11. These two schools are classified as priority education schools because the population meets the four parameters of the social reference index (a high rate of disadvantaged socio-professional categories, a high rate of students receiving scholarships, a majority of students residing in an urban policy district and a significant rate of students who have repeated a year before entering secondary school).

Schools in priority education are provided with specific resources, such as smaller class sizes and funding for outings and projects. From this point of view, the two schools set up numerous educational actions to promote learning: sensory-motor learning, individual development and collective fulfillment in kindergarten; learning of the fundamentals (reading, writing, counting, self-respect and respect for others) in elementary school. The links established with the environment are also forged in the context of sporting events or cultural outings to museums and theaters.

---

1 The ESPE has now become INSPE: Institut national supérieur du professorat et de l'éducation (French National Institute for Teacher Training).

2 To qualify as a priority urban policy district, a district must meet several cumulative criteria: it must be located in an urban area; it must have a minimum population of 1,000; and it must be characterized by "a gap in economic and social development, as assessed by a criterion of the income of its inhabitants. This gap is defined in relation, on the one hand, to the national territory and, on the other hand, to the urban unit in which each of these neighborhoods is located, according to terms that may vary according to the size of this urban unit".

Communication with families is carried out to inform them of the children's progress and to keep them informed of all the possibilities of participation in school activities. In addition to this ordinary communication that can be expected in any school structure, the teachers also strive to establish close ties with each parent.

1.1.2. Personalizing the relationship: a useful first step, but not enough

The ministerial measures in the framework of the city policy and priority education favor greater proximity with families so that bonds of trust are gradually established. To this end, several visits to the kindergarten are organized with the "early childhood" structures so that the young child can become familiar with their new environment. In the kindergarten, a personalized welcome for the child and their parents is set up as soon as the child registers (in April of the previous school year). The child's first day of school is prepared in advance with each parent to discover the facilities, the organization of the year and the various activities. Parents have the opportunity to spend some time in the structure at the end of the school year and at the beginning of the new year when their child will be welcomed.

Despite these measures, we note that it is always the same parents who are present and involved in the life of the school. Others, on the contrary, remain very distant and participate little: they come driving in to pick up the child, then leave immediately, limiting interactions.

The observations made show that some parents maintain a distance. This distance can be seen in the low level of communication with the teachers, even when the teachers write to them or come to them in the morning when the children are welcomed; it can also be seen in the low level of participation in the activities offered. It is always the minority of the most active parents who are present.

Several explanations were given by the teachers interviewed. If parents do not come to school or stay away as much as possible, it is because: "They don't feel comfortable in the school environment, they are afraid of us teachers"; "They have experienced failure and they feel, by coming here, that they are reliving the same difficulties"; "They don't understand the instructions"; "They don't want to interfere in our work, maybe because they think they are not competent enough"; "They are not interested in the progress of their child's schooling, it's too complicated"; "They expect us to be the ones to make decisions about everything academic anyway" (excerpts from the interviews with the teachers).

We can see that the misunderstanding between teachers and some parents persists and that attempts to bring them together do not work. The personalization implemented at the time of enrollment is probably not enough to establish lasting relationships of trust. In the end, this special time is rarely extended, due to the lack of availability of teachers who then address all parents, rather than each one of them. The parents who are most in tune with the school world and its expectations are often the parents who have experienced a smooth education and who have good memories of their time at school (in the interviews we conducted, "happy school memories" were strongly mentioned). For people who are less comfortable with school and its rules, the situation is much more complicated, distance sets in and gaps widen, even though the goal is the reduction of gaps.

If the school is an obstacle and the teachers are unable to establish solid and lasting relationships, new working methods are needed to try to change this initial pattern.

1.1.3. *Open and strengthened consultation, at the service of families and children*

We have noticed that when relationships with families are effective and peaceful, young children experience their schooling much better. These children are particularly receptive to the words and the looks that parents and teachers give each other. Even though they do not understand the precise content, they perceive very well the concern, the reproach, the disapproval and develop themselves, in this case, fearful behaviors in connection with the tensions that they observe. The degree of trust that is established between parents and teachers, apparent in speech and in non-verbal communication, is linked to the degree of acceptance of the school by the children.

Faced with this observation, which revealed a significant obstacle, the school staff, accompanied by their inspector, turned to two local structures to facilitate contact with the families. They contacted the social center in the neighborhood and the newly built media library to consider possible collaborations. Several meetings between these professionals took place to get to know each other better, to discuss the difficulties encountered and to try to overcome them together. In reality, the difficulties were shared, and the director of the social center explained that he had to go door-to-door with his colleagues to meet the inhabitants because some of them were so distrustful of "the social services" (Condette 2020a). Finally, the distance did not seem to concern only the school, but more broadly the institutions.

In order to face this difficulty together, the director of the social center, with the help of his team, and the media library librarians very quickly offered their services, the initial idea being to provide an information relay so that the parents who were furthest away from the school would agree to appropriate this educational space in another way.

1.2. Collaboration in action: initiating new know-how

A process of outsourcing the school has been implemented in an attempt to bring the school closer to the families and to be able to contact them in a different way by trying to establish mutual trust.

1.2.1. *Joint actions*

The director of the social center and his team, after the period of meeting the neighborhood's inhabitants, began to be well identified, recognized and then gradually appreciated. Thanks to this new notoriety, the director organized neighborhood parties (such as sports meetings, fairs, neighbors' day, etc.).

The drawings or other handicrafts that the children made at school were exhibited in the reception hall of the social center. In the same way, thematic exhibitions were organized at the media library: the children's work was thus showcased.

The parents who frequented the social center and the media library talked about these initiatives to their relatives. The information first circulated by word of mouth, then spread on social networks. Positive messages were circulated, and feedback was given to teachers by active parents who encouraged this transformation of the local space: "Before, in the neighborhood, there was not much going on [...] And now, there are many activities, for everyone, for the youngest as well as for adults" (excerpt from an interview with a mother involved in school life).

The teachers and the director of the media library have created reading areas for the children. Books were chosen by the pupils and studied at school; then they were made available to children and families at the library. Teachers came to the library to read the books: this reading was open to everyone, and parents had received an invitation beforehand.

New parents started to come to the library, especially as registration was free for local residents. At first, "it was just to come and see," as one mother said. They then borrowed books and board games. The librarians explained the rules of some of the board games so that parents could play with their children at home. "Storytime" was introduced, and more and more families came with their children to listen to these "beautiful stories", according to the toddlers. Some moms also brought the stories they knew or the books they had loved as children. Other parents, mostly moms, were present, but continued to stay in the background. Gradually, we discovered that they did not know how to read or had a very poor command of reading (some tried to memorize the story so that they could then tell it to their child).

Interconnection was established and solidarity was organized. Parents who read began to help non-readers. More generally, outside of these meeting times, they helped with administrative procedures and formalities.

A specific room dedicated to parents has been made available in the school. This has encouraged and multiplied discussion time between parents. In a few months, the number of "peer helpers" increased and a support group was formed (Condette 2020a). In the school, in this room reserved for parents, speakers were invited to discuss educational and health issues.

At the same time, thematic workshops were offered at the social center: cooking, sports and well-being workshops for parents. In the afternoons, specific sessions were initiated to help parents relearn, and thus fight against the illiteracy situations they had been suffering with for many years. After class, school support workshops were planned for their children in primary or secondary school.

The media library has continued and expanded its cultural activities by relying on local resources, regularly soliciting families to find out their needs and take their suggestions into account.

1.2.2. *Continuous redefinition of objectives and activities*

This joint work of the three categories of professionals, teachers, social workers and librarians was first built around targeted actions, then it was transformed into an overall educational project intended to welcome and solicit the inhabitants of the neighborhood, in particular the parents who remained in the background. The project, which was gradually developed, was based on an inventory of existing resources and needs, and on a shared diagnosis, involving several categories of actors. Various actions were co-constructed by the professionals, who were soon joined by local residents. The number of meetings and consultations increased, and new work habits were adopted. These meetings allowed for intermediate assessments of the actions carried out, for readjusting the project and for deciding together on the next steps to be taken.

The objective was to identify the real needs of the inhabitants and to bring adapted and concrete answers according to the unique situations. It was also a question, thanks to the exchange of views and complementary interventions, of encouraging interactions and giving or restoring the power to act to the people of the neighborhood, and in particular to the families who remained outside of social life.

After two years, we can see that groups have been formed to create links between the inhabitants of the neighborhood. The group of peer helpers seems to us to be a significant example of the *empowerment* sought, which has succeeded in taking shape in an evolving context where all new ideas and proposals are studied to allow the development of the neighborhood, and thus the fulfillment of the people who live there.

The local dynamic generates initiatives, the desire to act positively on their environment. In this context, everyone, according to their goodwill, their tastes, their skills, their availability, now feels authorized to contribute to the community.

This hopeful context acts as a virtuous circle: it leads to an increased participation of local actors and generates positive effects on the functioning of all local structures, and particularly on the school. Initially identified as a place that was not very accessible to the most disadvantaged, the school, through its interactions with other educational and cultural structures, has gradually become a space of trust at the service of the inhabitants.

In order to achieve the set objective, we note that several types of mediation were combined here, such as mediation by institutional actors and peer mediation. The symbolic mediations, which are the educational third places, and the resources made available (Maury et al. 2018), also hold a large place in the success of the project. Thus, objects, such as children's books and board games, offered by the media library, or initiatives such as door-to-door visits, exhibitions and festive events, are all mediations that create positive, rewarding situations and encourage the gradual participation of residents in the social and cultural life of the neighborhood.

1.2.3. *Change of mindset and values to promote*

The local actors, whatever their status, have strongly contributed to the renovation of this district, which is certainly underprivileged, but rich in its diversity and its inhabitants. The progressive nature of the actions carried out, based on the incentive to participate, has allowed these actions to gain momentum. Mistrust, absence and defection, which could be perceived as signs of disinterest, indifference or refusal, have been overcome and the continuous and persevering work carried out over a long period of time has modified behavior.

If the project approach is beneficial for the residents of this neighborhood, it is also beneficial for the professionals who then give meaning to their activity and envisage a brighter future for the residents, and also for themselves. The project has stabilized the staff of the three facilities studied: requests for transfers and geographic changes have decreased as staff feel that the work context is conducive to individual and collective ambitions.

Because the initial project is evolving, it mobilizes very different people, and it is precisely this diversity that brings added value. Everyone can find their place and make their availability, knowledge and know-how available. New skills emerge from working together and this gives or restores value to everyone. The people interviewed testify to this significant progress in terms of social recognition and self-esteem.

The project, as it has been elaborated and redefined to adjust to the needs, highlights operating principles based on welcoming otherness, trust and solidarity. Meetings and interactions develop communication and inter-comprehension and limit misunderstandings, as one inhabitant indicates: "It's true, today I'm talking to people I used to meet, but I didn't know them; I didn't want to be in contact, I didn't like them; I don't know why." Conflicts are not excluded, but they find ways of expression and regulation (Condette 2016). Social relations are structured around numerous actions during which solidarity and the interest in trusting each other are expressed.

If the needs are constantly increasing, the expectations are also expressed by the people involved. They expect a principle of reciprocity to be applied. They give their time and energy and in return they expect others to behave in the same proactive way. It is about increasing the number of participants, and also about engaging those who are usually on the sidelines by showing them the benefits of engagement. Getting involved means taking a more important part in community life and feeling truly integrated into the social group. Beyond sharing, getting involved also means gradually acquiring autonomy, increasing skills and developing better self-esteem. The notion of empowerment finds here the concrete modalities of its implementation.

1.3. Effects of collaborative work

If social ties are built, accentuating solidarity and mutual aid, the whole life of the neighborhood is modified. And we observe a re-enchantment of local life, where hope is reborn and initiatives multiply.

1.3.1. *Effects in terms of categorical rapprochement and interprofessionality*

This dynamic, promoted by the actors themselves and accompanied over a fairly long period of time, updates or renews the existing organization, provoking in this case a set of synergies.

The inhabitants do not only cross paths with each other at the entrance of the building or in the street, but they meet each other. They talk to each other, exchange and share ideas and help each other more. For example, we can observe an intergenerational reconciliation where the older ones take care of the younger ones, offering them activities, such as gardening. For example, there is an intergenerational bonding where older children take care of younger ones, offering activities, such as gardening, giving advice or calling them to order when they see potentially deviant behavior. Parents interviewed in this regard acknowledge that it is quite reassuring to know that children are being watched and cared for by older children.

Parents also organize themselves into solidarity networks, to accompany their children to activities and to support each other on educational issues. The new spaces that they have taken over, and particularly, the room dedicated to them in the school, allow them to meet and share experiences and knowledge among peers. This especially gives them the opportunity to de-dramatize school and to come into contact more easily with the teachers, who have become accessible or at least are perceived as being much more accessible.

For the professionals, the dynamic that has been set in motion is also generating positive progress. The collaborative work invites them to share experiences and knowledge in a multidisciplinary and multi-category approach. A gradual change in professional posture can be observed, where the approach is resolutely focused on the collective and a stronger sense of benevolence: everyone learns to put themselves in the place of the other, to be more attentive to all requests – explicitly, and also more implicitly – by making an effort to understand and translate these requests and by avoiding making judgments too hastily.

Teachers say they appreciate the opportunity to reach out to families in a different way, by soliciting parents who are already involved, and by relying on professionals outside their field of activity.

The multiplication of educational offers, through the existence of third places, such as the media library and the social center, opens up prospects for academic success for the children, but more broadly it leads to cultural contributions for the whole community. The professionals express their great satisfaction in promoting a quality service in education, by managing to help the children progress and weave social links.

1.3.2. *Systemic effects on the environment*

The district itself is being transformed. Changes are gradually taking place, both in the mindset of all the professionals who are inventing new ways of working and in their behavior, where the collaborative dimension is being deployed at all levels. Public action, thought out according to a systemic approach (Durand 2013), is implemented locally according to perceived expectations and expressed demands. But, by addressing all the inhabitants, it actually nourishes all sectors of activity, from public services to local shops.

Because numerous actions have been implemented, the feeling of insecurity is decreasing and residents are daring to make proposals to remedy the difficulties, for example, to regulate traffic and limit noise pollution. The general climate seems to be calmer, and we have noticed a decrease in neighborhood conflicts.

Local initiatives, such as peer helpers for families or intergenerational solidarity, are developing well beyond the school domain; they now affect the social organization of the neighborhood. New actions are appearing, supported by the municipality: a citizen's committee has been created to identify needs and provide concrete answers in a limited time. For example, gardens have been made available for vegetable gardening. An urban renewal plan is currently underway.

According to its inhabitants, the neighborhood has become a "village" where life is good, where people feel safe, and where they know they can count on others in case of need. The school,, like the social center and the media library,, is now perceived as a particularly welcoming learning place where people do not hesitate to trust their children and to invest in themselves.

In this proposed new organization, the problems have certainly not all been solved, but a process of continuous improvement, in the sense of Deming (2000), has been initiated in social life and only needs to be continued, with the active participation of the inhabitants and professionals of this district.

1.4. Conclusion: towards the construction of a local educational community

This research dedicated to the life of a neighborhood and the educational structures located there highlights the functioning of an ecosystem (Bronfenbrenner 1976) where the introduction of changes, based on a shared diagnosis, produces effects on the entire social organization.

The local partnership between the school, the social center and the media library, to which the municipality contributes, takes on its full meaning because it is built and led by the actors themselves. Professional collaborations are developed upon the occasion of the difficulties encountered to establish a consistent and durable social link based on the trust and involvement of the families. It is a policy of small steps that builds on local resources. This approach allows for gradual progress by integrating the ideas and proposals of the inhabitants, by encouraging and valuing the participation of all, starting with the achievements of small children.

Educational and cultural mediations are initiated to create meeting and dialogue spaces where recognition of each person and solidarity prevail. This progressive structuring of activities produces a new territorial dynamic centered on inter-knowledge, on reappropriation and on knowledge sharing. The feeling of belonging to a social group (Sainsaulieu et al. 2010) is strengthened a little more each day and becomes a vector for action. Action, in the extension of the Maussian conception of giving, is then thought of in the plurality of possibilities and in reciprocity where the giver can hope to receive in return (Mauss 2012).

In this new configuration, which brings together several structures, a local educational community is formed, promoting access to different types of knowledge. This local educational community also encourages *empowerment* that grants the right to act and that, at the same time, endows people with a real capacity to act.

These educational and cultural spaces, through their respective contributions, ultimately allow each person to learn a whole range of social skills that facilitate a harmonious life together and lead to the exercise of an equipped citizenship, in the service of a collective project.

1.5. References

Bronfenbrenner, U. (1976). The experimental ecology of education. *The Annual Meeting of the American Educational Research Association*, San Francisco, April 19–23, 91.

Condette, S. (2016). L'élève et sa relation conflictuelle à l'école : entre épreuves subjectives et réponses institutionnelles. In *Vivre les disciplines scolaires. Vécu disciplinaire et décrochage scolaire*, Reuter, Y. (ed.). ESF Éditeur, Paris.

Condette, S. (ed.) (2018). L'implication parentale dans le processus éducatif. Une étude sociologique dans plusieurs quartiers contrastés de villes du Nord de la France. Report, École supérieure du Professorat et de l'Éducation-Lille Nord de France/IA du Nord/ Laboratoire CIREL.

Condette, S. (2020a). L'offre de scolarisation précoce en France à l'épreuve des réticences familiales. In *Sociétés inclusives et reconnaissance des diversités. Le nouveau défi des politiques d'éducation*, Garnier, B., Derouet, J.-L., Malet, R. (eds). Presses universitaires de Rennes, Rennes.

Condette, S. (2020b). Validation et invalidation des acquis buissonniers au regard de la forme scolaire française. Tensions et enjeux pour la vie scolaire. In *Validation des acquis buissonniers. Vers une meilleure reconnaissance par l'institution éducative de l'expérience des professionnels, des étudiants et des élèves*, Baujard, C. (ed.). L'Harmattan, Paris.

Condette, S., Bailleul, M., Nyambek Kanga, F., Maréchaux, B., Obajtek, S., Ruffin-Beck, C. (eds) (2016). Les freins à la pré-scolarisation, étude qualitative sur six territoires de la politique de la ville dans le département du Nord. Report, Préfecture du Nord/Inspecteur Académique (IA) du Nord/Laboratoire CIREL [Online]. Available at: https://hal.univ-lille.fr/hal-01694255.

Deming, E.W. (2000). *Out of the Crisis*. The MIT Press, Cambridge.

Desgagné, S. (1997). Le concept de recherche collaborative : l'idée d'un rapprochement entre chercheurs et praticiens enseignants. *Revue des sciences de l'éducation*, 23(2), 371–393.

Dubet, F. (ed.) (2003). *École, familles : le malentendu*. Textuel, Paris.

Durand, D. (2013). *La systémique*, 12th edition. Presses universitaires de France, Paris.

Garnier, B. (2018). L'éducation informelle contre la forme scolaire ? *Carrefours de l'éducation*, 45, 67–91.

Lahire, B. (1995). *Tableaux de familles. Heurs et malheurs scolaires en milieux populaires*. Le Seuil, Paris.

Leclercq, S. (1995). *Scolarisation précoce. Un enjeu*. Nathan, Paris.

Luc, J.-N., Condette, J.-F., Verneuil, Y. (2020). *Histoire de l'enseignement en France XIXe-XXIe siècle*. Armand Colin, Paris.

Maury, Y., Kovacs, S., Condette, S. (eds) (2018). *Bibliothèques en mouvement. Innover, fonder, pratiquer de nouveaux espaces de savoir*. Presses universitaires du Septentrion, Villeneuve-d'Ascq.

Mauss, M. (2012). *Essai sur le don. Forme et raison de l'échange dans les sociétés archaïques*. Presses universitaires de France, Paris.

Meirieu, P. (2000). *L'école et les parents. La grande explication*. Plon, Paris.

Paillé, P. and Mucchielli, A. (2021). *L'analyse qualitative en sciences humaines et sociales*, 5th edition. Armand Colin, Paris.

Pétreault, G. and Buissart, M. (2014). Scolarité des enfants de moins de trois ans : une dynamique d'accroissement des effectifs et d'amélioration de la qualité à poursuivre. Report, IGEN and IGAEN [Online]. Available at: http://cache.media.education.gouv.fr/file/2014/11/3/2014043_Scolarite_moins_de_3_ans_345113.pdf.

Plaisance, E. (1986). *L'enfant, la maternelle, la société*. Presses universitaires de France, Paris.

Rayna, S., Rubio, M.-N., Scheu, H. (2010). *Parents-professionnels. La coéducation en questions*. Érès, Toulouse.

Sainsaulieu, I., Salzbrunn, M., Amiotte-Suchet, L. (2010). *Faire communauté en société. Dynamiques des appartenances collectives*. Presses universitaires de Rennes, Rennes.

Vincent, G. (ed.) (1994). *L'éducation, prisonnière de la forme scolaire*. Presses universitaires de Lyon, Lyon.

2

Expanding Roles for Community Institutions: US Public Libraries as Community Health Partners

With more than 320,000 outlets throughout the globe, aside from schools and museums there are few cultural and educational institutions as ubiquitous and universal as public libraries. Their geographic positioning and local embeddedness provide these unique organizations with the opportunity to respond to community needs while operating in local contexts. As their missions and roles adapt, public libraries are decreasingly static repositories whose primary function is to lend materials. With increased emphasis on services such as programs and outreach, there is an opportunity for these organizations to support and promote individual and community health in a rapidly changing world with large populations deprived of information access.

2.1. Background

Throughout the world, there are more than 320,000 public library outlets (Gates Foundation 2021). In the US, there are over 9,000 public library systems and over 16,000 public library outlets (Institute of Museum and Library Services, 2016). Before the Covid-19 pandemic, US public libraries boasted annual in-person visit rates of 1.5 billion (American Library Association 2015). Over the course of their existence, public libraries have adapted and expanded services to maximize their impact; these institutions provide a wide range of educational services and cultural opportunities to communities worldwide. No longer are they "just" books and

---

Chapter written by Mary Grace FLAHERTY.

materials repositories and lenders. Their geographic positioning and local embeddedness make public libraries unique organizations with regard to operating in local contexts and responding to local needs.

For decades libraries have served as centers for promoting literacy, and distributors of essential documents like income tax forms. Of late, changing missions and community roles have led to new approaches to service. For instance, in many communities, public libraries have served as safe havens during all types of natural disasters and social and civil unrest. During flood and wildfire emergencies, public libraries have provided shelter, and served as safe water and food dispensaries (Flaherty 2022). One coastal North Carolina public library uses their book drop for canned foods distribution in case of hurricanes (Flaherty 2018). When earthquakes and tsunamis struck Japan in 2011, librarians adapted by setting up libraries at shelters so that they could continue to provide support and patron services (Suzuki and Miura 2014). The Elliot Lake Public Library in Ontario, Canada, used disaster as an opportunity when their facility was demolished due to a mall collapse. With the support of their community, they rebuilt with improved services (Stewart 2014).

When the city of Ferguson, Missouri, in the US was beset by violent protests in response to the police killing of unarmed Black man Michael Brown, the library stayed open and helped the community return to stability (Chiochios 2016). The sign that greeted patrons at the library's entrance read "During difficult times, the library is a quiet oasis where we can catch our breath, learn and think about what to do next. Please help keep our oasis peaceful and serene. Thank you!" The Ferguson library director, Scott Bonner, made the point that although this was a "dramatic moment, and a dramatic circumstance … this is what libraries do every day" (Zeman 2015). A similar response took place in Baltimore, Maryland, USA when riots erupted after the police killing of Freddie Gray. The city was overcome by violent protests; there were cars and shops set on fire; some neighborhoods resembled war zones (Yan and Ford 2015). Schools suspended classes, yet the public libraries stayed open. The library facilities were unharmed and provided a safe space for community members (Cottrell 2015).

Public libraries also serve as support centers for newly arrived refugees with services like language instruction, civic instruction and computer classes (Varheim 2011). They serve as settings for mobile health services and vaccine clinics and offer employment counseling centers and gathering places (Flaherty 2018). Their mission continues, public libraries serve as information providers and can be vital, essential community centers.

Though library roles and functions are varied and myriad, here we will focus specifically on the expanding role of public libraries with regard to opportunities for supporting and promoting individual and community health.

2.2. US public libraries and health

Public libraries are often characterized as organizations that help to level the playing field. That is, they routinely provide access to materials and opportunities without membership requirements or fees. They have also been identified as potential meso-level community resources that can promote overall population health and help reduce health inequality (Philbin et al. 2018). In fact, in their scoping review, Philbin et al. (2018) found that US public libraries routinely address social determinants of health inequality, such as health care access, addiction, stress, food, early life, social exclusion, employment, disaster response and social support. For each of these categories, the researchers provide examples where libraries and library staff support health, largely through service and program provision. Examples include offering weight loss, fitness and yoga programs; hosting vaccine clinics; providing needle disposal facilities; hosting nutrition workshops and giving out free meals during summer holidays; offering outreach in homeless shelters; providing job training and resume help; serving as evacuation sites and as voter registration outlets (Philbin et al. 2018).

2.3. Shifting missions and responsibilities

Although public libraries do support health activities, research has also found that some public library staff can feel unprepared to help patrons when it comes to health issues and health information (Smith 2011). At times, new services evolve as a response to community members' needs, problems and struggles. Thus, the public library's role and community expectations in terms of expanding services can thrust new duties upon already over-stretched workers. In addition, this shifting role can require administrators to respond to pressures in a reactive, rather than proactive manner.

In the US, the opioid epidemic provides a stark example of the extremely varied types of social safety net the public library has become. The problem came to the forefront when the McPherson library branch in Philadelphia, Pennsylvania had to close because their bathroom pipes became clogged with needles; patrons were using the bathrooms as places to inject drugs (Ford 2017). Since that time, the library has new policies that require identification cards and time limits on bathroom use, with security guards who regularly monitor; they have also installed needle disposal boxes, and staff are trained to administer recovery drugs such as naloxone (Ford 2017).

The state of North Carolina has also been particularly hard hit by the opioid epidemic, and earned the unfortunate place as "number one," due to its high rate of opioid-related deaths compared to the national rate (More Powerful NC 2019). In 2019–2020, a statewide survey of North Carolina public library directors found a wide range of organizational responses and willingness to engage in opioid epidemic response. Some directors reported patrons and library staff would be put at risk if the library was engaged in any type of acknowledgment of the crisis; others provided training for staff to administer a life-saving recovery drug (naloxone) in cases of overdoses (Wrigley et al. 2020).

In another statewide survey, this time with Pennsylvania library directors, researchers found almost 12% of respondents reported witnessing a drug overdose at the library in the past year; most respondents felt their professional training was inadequate for their interactions with patrons on health and social issues. In addition, there was a perceived need for more resources and training through cooperative and collaborative efforts with public health partners (Whiteman et al. 2018).

While some library workers may have reservations about administering recovery drugs in an overdose situation and view this activity as beyond their job duties (Ford 2019), one obvious and practical service that is likely within their perceived job scope is to provide assistance with accessing information and with evaluating the veracity of online information, including health.

2.3.1. *Health information providers*

With the advent of the Internet, access to all types of information has become pervasive, particularly in privileged and wealthier nations. Librarians are no longer the primary gatekeepers of resources and information they once were. With this change, the librarian's role has shifted to information interlocutor; that is, someone who can aid in accessing and evaluating the torrent of (often contradictory) information individuals are exposed to everyday. In fact, library users have identified public libraries as highly trusted resources for health information, and libraries have been characterized as important community partners for providing high-quality health information (Becker et al. 2010).

In almost half of in-person library visits (42%), patrons reported using the libraries' resources to find health information (Horrigan 2015). Another study found more than a third of reference inquiries included questions related to health (Shubik-Richards 2012). The role of the public library as health information provider makes sense. As educational organizations, improving literacy is what libraries do, and literacy is key to lifelong health (Whiteman 2018). Furthermore, in some communities, such as rural upstate NY, there are more library outlets than hospitals or health clinics, signifying an opportunity for libraries to act as an important health information resource in under-resourced geographic areas (Flaherty 2013).

Many of the essential health information services libraries can provide do not require medical training or knowledge, just knowledge about what is considered a credible source. Being able to refer patrons to a local or national government website, and referring them to a credible source may be sufficient to neutralize the harm of misinformation acquired from less credible sources. A trivial but insightful example arose in the past decade highlighting the medical information shortfalls of Google searches. In August of 2011, if one Googled "Rx for Lyme Disease" in the US, 7 of the top 10 hits suggested medically unproven folk treatments such as honey or salt and vinegar. By August of 2014, the misinformation problem appeared to be addressed, as the same search provided antibiotic-based treatment, in line with the Centers for Disease Control guidelines, for the top 34 returns. But, by September 2015, apparent changes in algorithms resulted in non-authoritative non-antibiotic-based treatments for the top two hits, and these hits were now paid advertisements (Flaherty 2016). These sorts of credibility issues with the Internet and social media largely disappear if librarians can guide patrons to credible, medically accepted sources.

For many, this credible source provider role was kicked into overdrive when the Patient Protection and Affordable Care Act, which provided health insurance to US citizens and legal residents, was passed. In many places, public library workers were tasked with helping patrons negotiate the online insurance sign-up system; they responded by holding workshops and hosting trained "navigators" who assisted patrons with form filling and questions (Vardell and Wang 2020). Beyond inviting and hosting experts to assist with health insurance forms, guiding patrons to accurate health information can be as simple as prominently providing links on the library's homepage to vetted consumer health and medical websites, such as the US National Library of Medicine's easy to use MedlinePlus (medlineplus.gov), the US Centers for Disease Control and Prevention (cdc.gov) and the Mayo Clinic (mayoclinic.org), as well as national, state and local health departments.

2.3.2. Pandemic response

During the Covid-19 pandemic, we have witnessed heroic responses to community crisis by library workers. When almost all libraries abruptly closed to in-person patrons, library staff coordinated with local agencies to ensure service provision, such as by finding alternative safe gathering places (e.g. empty conference centers) for homeless patrons (American Library Association 2020a). When mask and personal protective equipment shortages became apparent, library workers started using their 3D printers to create face shields for hospital workers (American Library Association 2020b). As school and college classes shifted to online, public libraries provided virtual homework help, and mobile Wi-Fi hotspot lending for Internet access. When most libraries were physically closed, online services expanded, virtual programming became common and library workers adapted in creative and thoughtful ways (American Library Association 2020a). A nationwide survey of librarians in all types of settings in the US found that the majority reported the pandemic also engendered new partnerships, with new community foci, such as addressing food insecurity, and sharing accurate information about community resources (American Library Association 2020b).

2.3.3. *Seizing opportunities*

Community partnerships can enhance public libraries' capabilities to offer health activities through programs. While some public libraries in the US have hired licensed social workers and public health nurses to assist with social welfare support (Flaherty 2013); for smaller libraries, hiring additional staff may not be possible. Establishing collaborations with local health providers, local health departments or their equivalent and other community organizations can yield similar social benefits. Figure 2.1 (adapted from Flaherty 2018) is included to portray the array of potential health program collaborators and partners for public libraries who are considering outreach initiatives. This list is not exhaustive, it is meant to be a conceptual jumping off point and can be tailored to specific settings.

The library can serve as a forum for workshops on how to identify misinformation and disinformation around health issues. Community panel discussions could be employed using local resources; for example, the local pediatrician could be invited to a health panel where they explain the benefits of vaccination for children. This approach could be augmented with a companion program such as the one offered at the Jaffrey Public Library in New Hampshire recently, a "vaccine clinic" where children could have their dolls and stuffed animals "vaccinated". The doll clinic program was an intentional effort to include health literacy as part of lifelong learning, a cornerstone of the library's stated mission. Other health literacy initiatives at the Jaffrey library have included handwashing activities for small children using rubber duckies, science focused book clubs and microscope kits and a human body skeleton available for checkout. Thus far, these efforts have been positively received by the library's community (Monadnock Ledger-Transcript 2021).

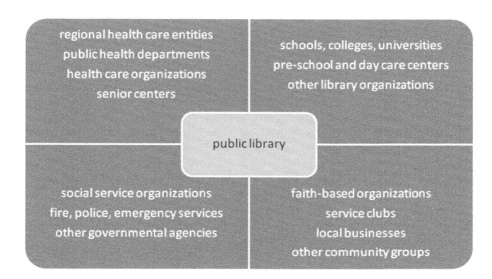

Figure 2.1. *Potential health outreach collaborators*

Another area where public libraries can become involved around health promotion is by assisting health departments with collecting and interpreting data in order to perform community assessments of health indicators. For instance, the librarian can use their information search skills to help codify prominent health challenges and provide that data to local health partners. Agencies can then work together on educational campaigns and tie library programs to relevant educational initiatives.

As global climate change has been recognized as an imminent crisis, and sustainability efforts are finally at the forefront of national and local agendas, public libraries are well positioned to provide education and a forum for community discussions of preparation and resilience. To that end, community gardens, pollinator gardens and greenways (undeveloped land set aside for environmental and recreational use) are cropping up adjacent to public libraries, and libraries have been identified as supporting walkable neighborhoods (Lenstra 2019). In Massachusetts, the Blue Marble Librarians group has been created to engage in and promote ongoing climate preparedness programs and events throughout the state (Massachusetts Library System 2021).

2.4. Final thoughts

All of these efforts require ensuring that community needs and expectations are being met, and that the library staff are engaged in planning and executing strategies and activities. On every health problem to be addressed, major conscious decisions should be made: are we better informing the community as a whole or the individuals who walk in, is our mission to provide credible medical information or to provide links to services or both? It is likely that different libraries will take different approaches and that different health issues will beckon different approaches in the same place. But in every case, credible or best available information exists, and libraries are uniquely well suited to be the interlocutor between that information and their community. Open communication and clear feedback loops are necessary to inculcate success. On-going training and continuing education activities are necessary for staff to be prepared to engage with their communities around health and health issues.

In the US, the Federal Emergency Management Agency has recognized the important support role that public libraries play, through their designation of libraries as fulfilling essential community functions during emergencies (Stafford Act 2011). As access to information becomes more of a commodity rather than a right, public libraries are one of our last free information outlets. As the stereotype of book repository recedes and libraries are noted as vital community centers, their core mission remains the same: "We exist for the betterment of communities. We support literacy and learning. We want all our resources to be free and everyone to feel welcome" (Grant 2021; quoting Ramiro Salazar, former president of the Public Library Association).

2.5. References

American Library Association (2015). *Public Library Use*. American Library Association, Chicago [Online]. Available at: http://www.ala.org/tools/libfactsheets/alalibraryfactsheet06.

American Library Association (2020a). Public libraries respond to COVID-19: Survey of response and activities. *Public Library Association*, 23 March.

American Library Association (2020b). How public libraries are responding to the pandemic. *American Libraries Magazine*, 9 April.

Becker, S., Crandall, M.D., Fisher, K.E., Kinney, B., Landry, C., Rocha, A. (2010). *Opportunity for All: How the American Public Benefits from Internet Access at US Libraries*. Institute of Museum and Library Services, Washington.

Chiochios, M.E. (2016). The Tweets heard around the world: Ferguson Municipal Public Library's Twitter use around the 2014 civil unrest and its role in supporting community disaster resilience. Master's Thesis, University of North Carolina, Chapel Hill.

Cottrell, M. (2015). Baltimore's library stays open during unrest: Q&A with CEO Carla Hayden. *American Librairies Magazine*, May 1st.

Flaherty, M.G. (2013). The public library as health information resource? *Syracuse University* [Online]. Available at: http://surface.syr.edu/cgi/viewcontent.cgi?article=1081&context=it_etd.

Flaherty, M.G. (2016). Good value: Health information and the MSLS librarian. *The Bottom Line*, 29(3), 173–179.

Flaherty, M.G. (2018). *Promoting Individual and Community Health at the Library.* American Library Association, Chicago.

Flaherty, M.G. (2022). *The Disaster Planning Handbook for Libraries.* American Library Association, Chicago.

Ford, A. (2017). Saving lives in the stacks: How libraries are handling the opioid crisis. *American Libraries Magazine*, 21 June [Online]. Available at: https://american librariesmagazine.org/2017/06/21/saving-lives-in-the-stacks/.

Ford, A. (2019). Other duties as assigned: Front-line librarians on the constant pressure to do more. *American Libraries*, 50(1/2), 40–47.

Gates Foundation (2021). *Global Libraries.* Bill & Melinda Gates Foundation, Seattle, Washington.

Grant, R. (2021). How Memphis created the nation's most innovative public library. *Smithsonian Magazine*, November.

Horrigan J.B. (2015). *Libraries at the Crossroads.* Pew Research Center, Washington.

Institute of Museum and Library Services (2016). Public Libraries in the United States survey: Fiscal year 2013. Report, Institute of Museum and Library Services, Washington.

Lenstra, N. and Carlos, J. (2019). Public libraries and walkable neighborhoods. *International Journal of Environmental Research and Public Health*, 16(10), 1780. doi:10.3390/ijerph16101780.

Massachusetts Library System (2021). Climate preparedness week: Blue marble librarians: Get Support. Massachusetts Library System.

Monadnock Ledger-Transcript (2021). Monadnock Doll Hospital returns to Jaffrey Public Library. *Monadnock Ledger-Transcript*, 23 February.

More Powerful NC (2019). The impact of opioids [Online]. Available at: https://www.morepowerfulnc.org/get-the-facts/the-impact/.

Philbin, M.M., Parker, C.M., Flaherty, M.G., Hirsch, J.S. (2019). Public libraries: A community-level resource to advance population health. *Journal of Community Health*, 44(1), 192–199.

Robert, T. (1988). Stafford disaster relief and emergency assistance act. Law, The Public Health and Welfare.

Shubik-Richards, C. and Dowdall, E. (2012). *The Library in the City: Changing Demands and a Challenging Future*. The Pew Charitable Trusts Philadelphia Research Initiative, Philadelphia.

Smith, C.A. (2011). "The Easier-To-Use Version": Public librarian awareness of consumer health resources from the national library of medicine. *Journal of Consumer Health on the Internet*, 15(2), 149–163.

Stewart, A. (2014). When disaster strikes: Opportunities for community and institutional renewal at Elliot Lake Public Library. *Public Library Quarterly*, 33(4), 304–329. doi: 10.1080/01616846.2014.970111.

Suzuki, S. and Miura, T. (2014). The librarians of Fukushima. *Journal of Library Administration*, 54(5), 403–412. doi:10.1080/01930826.2014.946755.

Vardell, E. and Wang, T. (2020). Public librarians connecting communities to health insurance information. *Public Library Quarterly*, 9 November, 1–28 [Online]. Available at: https://doi.org/10.1080/01616846.2020.1844535.

Varheim, A. (2011). Gracious space: Library programming strategies towards immigrants as tools in the creation of social capital. *Library and Information Science Research*, 33(1), 12–18. doi:10.1016/j.lisr.2010.04.005.

Whiteman, E.D., Dupuis, R., Morgan, A.U., D'Alonzo, B., Epstein, C., Klusaritz, H., Cannuscio, C. (2018). Public libraries as partners for health. *Preventing Chronic Disease*, 15, 170392 [Online]. Available at: https://doi.org/10.5888/pcd15.170392.

Wrigley, J., Kennedy, C., Flaherty, M.G., Ponder, M., Foster, M., Akman, J. (2020). A statewide analysis of North Carolina public libraries and their response to the opioid epidemic. *Public Library Quarterly*, 39, 421–433.

Yan, H. and Ford, D. (2015). Baltimore riots: Looting, fires engulf city after Freddie Gray's funeral. *CNN*, 28 April.

Zeman, M. (2015). The little library that lent a hand: Ferguson municipal public library. *Public Libraries Online*, 12 February.

3

Regarding the School Form: Critical Reflections

Victim of its success, the notion of the "school form" is today experiencing such semantic inflation that, as Guy Vincent, Bernard Lahire and Daniel Thin note, the expression tends to become a "pseudo-savant term used in place of the common term school" (Vincent et al. 1994, p. 11). Any change in the school, any pedagogical reform, any reorientation of the school's aims and of the values that support them is too readily translated in terms of "transformation of the school form", which then loses in understanding what it gains in extension.

This is why, when we speak of the "school form", we must begin by giving, or rather restoring, a precise conceptual meaning to the expression. It will then be possible, in a second step, to critically examine what this concept brings, that is, in what way we can clarify the historical and sociological analysis of school phenomena, and also what the limits of this clarification are. In short, first, thinking of the school form, then asking ourselves what the school form allows us to think.

3.1. Thinking about the school form

As we know, the concept of the school form was put forward by G. Vincent in his book *L'École primaire française* published in 1980. "L'École" (the school) is here an adjective that qualifies a *form of socialization* of childhood and youth, implicitly opposed to other historical or possible forms of socialization. In its most rigorous formulation, the concept proposed by G. Vincent is that of "school form of socialization", the expression "school form" being, after all, only a shortcut: an

Chapter written by Pierre KAHN.

equivocal shortcut that partly explains the immoderate use of such a term to designate everything that has to do with school or everything that happens there.

It is a form of socialization in that it brings about a social transformation in the child: their transformation into a schoolchild, at the end of which they are supposed to have acquired all the moral qualities and habits of a good student: "Acceptance of effort, attention, meticulousness, etc." (Vincent 1980, p. 41). To transform the child into a schoolchild is thus to subject them, under the constant gaze of the teacher, to a set of rules, on the impersonality of which G. Vincent and, following him, B. Lahire and D. Thin have constantly insisted on (Vincent 1980, p. 43; Vincent et al. 1994, pp. 11–48). In a word, it is to discipline the student. The school form is in essence disciplinary, and the "disciplines" taught in school bear this name first of all in that they contribute to this enterprise of disciplining (Vincent 2004, pp. 112–113), as do the distinctive characteristics of such a form: enclosure of space (Vincent 1980, p. 21), squaring of the timetable (p. 40), repetition and artificiality (in the sense that they are disconnected from any practical use or destination) of the exercises (p. 41). By making discipline the "morality of the class", and thus an educational end in itself, and not a simple means to better learning, Durkheim (1963, pp. 125–126)[1], to whom G. Vincent often refers (see, for example, Vincent 2004, p. 113), insisted on this essential "socializing-disciplinary" dimension of the school, and his sociology of education can in this respect be understood as a theoretical justification of the school form.

This school form of socialization has a double character: it is both historical, that is, its emergence can be dated – and continuous – that is, it can be found in different types of school organizations. To think of the school form is, in other words, to think of both its historicity and its "transhistorical" unity:

> The use of the term "school form" in the singular could have the advantage of making it possible to identify [...] on the one hand, the novelty in the 16th and 17th centuries of a form of transmission, and on the other hand, the continuity from that time up to and including our own of a certain number of easily observable traits (Vincent 1999, p. 3).

3.2. Historicity of the school form

Of these two dimensions, historicity is undoubtedly the least problematic to understand: "The complementary concept of socialization [...] is that of historicity" (Vincent 2004, p. 121 [translation]), and it is moreover this historicity that leads

---

1 First published in 1934.

G. Vincent to prefer the term "form" to that of "structure" (Vincent 2012a, p. 113). What G. Vincent calls the "school form" appeared in the 16th and 17th centuries; the sociohistorian identifies its emergence in the creation of the "little schools of the poor" in Lyon, by Abbé Charles Démia, and he sees its most elaborate codification in the work of Jean-Baptiste de La Salle and the various reissues of the *Conduite des écoles chrétiennes* (Conduct of Christian schools). But this new form was not peculiar to the elementary school and, from the end of the 16th century, the same disciplinary concern, the same demand for obedience to impersonal rules, was already being observed in the Jesuit colleges (Vincent et al. 1994, p. 15). Another form of socialization, based on the existence of personal relations between the educator and the educated, consisting of doing, seeing and hearsay and involving the child's participation in the activities of the house, the workshop or the farm, gradually disappeared (and not without resistance) (see also Vincent 2012a, p. 112).

It is thus a question, with the concept of the school form,, of thinking of the school as a singular historical institution, introducing children into a specific closed universe of rules aimed at disciplining them. The specificity of the school form is then to make education, contrary to the previous forms of socialization, *a goal in itself*, that is separated from the activities for which it could be given. When Rousseau, at the beginning of *Émile*, writes that it is a question for him of forming a man in general, and not an individual with particular social functions[2], he formulates, at the foundation, the very principle that the school form has imposed in relation to the forms of socialization that preceded it.

Now, this thinking about the school clashes with a contrary thinking, relayed today by a willingly alarmist discourse on the contemporary evolutions of the school in France, denounced as so many "pedagogical" excesses marginalizing, or even tending to make disappear, the function of instruction, which is nevertheless constitutive of the very idea of school. By denouncing these excesses, such a discourse, which we will call "instructionist", is as if naturally led to advocate the restoration of a school order based on this transmission,, and at the same time to justify some of the major characteristic features of what G. Vincent calls the *school form*. This is why, it is interesting to confront these two thoughts about the school, which in fact refer to two diametrically opposed meanings of the idea of "school form". To do this, let us start with one of the most representative and most elaborate texts of this current: the beginning of Jean-Claude Milner's book, *De l'école* (1984a):

> That the school exists is, in truth, to say only this: in a society, knowledge exists and this knowledge is transmitted by a specialized

---

2 "When he leaves my hands, he will be, I agree, neither a magistrate, nor a soldier, nor a priest; he will first of all be a man" (Rousseau 1966, p. 42).

body in a specialized place. To speak of school is to speak of four things: (1) knowledge; (2) transmissible knowledge; (3) specialists in charge of transmitting knowledge; (4) a recognized institution, whose function is to bring together, in a regulated manner, the specialists who transmit and the subjects to whom one transmits (p. 9).

Several remarks can be made about this short text in particular and about current "instructionalist" conceptions of the school in general:

– The school that Milner defines here is indeed also a form; the form of any school, whatever the society in which the school exists, whatever the nature and content of the knowledge transmitted and whatever the institutional organization adopted. This form is that of any institution aiming at dispensing knowledge in a regulated way.

– For all that (and here, the opposition with the school form of which G. Vincent speaks is frontal), it is a *timeless form;* it cannot be understood from a historical social and political state. If, for Milner, the school is a form, it is so in the sense of the Platonic *eidos*: the four conditions that constitute it define it in *essentia*. Beyond Milner, this essentialism is a characteristic of all the texts (and they are numerous) which see in the evolution of the current school not only the abandonment of an old and regretted school order but also the death of the school as such.

– This "essential" school order is itself defined by the attributes by means of which G. Vincent qualifies the school form: sanctuarization of the school space, separation of school and life, decontextualization of knowledge, substitution of impersonal rules for interpersonal or community educational relationships[3]. In the instructionalist discourse, these attributes are the necessary conditions of the instructional function that defines the school. They thus become attributes of *the school in itself;* they are deduced from the very idea of school. In this way, the "instructionalist" discourse naturalizes the school form.

– From then on, *the school order can no longer be a form of socialization*, as a form of socialization is always historical. The naturalization of the distinctive signs

---

3 We find these themes developed at length in all the "instructionist" literature that has flourished since the 1980s, notably by Catherine Kintzler (*La République en questions*, Minerve, Paris, 1996), Jacques Muglioni (*L'École ou le loisir de penser*, CNDP, Paris, 1993), or Henri Pena-Ruiz (*Qu'est-ce que l'école?*, Folio Gallimard, Paris, 2005). But they can already be found in Alain's *Propos sur l'éducation*, which was published in book form in 1931. By confessing to wanting to like the "bare walls" of the classroom (Presses universitaires de France, Paris, 1961, VI, p. 13) and by distinguishing the student from the apprentice (XXIX, p. 63), Alain's thought on education can be understood as a philosophical legitimation of the school form.

of the school form is thus accompanied by an inversion of their meaning. The sanctuarization of the school, the decontextualization of school learning, the impersonality of the rules no longer signify the entry of the child into the disciplinary universe of a specific educational institution, but, on the contrary, thanks to the instruction they receive, the promise of the formation of their free and enlightened judgment, the condition of their emancipation. The "school disciplines" themselves are "naturalized", as if they resulted from the very order of knowledge and deserved the name of "discipline" only because they give, as Descartes would have said, "rules for the direction of the mind". The inversion of G. Vincent's theses is complete here: the school is thought of from Condorcet, and not from the Frères des écoles chrétiennes (Brothers of the Christian Schools); it is defined by instruction, not by education; it is less a form of socialization than the privileged place where children have the "leisure to think" (Muglioni 1993) and where it is the *individual* who builds themself up by learning to think for themself.

The weakness of this approach is, of course, its essentialism,, or more precisely the articulation it makes between this essentialism and the emancipatory ideal then conferred on the school, even though this ideal could only be formulated in particular conditions and by historical actors (it was hardly formulated before the French Revolution). We could certainly object to this because the "instructionalist" thinking of the school responds less to a question of fact than to a question of right, that it is a construction and not a nostalgia, that it thinks of an ideality and not a past[4]. But by what coincidence then does this pure construction find the components that G. Vincent identifies in the historical school form? To see in the enclosure of the school space or in the dissociation between school activities and adult social life the formal conditions of the formation of a free and enlightened mind is problematic, even not very credible, if these alleged conditions are observable in a singular historical configuration which, at the time of its constitution, was in no way concerned with emancipating individuals.

In other words, the socio-historical analysis of the school form as proposed by G. Vincent disenchants the "instruction" discourse on the school. It shows that, by proclaiming its attachment to the characteristic features of a school form that appeared around the 16th–17th centuries, this discourse confers on these features an ideal meaning that is far removed from their real historical meaning. It is only ever the *romance* of the school form, or, if we prefer to express ourselves in a language borrowed from Marxism, the idealized consciousness that it can take of itself and of its value.

---

4 Milner. J.C. (1984b). Réponse de J.C. Milner. *Le Débat*, 31(4), 48–56.

3.3. Transhistorical continuity

In short, it could be said that for Vincent, thinking of the school in terms of a "form of socialization" serves three purposes. The first, as we have just seen, is to avoid the naturalization and idealization of the constituent elements of this form. The second function, about which a few words must also be said, is to understand that this is a *new type of social relationship in general*, which can be described in terms of an extension of the pedagogical relationship outside the school. The "schooling" of the catechism, from the 17th century onwards, is one of the most significant illustrations of this, but we can also evoke, from the 19th century onwards, the way in which cultural practices are approached, or again, today, the tendency to pedagogize the relationship between parents and their children (Vincent 2004, p. 124). As for the third function of the concept of "form of socialization", it is to be able to grasp, thanks to it, the profound unity of several types of organization of the school corresponding to different historical moments. It is, moreover, with regard to these last two functions that we can consider that education is "imprisoned by the school form". As G. Vincent, B. Lahire and D. Thin in the book that bears such a title (admittedly in the form of a question): *Des écoles des Frères à l'école de la République, bien des choses changent, mais sans doute pas ce par quoi nous avons défini la forme scolaire* (From the Brothers' schools to the school of the Republic, many things change, but probably not what we have defined the school form by) (Vincent et al. 1994, p. 13). In other words, from one school to another, from the 16th to the 19th century, we would have to deal with what G. Vincent called, in his founding work of 1980, "variants" of the same school form. Now, as much as we can give him "a pass" when he establishes the historicity of the school form, the thought of its unity or of its transhistorical continuity poses a problem.

The "live issue" at stake here is that of the "republican school", as it was set up by J. Ferry and the republicans of the early Third Republic, and of which certain discourses – and in particular the one we have called "instructionalist" above – tend to emphasize the break it makes in the history of the school and to celebrate its formative, even emancipatory value. However, G. Vincent takes this thesis in the opposite direction. To say that the school of the Third Republic was a "variant" of the school form is in fact to maintain that, beyond the reform discourse that it held about itself ("the new school regime" as J. Ferry put it), it was in the end only another way of disciplining students. By seeking to impose itself as a law of reason that everyone can recognize, the rule becomes internalized, but does not disappear. So that "the respectful and obedient citizen, knowing their rights, but above all their duties, that the school of the Third Republic intends to form, is still a *schoolchild* (emphasis in original)" (Vincent et al. 1994, p. 15). The apparent novelty of the republican school is, in other words, a kind of "ruse of disciplinary reason"; we could even say better: The appeal to "reason" is only a "ruse of the rule" to better impose itself. This is an understanding of the history of the school that owes much to

Michel Foucault. Just as Foucault, in his *Histoire de la folie à l'âge classique* (1961), saw in Pinel's liberation of the alienated at the end of the 18th century another way of controlling their deviances, so the school of the Third Republic is fundamentally, despite its progressive discourse, a new way of subjugation:

> What has been called the revolution – the pedagogical one – of 1880 should probably be conceived less as the more or less open door [...] to the Enlightenment, to Liberty and Happiness than as a new way of subjugating: this school [...] which, instead of demanding blind obedience to the rule, seeks to make its necessity understood, which demands adherence and no longer simple submission, appeared to a fraction of the bourgeoisie, from the beginning of the 19th century, as the only adequate one, because the only one capable of diverting and using instead of repressing the collective wills (Vincent 1980, p. 96).

In short, "it is no longer a question of training, but it is necessary to regulate" (Vincent 1980, p. 98) and "the reason of the pedagogues is a discipline, more precisely self-discipline" (p. 99). This leads G. Vincent to a *double reading* of Ferdinand Buisson's *Dictionnaire de pédagogie* (noted "DP"), of which he unduly makes "the Bible of the school of the Third Republic" (p. 37). In *L'École primaire française*, the references to the DP are the object of a real montage: entries favorable to the thesis of the "variant" of the school form are systematically called upon ("School discipline", "School furniture", for example[5]); on the contrary, the entries that would have been likely to contradict it, and which are not the least numerous ("Activity", "School correspondence", "Childhood", "Enthusiasm", "Play", "Recreation", etc.), are not mentioned. So that when G. Vincent, B. Lahire and D. Thin write that, between the école des Frères and that of the Third Republic, the changes may be important, but not from the point of view of the school form, one is entitled to ask whether, from one school to another, it is the unity of form or the importance of the changes that is most significant. We can, of course, identify this unity of the school form in the school of the Third Republic (as attested to in particular by the photographic evidence it has left us). But if we are concerned, as G. Vincent himself never ceases to characterize his work, with making a "comprehensive" sociohistory of the school, we can also consider that the transformations brought about by J. Ferry's school are ultimately more significant than the permanencies to which it bears witness in relation to the école des Frères, and that in the end it produced results that were much more ambiguous and

---

5 He could have added others: "Emploi du temps", for example, or the article "Attention"., written by Michel Bréal, which defines attention, in a very "Lassalian" way, as the capacity for students to react to the finger and eye without the teacher even needing to speak.

contrasted than the self-disciplined and self-regulated citizen it was supposed to form.

3.4. School form and democratic form of socialization, historicity versus continuity?

This is an objection that G. Vincent ended up making to himself. The concept of "variants of the school form", he wrote 20 years after publishing *L'École primaire française*, was too weak; it underestimated the differences that could be observed from one period to another in the history of the school (Vincent 1999, p. 4). This underestimation is even, confesses G. Vincent, a "mistake" in that the transhistorical continuity of the school form, when too strongly asserted, ultimately comes to contradict its historicity (Vincent 2012a, p. 120). This will lead him to consider the emergence of a new form of socialization, the "democratic form of socialization" (Vincent 1999, 2004), illustrated, on the theoretical level, by Condorcet's thought and, on the practical level, by the creation of the Ecole Normale de l'An III, and also, in our own day, by the effort of the municipality of Saint-Fons to build a new educational space on the scale of the city (Vincent 2004, pp. 126–129). This form of democratic socialization, G. Vincent names it, precisely to distinguish it from the school form and in explicit reference to Condorcet, the form "public instruction" (Vincent 1999, 2004). To speak of a new form of socialization other than the scholastic form, it should be noted, does not mean that G. Vincent is approaching Ivan Illich's thesis on the "society without school[6]" (Vincent 2004, p. 131). It is simply a question of trying to think about the possibility of a school not constituted by the school form. From then on, we can return to the question of knowing if education in general (even non-school education) is "prisoner of the school form", that is, we can ask ourselves if the school itself cannot free itself from this form.

This new "democratic" form of socialization, by the way, does not make the school form disappear; it simply constitutes an alternative that is both possible and emerging. Nevertheless, such an evolution in G. Vincent's work leads him to restrict quite considerably the field of application of the concept of school form to the 17th century (Vincent 2004) and to the school of Jules Ferry.. In this, he unexpectedly joins the historical analysis proposed by Claude Lelièvre and Christian C. Nique[7], G. Vincent then comes to oppose the "democratic" model of "public instruction" of the First Republic to the school of the Third Republic, still "prisoner" of the school form.

---

6 Illich. I. (1971). *Une société sans école*. Le Seuil, Paris.

7 Nique, C. and Lelièvre, C. (1993). *La République n'éduquera plus. La fin du mythe Ferry*. Plon, Paris.

Compared to his first works, the reversal is spectacular: "reason" (Condorcet) is no longer a ruse of the rule, but its antonym (Vincent 2004, Chapter V, "La règle et la raison", pp. 81–109). Basically, G. Vincent dissociates what the instructionalist discourse had a tendency to associate, even to confuse. Indeed, the latter saw in the school form the very model of the school of knowledge, of reason and of emancipation; G. Vincent sees precisely the opposite. Nevertheless, he gives this school ideal a certain effectiveness, by making it endorsed by a non-school form of socialization whose first expressions appear, according to him, in the century of the Enlightenment and the Revolution. The instructionism of J.C. Milner, or even of C. Kintzler, who devoted a remarkable study to the concept of public instruction in Condorcet[8], is certainly "denaturalized", historicized, but the theses he defends are "re-enchanted" in a way: they find, in the eyes of G. Vincent, a certain value and legitimacy.

3.5. Conclusion: the concept of school form, a useful concept?

There is food for thought here: by finally wanting to limit the field of application of the concept of school form, does Vincent not mark the limits of the concept itself, that is, make its sociological interest problematic? Indeed, it is one of two things. Either the school form is a concept thanks to which it is possible to think not only of a historically situated and dated reality (l'école des Frères, the colleges of the Ancien Régime, the Napoleonic lycée, the school of the Third Republic), but more profoundly, of a general type of social relationship, still at work today, in school as well as outside of school; but what then of the radical social transformations that the socialization of youth has undergone since the 17th century? Or – this is the second term of the alternative, and also the final position of G. Vincent – the school form is a concept that is not yet fully understood. Vincent's last position, the school form is a concept that must be limited to the thought of a social reality to which ours is very far from being reduced, but then the essential of its interest is historiographical, and it allows us to understand much more what separates us from the forms of socialization at work in the école des Frères in the 17th century than what brings us closer to them or what continues to be the case with them in us: a paradox that distances G. Vincent's last work from its first ambition.

In truth, it would be very difficult to recognize in the present school the disciplinary universe proper to the school form. Its opening to the outside world means not so much the general schooling of social relations as what we might call

---

8 Kintzler, C. (1984). *Condorcet. L'Instruction publique et la naissance du citoyen.* Folio Essais, Paris.

the "de-schooling" of its own mode of socialization. It is no longer the school that informs the social, but the social of contemporary democratic individualism which, with parents, cell phones, "youth culture", the recognition of the child "behind" the student and the submission of the disciplinary regime of the establishments to the ordinary rules of the law, penetrates the school and contributes to its deinstitutionalization. But the same could be said of the "democratic" form of socialization, the "public instruction" form, which is hardly to be found in the school of today and only has meaning as a thought of a school ideal (what the school should be), and not as a sociological concept allowing us to understand what it is.

This leads to a rather radically critical conclusion. Indeed, what does the concept of school form, even enriched by its distinction from that of "form of democratic socialization", ultimately allow us to think? The école des Frères of J.B. de La Salle or the colleges of the Ancien Régime? No doubt. The school of Jules Ferry? That is already much more ambiguous. The current school? We do not believe it.

3.6. References

Durkheim, E. (1963). *L'Éducation morale*. Presses universitaires de France, Paris.

Foucault, M. (1961). *Histoire de la folie à l'âge classique*. Plon, France.

Kintzler, C. (1984). *Condorcet. L'instruction publique et la naissance du citoyen*. Folio Essais, Paris.

Milner, J.-C. (1984a). *De l'école*. Le Seuil, Paris.

Milner, J.-C. (1984b). Réponse de J.-C Milner. *Le Débat*, 31(4), 48–56.

Muglioni, J., (1993). *L'École ou le loisir de penser*. La Commission Nationale du Débat Public, Paris.

Nique, C. and Lelièvre, C. (1993). *La République n'éduquera plus. La fin du mythe Ferry*. Plon, Paris.

Rousseau, J.-J. (1966). *Émile ou de l'éducation*. Garnier-Flammarion, Paris.

Vincent, G. (1980). *L'École primaire française. Étude sociologique*. Presses universitaires de Lyon, Lyon.

Vincent, G. (ed.) (1994). *L'éducation prisonnière de la forme scolaire ?* Presses universitaires de Lyon, Lyon.

Vincent, G. (ed.) (1999). Postface. In *L'École primaire française*, 2nd edition. Presses universitaires de Lyon, Lyon.

Vincent, G. (2004). *Recherches sur la socialisation démocratique*. Presses universitaires de Lyon, Lyon.

Vincent, G., Lahire, B., Thin, D. (1994). Sur l'histoire et la théorie de la forme scolaire. In *L'éducation prisonnière de la forme scolaire ?* Vincent, G. (ed.). Presses universitaires de Lyon, Lyon.

Vincent, G., Courtebras, B., Reuter, Y. (2012a). La forme scolaire. Débats et mises au point. Premier entretien. *Recherches en didactique*, 1(13), 109–135.

Vincent, G., Courtebras, B., Reuter, Y. (2012b). La forme scolaire. Débats et mises au point. Deuxième entretien. *Recherches en didactique*, 2(14), 127–143.

Museums and the School Form: What are the Interactions?

Introduction to Part 2

"Museums and the School Form: What are the Interactions?", the second part of this book, involves identifying the role of museum institutions in the school educational dynamic. It invites the actors concerned by these two spheres (cultural and educational), as well as the institutions within which they work or are called to work. This part seeks to examine the central notions of mediation and mediatization of patrimonial knowledge, by focusing, in particular, on the cultural education policies that underlie them, as well as the institutions that support them.

From an etymological point of view, the term "mediation" refers to the action of the mediator, to the fact of serving as an intermediary. The mediator is themself defined as the one who accompanies and guides an encounter between the visitor (public) and the work (cultural good) through a variety of devices likely to give them greater autonomy. Cultural mediation, indissociable of the wills of culture democratization, aims to provide access to cultural and patrimonial values to the largest audience. Mediatization is understood through the notions of mediatizing (indirect action) and mass media (an intermediary device to access large audiences), making the question of technical and/or technological supports unclear.

From the point of view of learning, mediation could replace the terms transmission-diffusion, in order to take into account in a more striking way the position of the learner. As for mediatization, it necessarily encompasses the influence of the medium(s) on learning (Jacquinot 2003). While school remains today the main means of acquiring knowledge and culture, it is impossible not to recognize the actuality of non-school forms of acculturation that determines "the possibility for everyone to learn new knowledge and to cultivate themselves without school or outside of school" (Jacobi 2018, p. XV). The establishment of the boundaries between formal, informal and non-formal still remains at times unclear,

Introduction written by Anik MEUNIER.

and that of the roles that schools and cultural institutions, respectively, play in this transmission and mediation of patrimonial knowledge is increasingly protean. Attempting to reach audiences or users who are still little or not coveted by the authorities legitimizing the forms and accesses of culture, and little concerned by the cultural proposals as they are presented, questions arise. Do cultural education policies participate in the project of formal and non-formal education or, even more broadly, in cultural democratization? Do these policies guarantee access to culture for all, to forms of cultural democracy? Is there such a thing as artistic and cultural education? If so, in which environments and contexts is it best represented? The following chapters will raise issues of partnership between the cultural and educational worlds and address some of these questions.

According to the perspective of transmission, the roles assigned to each of the actors involved are likely to vary and to be redefined. Indeed, this redefinition of the roles granted to the ones and to the others in this relationship to culture and to education is in the heart of the logics of the mediation. To put it simply, museum and school actors now share what is considered to be a role of mediator of culture and knowledge. In Quebec, the recent referential of professional competencies, of the teaching profession[1], directs teachers to develop skills related to culture and to take on the role of mediator of elements of culture. Does this role in the sharing of professional dynamics (school and cultural) bring them into conflict or into healthy complementarity with each other? Do school educational staff and cultural mediators become accomplices or competitors? And then what are the implications of these partnerships for the audiences concerned?

Is the dichotomy between culture and education, although complementary, tend to soften and fade little by little? Could new dynamics be envisaged? They have long been desired.

Chapter 4 is written by Géraldine Barron, curator of libraries, doctor of history and deputy director of the library of the Université du Littoral Côte d'Opale (France). She is also a researcher associated with the ICT laboratory at the University of Paris. Her text addresses the question of technical culture through the transmission of technical knowledge in 19th-century France through the prism of collections of objects gathered in two Parisian institutions emblematic of the issues of teaching and popularization, the CNAM (Conservatoire des arts et métiers) and the Musée de Marine. Since the Enlightenment, the commercialization and display of technical objects, as well as the development of a specific literature and museum collections, have contributed to the transmission of technical knowledge outside of the corporation and the school or university institution. From then on, this work was

---

1 https://cdn-contenu.quebec.ca/cdn-contenu/adm/min/education/publications-adm/devenir-en seignant/referentiel_competences_professionnelles_profession_enseignante.pdf?1606848024.

officially carried out outside instituted educational frameworks, and these two institutions followed intersecting paths. In the case of the CNAM, its vocation encourages it to transmit know-how through the demonstration and exhibition of the most recent inventions, while gradually converting its machines into museum collections, without losing its teaching function. As for the Musée de Marine, it is around learning models that it progressively becomes a conservatory of naval art, while its teaching function remains foreign to it, even though it plays a major role in the transmission of technical knowledge and the popularization of maritime culture.

Chapter 5 is written by Marion Trannoy Voisin, head of mission at the Citadelle de Corte and responsible for the renovation of the citadel. This contribution gives an account of the project of transforming the Musée de la Corse, installed in the Citadelle de Corte and opened in 1997, as a museum of society. The text engages a critical reflexivity on the practices and on the capacities of interactions with the other cultural actors. These determining stakes were in the heart of the renewal of the museum establishment. Through the realization of the installation *A citadella di Corti*[2], the text questions the processes of construction and transmission of meaning and knowledge at work in this institution. New approaches to the conception of museography and mediation, desired to be more open and inclusive, were experimented with and put to the test. This project of renewal of the orientations of the Musée de la Corse and the Citadelle de Corte has shaken the codes of the professionals in charge of the conception of the exhibition. This approach revealed unusual scenographic and expographic processes and induced a new relationship with the space and the site, which shelters the buildings of the museum. From this experience, all the possibilities of the future of the Citadelle de Corte were revealed and criticized. Questions are raised, among which: How do visitors appropriate these various possibilities? Is a co-construction of this future possible? What is the efficiency of this bet on collective intelligence for the future of this place of knowledge sharing?

Chapter 6 is written by Nathanaël Wadbled, associate researcher at the Université de Lorraine. He is interested in the world of heritage and school education t, considering that these two environments maintain different relationships to knowledge, but whose actors are brought together during school visits. The pupils are then entrusted to a guide-lecturer, who offers them a mediation adapted to the museum space and the pupil visitor, accompanied by the guide, enters into a relationship with the subject. While in the classroom, the pupil receives knowledge from the teacher that must learn in a different form and according to different modalities. For the teacher, this raises the dual question of their relationship with the guide-lecturer and the way in which their professional identity is affected by the

---

2 *A citadella di Corti*, "A Citadel for a Horizon" (November 2015).

pupils' new relationship to knowledge. This text examines this dynamic from two study fields carried out according to two different methods. On the one hand, comprehensive interviews were conducted with pupils and their various supervisors during a research project on the experience of visiting the Auschwitz-Birkenau memorial museum. On the other hand, participative observations as a tour guide were conducted during a professional internship on the battlefields of the Somme. These two case studies illustrate the complexity of the relationships between the transmission of historical knowledge on a patrimonial site and the teaching skills.

Chapter 7 is co-authored by Anik Meunier, a full professor in museology and education at UQAM, and Camille Roelens, a researcher at the Centre interdisciplinaire de recherche en éthique at the Université de Lausanne. They are interested, in a diachronic perspective and in response to social demands, in museum institutions that have evolved and diversified. These major transformations within cultural facilities, as well as the creation of new structures (permanent or temporary) to exhibit content (artistic, scientific, socio-historical) and to raise awareness of current issues, cross several fields and disciplines. In this regard, some questions are raised. What are the impacts of interactions with audiences on the production and dissemination of discourses and the functioning of mediation devices? What are the modalities and the scope of cultural transmission defined as a transfer of conserved objects, knowledge and values? How do these interactions, increasingly asserted and desired between publics and institutions, influence the effects of mediation and educational intentions in a non-formal context? In particular, the text uncovers the interactions between non-formal education and cultural transmission in order to analyze the reception of museum mediation devices used to enshrine the patrimonial value of objects or practices in order to communicate with audiences.

Chapter 8 is written by Corinne Baujard, a university professor of education and training at the Université de Lille. This chapter deals with a case study on the management of organizations for the *agrégation externe du second degré* (a competitive examination for the recruitment of professors in France to teach in high schools, preparatory classes, universities and grandes écoles; it is the only example in the world of a body that is present in both the secondary and higher education systems). The text questions the space of training in the museum confronted with actions of modernization. It deals with the digitization of activities offered to the public. Several innovative pedagogical initiatives support the reflection of the uses by the visitors and the various facets of the cultural spaces of training question the rapport of the cultural knowledge in universe of sense for the future professors. How can the digital museum be a cultural space for training? What does the museum reveal about pedagogical practices? The approach put forward invites to focus on new educational programs in interaction with the actors of the cultural environment.

References

Jacobi, D. (ed.) (2018). Avant-propos. In *Culture et éducation non formelle*. PUQ, Quebec.

Jacquinot, G. (2003). Médiation, médiatisation, un entre-deux : pour une autonomisation de l'apprentissage. *Notions en questions*, 7, 127–136.

Rogers, A. (2005). *Non-Formal Education. Flexible Schooling or Participatory Education?* University of Hong Kong/Kluwer Academic, Hong Kong/New York.

Seguy, J.-Y. (ed.) (2018). *Variations autour de la "forme scolaire". Mélanges offerts à André D. Robert*. Presses universitaires de Lorraine, Nancy.

Vincent, G. (eds) (1994). *L'Éducation prisonnière de la forme scolaire. Scolarisation et socialisation dans les sociétés industrielles*. Presses universitaires de Lyon, Lyon.

4

The Transmission of Technical Culture in France in the 19th Century via Collections of Objects

After a long period of neglect, in which it had been unjustly kept, the history of technical education was given renewed interest in the 1990s (Marchand 2005). The role of industrial exhibitions, particularly universal exhibitions, in the training of workers is no longer in question, and the role of the Conservatoire des arts et métiers (French Conservatory of Arts and Professions) in the organization of technical education is well known (Lembré 2021). The articulation between technical training and the construction of collections, whether educational or museum-related, is still an area that needs to be explored. To focus on the place of collections in the transmission of technical culture means questioning practices rather than teachings, joining the active current of the history of techniques, which has undergone a cultural turn in recent years, focusing more and more on the construction and place of technical knowledge in society. Two institutions and collections have been the subject of recent studies that allow us to question the links between collections and learning in a new way; in keeping with the theme of the book, this chapter proposes to take a look in the rearview mirror, in order to give scope to the current concerns of teachers and professionals in museums, archives and libraries, and to question practices over time. The ideas and principles underlying the creation of the Conservatoire des arts et métiers and the Musée naval de Paris (Paris Naval Museum) have many similarities; however, over the course of their first century of existence, these two institutions have followed very different paths, which illustrate

Chapter written by Géraldine BARRON.

the ambiguity of the initial project of public spaces for techniques. The study of the constitution of their collections is still recent, but rich in lessons[1].

4.1. Crossed histories

The origin of the objects and ideas that gave birth to the Conservatoire des arts et métiers and the Musée naval de Paris is rooted in the Age of Enlightenment: in the second half of the 18th century, scholars who were members of the Académie royale des sciences (Royal Academy of Sciences) built up collections of machines and models that they wished to use for teaching purposes. In 1748, Duhamel du Monceau, Inspector General of the Navy, offered the king his collection of models of ships and equipment. Seven years earlier, he had founded a school intended to provide theoretical instruction to student naval engineers and builders, in addition to the practical training they received at the ports. The collection was deposited in the Louvre, initially as an annex to the school; it was soon after transferred to the "salle de Marine", near the session room of the Académie des sciences, where many questions related to navigation and shipbuilding were discussed. A few years later, in 1782, Jacques Vaucanson bequeathed to the king the collection of automatons, machines and instruments that he had built and assembled in the Hôtel de Mortagne. This collection formed the basis of the Conservatoire des arts et métiers and was transferred to the former priory of Saint-Martin-des-Champs at the beginning of the following century.

Although both institutions are daughters of the Enlightenment, it is necessary to look at their genesis to understand why and how their history diverges.

4.2. Conservatoire des arts et métiers

The Conservatoire des arts et métiers was founded by decree on 19 Vendémiaire year III (October 10, 1794) on the initiative of Abbé Grégoire with the following motivation:

> The creation of a conservatory for the arts and professions, where all the new tools and machines invented and perfected will come together, will arouse curiosity & interest, and you will see in all matters very rapid progress. [...] It is necessary to enlighten ignorance, which does not know, and poverty, which does not have the means to know. [...] In the conservatory, there will be an exhibition room where all new inventions will be gathered. This means, absolutely similar to what is

---

1 See, in particular, the work of Marie-Sophie Corcy and Lionel Dufaux for the Conservatoire, and Géraldine Barron for the Musée naval.

practiced in the Louvre for painting and sculpture, seemed to us very appropriate to fertilize genius (Gregoire 1794).

Grégoire gave substance to a triple ambition in the service of progress: to enhance industry, to educate and to promote innovation. The Vaucanson collection represented only a part of the numerous objects previously scattered in different places in the capital and gathered in the priory of Saint-Martin-des-Champs. The function assigned to this collection was the transmission of knowledge by sight, as expressed by the deputy Alquier in 1798:

> Those who come to the Conservatoire will all be workers, whose conceptions must not be obscured by abstract or scientific speeches: they must be made to see more than they must be told. The play of a machine, set in motion before their eyes, is often for them the best demonstration[2].

Several elementary school projects, based on learning by observation, sometimes called "elementary school of reasoned industry", were born in the first years of the Conservatoire, but did not last long, while the exhibition galleries were opened to the public in 1802. It was during the Restoration that a new proposal emerged: rather than ensuring the initial training of children or young workers, it was a question of allowing workers to deepen their knowledge in order to perfect their practice, in other words, a lifelong training offer ahead of time. The education was to be public, free and taught by scholars who promoted the application of science to the industrial arts. The first three courses were instituted on the initiative of Charles Dupin by the royal order of November 25, 1819: Dupin himself taught applied mechanics, Nicolas Clément-Desormes applied chemistry and Jean-Baptiste Say industrial economics.

The teaching offer expanded with the creation of a chair of applied physics in 1828 and six new chairs in 1839. The professors proposed to pass on to their "listeners" the theoretical elements and, above all, the practices necessary for the application of industrial processes. This teaching was still based on collections of objects and machines, but the professors replaced the demonstrators, the amphitheater replaced the gallery, and the high level of oral teaching replaced the teaching *de visu*[3]. Collections were built up as faculty members needed them,

---

2 Cited by (Dufaux 2017, p. 99); (Alquier 1798).

3 "Report made by Mr. Cunin-Gridaine, on behalf of the Committee on Supplementary Appropriations on the bill requesting an extraordinary appropriation of 134,263 francs for the cost of installing and furnishing the galleries of the Conservatoire des arts et métiers," *Compte-rendu des séances de l'Assemblée nationale législative*, vol. 10, from July 30 to December 15, 1850, pp. 83–86.

following a principle of thematic and chronological series, to illustrate the march of progress, but the relationship between collections and teaching remains ambiguous (Dufaux 2017). Exhibition and demonstration spaces were distinct, and objects were more mobile than teachers and listeners. In 1850, an inventory counted 7,000 poorly displayed machines in the galleries: at this time, the Conservatoire was working to upgrade its exhibition spaces so that all of its collections could be seen and appreciated by the public. It also began to consider retrospective acquisitions to complement the "novelties": the galleries gradually became a museum. Some machines could be set in motion, to demonstrate mechanical or physical principles, as in the nave of the church of Saint-Martin-des-Champs (Corcy et al. 2017), and also in Arthur Morin and Henri Tresca's experimental laboratory of mechanics, created to experiment with the machines of industry and spark innovation. Although increasingly distinct, museums and education continued their interaction.

4.3. Musée naval

With the Revolution, Duhamel du Monceau's collection became dormant, but it formed the basis of the Musée naval, also called the "Musée Dauphin" and the "Musée de Marine", whose creation was decided in 1827. Like the Conservatoire, the Musée naval made it possible to bring together collections that were scattered, poorly used and poorly maintained. The project is formulated as follows:

> The Musée Dauphin will contain models of warships of all ranks, and, as far as possible, those of merchant ships of various sizes; relief maps of the ports and of our principal maritime establishments; apparatuses and machines especially in use in the arsenals; instruments used for navigation, and curious products of newly discovered countries (Musée naval 1828, p. 199).

The requirement of novelty is less preponderant than at the Conservatoire. It is rather a question of making known a technical environment foreign to the capital. A workshop for the construction and restoration of models was attached to the museum, and the royal decision stipulated that the curator who directed this miniature arsenal had to belong to the corps of naval engineering officers, which had replaced that of engineer-builders[4]. The Museum in Paris was developed by taking from the collections of the different military ports of the kingdom. These collections predate the Musée naval project, as they originated in Colbert's 1679 ordinance that prescribed the construction of scale models of the various types of ships designed in

---

4 The engineer-builders, civil officers, became military officers of the Marine Engineering in 1800.

the arsenals. In Toulon, Charles Dupin opened the first naval museum in 1814 around these collections and a school of drawing and modeling (Cros and Baron 2013), which was not unlike the initial projects of the Conservatoire. In Paris, however, there was no teaching function, even though the mission of the museum, marked by proselytism, did not neglect the educational aspect:

> The usefulness of such an establishment will be keenly felt by all those who know the needs of the navy, and the obstacles that oppose the prosperity of this so important portion of the public force. […] It is felt that it is by popularizing the ideas relating to the navy, by making these ideas penetrate our morals and our education, that we will end up interesting the whole nation in our successes at sea (Musée naval 1828, p. 199).

The engineer-curator Apollinaire Lebas considered that the museum should be something more than a simple instrument of propaganda. The collection "must not only offer a complete image of what is done today, it must reproduce at least an idea of what was done in the past, by presenting the series of improvements that are reserved for future works[5]". However, he added, "From this point of view, the Musée naval is a true conservatory", which nevertheless envisages the demonstration of progress over a longer period of time than Gregoire had done. Engineers, sailors and architects were encouraged to deposit their archives there and the museum aimed to remain the training ground it was in the 18th century, although it was no longer attached to a school. The school of maritime engineering, established in Paris in 1795, moved around a lot: to Brest in the year X, then to Lorient; it returned briefly to Paris between 1854 and 1872, at a time when the museum was no longer directed by a man of the Navy, but by a painter, and was no longer dependent on the French Ministry of the Navy, given that the reform of the national museums in 1848 had placed it under the supervision of the Fine Arts Department. The enrichment of the collections and their legitimacy in the Louvre palace suffered from this change of administrative supervision; the museum received more exotic objects transported by the ships of the Royale than properly maritime objects, looking more like a cabinet of curiosities than a museum of navigation techniques. It was not until the dawn of the Third Republic that a retired naval officer took over the command of this fleet in miniature and the project of a conservatory of naval art, developing the technical collections, as well as the written and graphic documentation. Acquisitions became more systematic, based on the principle of series as at the Conservatoire, aiming at exhaustiveness and encyclopedism in the field of navigation (Barron 2019). Unfortunately, the École du génie maritime (school of maritime engineering) moved to Cherbourg at this time.

---

5 Archives nationales, archives des musées nationaux, 20144780/1, Apollinaire Lebas, "Note pour Monsieur le Directeur des Musées nationaux", July 25, 1848.

4.4. Collections and audiences: outline of a differentiated transmission

The same categories of actors contributed to the creation and development of the Conservatoire and the Musée naval: military officers and engineers, pillars of the learned institutions born of the Revolution, most of them from the École polytechnique and members of the Académie des sciences. They shared an ideal of progress and the diffusion of knowledge of the "arts" at all levels of society, which continued when science and technology began to diverge towards the middle of the century[6]. The collection of objects served as a support for learning by observation and demonstration. At the Musée naval, as at the Conservatoire des Arts et Métiers, the ambition to maintain France among the great nations underlaid more social motivations of control and moralization of the working population. It was a question of fighting against the idea of a decline in workers' know-how in a context of abolition of guilds and rapid industrialization (Lembré 2021): in land-based production as in the navy, battles with England were fought and won through innovation and no longer by cannon fire. The dissemination and publicization of knowledge was not only through objects but also through the gathering and provision of important documentation on and around the collections to professionals who wished to improve their skills. At the Conservatoire as at the Musée naval, books, drawings, maps and other technical manuals were systematically collected: the library was inseparable from the collections of objects and was also open to the public.

The gap between the initial intention and the actual realizations tended to widen throughout the 19th century. The relationship between objects and teaching was ambiguous, to say the least, and the collections tended to become autonomous and "museumized". However, if we know the why and the how of the constitution of these collections, it is more difficult to comprehend the "for whom?" While today, visitors and their practices are at the heart of the concerns of museums, and attendance statistics and public surveys are becoming more widespread, visitors are curiously absent from the archives of the 19th century. However, we can see them in the background, in the regulations and schedules, and then, more clearly in the second half of the century, in the tourist guides and in the press.

Samuel Hayat proposes a categorization of the Conservatoire's audience into two figures (Hayat 2017):

– the professionals;

– the general public.

---

6 On these issues of science, technique and technology (see, in particular, Carnino (2015) and *Artefact* (2021)).

At the Musée naval, the first category was excluded because of its geographical distance from the ports, even though professionals were committed to enriching the collections through a significant practice of donations. At the Conservatoire, these audiences were served by distinct spaces: amphitheater and gallery. The amphitheaters are where evening and Sunday classes were held. When it was created, the Conservatoire was aimed at a working-class public with a view to disincorporating technical knowledge and providing universal access to knowledge, technical culture and its tools and machines. According to Abbé Grégoire, the depository of machines should arouse "the feeling of beauty [...], the genius of the arts" (Guillaume 1804, p. 62) in order to encourage the work of workers. In 1819, with the creation of the Conseil de perfectionnement and the first teaching chairs, it was aimed at a wider range of professionals, craftsmen, workers and entrepreneurs. In the dedication "To the French workers" of his geometry course, which was held twice a week at 8 pm in a crowded amphitheater (Chatzis 2009, p. 105), Dupin nevertheless reiterated the ambition of knowledge for all that would feed innovation:

> French workers, raise your soul to the happiness of such a hope! If you study the application of geometry and mechanics to your arts and professions, you will find in this study a means of working with greater regularity, precision, intelligence, ease, and speed. You will do better and faster; you will learn to reason out your work and your inventions (Dupin 1825, p. VI).

The universalist ideal diminished as chairs were created that were no longer dedicated to a discipline (chemistry, industrial economics, mechanics), but to a professional field, to a production (agriculture in 1839, ceramics, dyeing, spinning, etc.). The teaching at the Conservatoire was an intermediary between the arts and professional schools and the engineering schools: highly practical, based on example and demonstration, it was neither an initial training nor a purely theoretical education, but a means of perfecting oneself for "men of art". A journalist of the magazine *La Nature* related, in 1883:

> We recently visited the Conservatoire des arts et métiers in Paris, and the learned director, Colonel Laussedat, was kind enough to honor us himself with the new and interesting gallery of civil constructions that we owe to his intelligent initiative. Everything related to the art of building, from samples of raw materials, stones, marbles, etc., to models of modern houses, large tubular or suspended bridges, everything that is used to build these constructions, tools, machines, etc., is brought together, and forms a whole of powerful interest,

where the architect, the engineer, and the worker will find very instructive documents[7].

The collections were therefore aimed at professionals, first workers, then increasingly foremen and engineers, but they retained their edifying role. This preoccupation with publicizing technology and exhibiting the diversity of industrial products is found in the great ephemeral events, such as industrial exhibitions and universal exhibitions, which also attract professionals, as well as the simply curious and democratize access to these technical objects; it would therefore be better to make a distinction between those who attend the courses and the indistinct but eminently diverse mass of visitors to the galleries, this general public "fictitious receptor" (Jacobi 2017) and a priori undefined, if not by its opposition to the specialists of the technique.

At the Conservatoire, the galleries were open during the day, first on Thursdays and Sundays, to the "general public" and by permission on other days, and then more and more widely as lighting and tourism progressed. The Musée naval was only open to the public by invitation until 1837, then on Sundays for everyone and by invitation during the week[8]. It was only in 1855, on the occasion of the Universal Exhibition, that this restriction was lifted (Bresc 2000, p. 184). The universal exhibitions found a natural extension in the museums, both in terms of collections and visitors. The attendance increased considerably and was counted in thousands[9]. The Musée naval was packed, especially on Thursdays, children's day, and on Sundays, attracting "good peasants, simple mothers, young girls with little education [...] and young men and children" (Méa 1884). One journalist even estimated that it alone attracted a third of the Louvre's visitors, even though it was not very visible, relegated to the second floor, and poorly served by a narrow staircase[10]. As the industrialist Charles Laboulaye wrote (1867), "the walk at the Conservatoire has determined more than one vocation, has lit the sacred fire in many children who are today our best engineers, our most skillful industrialists". The use of the term promenade and the summoning of children clearly underline the gap between the gallery and the amphitheater, between the professionals and the general public. At the Louvre, the fine arts competed with the useful arts, which were nevertheless accessible to:

> [those] who know neither Apollo, nor Diana, nor all the marble divinities of the first floor, who do not understand the difference

---

7 *La Nature, revue des sciences et de leurs applications aux arts et à l'industrie.* December 1, 1883, p. 66.

8 As of 1843, it is open from Tuesday to Sunday from 10 to 4 pm.

9 AMN, *1BB24, meeting of December 22, 1881.

10 Sabine Méa, "Le Musée de Marine", *Le Journal des Arts*, December 1884, p. 1. *Journal des débats*, December 19, 1911.

which exists between a cut crystal and a four penny glass, but who contemplate for a long time with tenderness a piece of tarred cable, a steel pulley, a lighthouse lantern, a beautiful vessel, which seems to advance towards them under all its sails spread out in the shape of wings – or who sometimes look, alas! with a very sad air the debris of a shipwreck. [...] And the young people and the children, would you count for nothing what they learn there? What sentences would these examples be worth in kind? Are they not the complement, the clarification of their travel books; are they not the stimulus that made them work with application all week in order not to miss their outing and to drag their grandfather or their mother to the Musée de Marine (Méa 1884).

We might doubt the veracity of these words written in order to defend the maintenance of the Musée de Marine in the Louvre, where its presence was constantly questioned by the curators of fine arts. It is, however, supported by firsthand accounts:

It is not without tenderness that I remember the time [...] of my childhood when my good grades in high school were rewarded by a visit to the Musée de Marine, in the Louvre. On Thursdays or Sundays, passing with contempt in front of the entrance to the painting galleries, I would cheerfully climb the two floors and the steep staircase leading to the goal of my schoolboy dreams. There, in long, low rooms, the most attractive objects for a child's soul were and still are displayed. [...] It seemed to me that I was in an immense toy store[11].

At the Louvre, even though the museum is not designed for demonstrations, unlike the Conservatoire, the curators made an effort to stage their collections: lighting a lamp in a lighthouse model to illustrate the operation of an eclipse lighthouse[12]; to put a relief map of the Suez Canal next to the models of the dredges that were used to dig it; to write notices that do not water down the data of the objects exhibited. The admiral curator remarked, in the article he devoted to the museum in the *Revue maritime et coloniale*: "One has little idea of the number of men and especially of workers who read or browse through these legends and of the number of fathers or teachers who find answers to their children's curiosity there" (Pâris 1881, p. 268). The number of lexical occurrences of the educational theme ("instruction", "instruire", "école" and "populariser") in this article is indicative of this desire (Pâris 1872).

---

11 *Journal des débats*, May 5, 1893, p. 2, "Correspondance" section.
12 AMN, *1BB22, meeting of February 4, 1875.

The Musée de Marine also responded to a political objective, which was to mobilize public opinion on the military and technical issues of the Navy. This was the wish expressed by the historian and tactician Grivel in 1869:

> To popularize progress in its many applications, to call on public opinion and common sense, to pronounce on questions that have been almost inaccessible until now, for most military and sailors! [...] Through the press, through the platform, through books, in our daily conversations, let's work to educate our nation about the sea (Grivel 1869, pp. 247–248, 280).

4.5. Conclusion

If the two institutions share a common origin, the nature of their creation diverges: the Conservatoire was first and foremost a place of training and remained so even when its galleries welcomed collections that were more and more unconnected to teaching, while the Musée naval was above all a place of conservation. Nevertheless, the two institutions had to valorize the technical object, to disincorporate and democratize knowledge, in order to favor the industrial development of France. This educational mission was twofold: the continuous training of professionals to encourage their improvement and innovation; the edification of workers and youth in the service of a secular religion of industrial progress in a context of strong international competition.

Over the course of the century, two trends were implemented in the service of this intention: an increase in the number of opening days and hours and an increase in the number of collections. The Conservatoire, which managed its own premises, had more latitude than its naval counterpart (from 11 rooms in 1849 to 39 in 1869, and continued to expand[13]). From 1851 onwards, the universal exhibitions were an undeniable driving force both in the growth of collections and in the attraction of the public. The multiplication of travel guides and catalogs of the collections encouraged and guided visitors. This development was part of the movement of scientific popularization and positivism.

The description of the audiences of these technical collections highlights the educational principles that underlaid the presentation of the objects. However, we cannot speak of pedagogy through the object, because putting it in a collection does not really allow for its pedagogical use, even at the Conservatoire, where the distinction between teaching and collections is becoming increasingly clear. As Édouard Charton wrote in the *Magasin pittoresque* about the Conservatoire, "the

---

13 *Annales du Conservatoire des arts et métiers*, volume 8, 1868, p. 332.

gathering in the same place as machines, models, and the most useful objects for industry, constituted a first teaching, teaching by sight. The Conservatoire was a museum. It was necessary, next to the museum, to open, a *school*". However, the small school quickly disappeared in front of the rise of primary education; only higher education remained, more intended for the "executives" of industry than for the workers. The audiences of the galleries are considered less attentive than the listeners of the courses, more picker than hunter, in search of an emotion more than of learning. The sight of these objects and the way they were set in motion aroused curiosity and wonder, as all the accounts report. Literature and the proponents of popular science participated in this movement, from Jules Verne to Camille Flammarion: in the intention of popularization, wonder did not prevent the appropriation of knowledge, quite the contrary. Distilled knowledge can be considered superficial, but it is in no way simplistic or reductive, as the catalogs raisonnés and descriptive notes testify. Spaces of informal education (Garnier and Kahn 2018), these museums constituted in the 19th-century places of knowledge and responded to a desire for popular education, social progress through work and instruction, and also of scientific popularization and valorization of industry. Paradoxically, the "general public" could be considered as dangerous for the collections because it was a mass of people: over-attendance was harmful to the collections and imposed a physical distancing in the form of showcases and cords, which had not initially been desired. Despite this, it encouraged the rationalization of the presentation in the form of chronological or thematic routes.

All these approaches and perceptions are indicative of the origin of the leaders of these institutions, who were part of a bourgeoisie trained in schools that valued the complementarity between theory and application, and who inherited from the Enlightenment and the Revolution the values of encyclopedism and universalism. We find them as much in industrial innovation as in the emerging human sciences (archaeology, ethnography), centered on the object and its analysis, using analogy and comparison. Nevertheless, it must be admitted that the analysis of technical collections and their audiences as presented here is biased by much more contemporary questions. Indeed, the profiles of curators and their reflections on collections and their uses have evolved considerably, as have their professional training and specialization. Increasingly advanced research in museology and a heightened interest in audiences combine with economic and competitive issues, in order to make museums more attractive and visitors more like actors; the question of learning and the transmission of informal knowledge mobilizes at the same time the attention of researchers (Jacobi 2018). These intentions of seducing and instructing the public can be contradictory and generate tensions between intention and realization.

4.6. References

Alquier, C.J.-M. (1798). *Rapport fait par Alquier sur une résolution du Conseil des Cinq-Cents relative au Conservatoire des arts et métiers, séance du 27 nivôse an 6.* Imprimerie nationale, Paris.

Barron, G. (2019). *Edmond Pâris et l'art naval : des pirogues aux cuirassés.* Presses universitaires du Midi, Toulouse.

Barron, G., Camolezi, M., Deldicque, T. (eds) (2021). Technique, technologie. *Artefact. Techniques, histoire et sciences humaines*, 15 [Online]. Available at: https://doi.org/10.4000/artefact.11161.

Bresc, G. (2000). *Mémoires du Louvre.* Gallimard/Réunion des musées nationaux, Paris.

Carnino, G. (2015). *L'invention de la science : la nouvelle religion de l'âge industriel.* Le Seuil, Paris.

Chatzis, K. (2009). Charles Dupin, Jean-Victor Poncelet et leurs mécaniques pour "artistes" et "ouvriers". In *Ingénieur, savant, économiste, pédagogue et parlementaire du Premier au Second Empire*, Dupin, C. (ed.). Presses universitaires de Rennes, Rennes.

Corcy, M.-S., Dufaux, L., Ferriot, D. (2017). Arts et Métiers : polysémie et dynamique d'une collection. *ICOM International Committee for University Museums and Collections*, 9, 71–84.

Cros, B. and Baron, C. (2013). *Toulon, l'arsenal et la ville.* Musée national de la marine.

Dufaux, L. (2017). *L'amphithéâtre, la galerie et le rail : Le Conservatoire des arts et métiers, ses collections et le chemin de fer au XIXe siècle.* Presses universitaires de Rennes, Rennes.

Dupin, C.-F. (1825). *Géométrie et méchanique des arts et métiers et des beaux-arts : cours normal... professé au Conservatoire royal des arts et métiers.* Bachelier, Paris.

Garnier, B. and Kahn, P. (2018). *Éduquer dans et hors l'école : lieux et milieux de formation. XVIIe–XXe siècle.* Presses universitaires de Rennes, Rennes.

Grégoire, H. (1794). Rapport sur l'établissement d'un conservatoire des arts et métiers. Séance du 8 vendémiaire, l'an 3 de la République une et indivisible, imprimé par ordre de la Convention nationale [Online]. Available at: https://gallica.bnf.fr/ ark:/12148/btv1b1 0538212s.

Grivel, R. (1869). *De la guerre maritime avant et depuis les nouvelles inventions. Attaque et défense des côtes et des ports, guerre du large. Étude historique et stratégique.* Maison Arthus Bertrand/Librairie J. Dumaine, Paris.

Guillaume, M.J. (1804). *Procès-verbaux du Comité d'instruction publique de la Convention nationale.* Imprimerie nationale, Paris.

Hayat, S. (2017). Les savoirs et leurs publics : l'exemple du conservatoire des arts et métiers (XIXe–XXe siècles). *Innovations*, 52(1), 139–160.

Jacobi, D. (2017). *Les musées sont-ils condamnés à séduire ? Et autres écrits muséologiques.* MkF, Paris.

Jacobi, D. (ed.) (2018). *Culture et éducation non formelle.* Presses de l'Université du Québec, Quebec.

Laboulaye, C. (1867). Conservatoire des arts et métiers. *Paris-Guide par les principaux écrivains et artistes de la France.* Librairie internationale, Lille, 196–210.

Lembré, S. (2021). Des travaux et des cours. Industrialisation et enseignement industriel en Europe occidentale des années 1830 aux années 1930. *Artefact. Techniques, histoire et sciences humaines*, 13, 335–359 [Online]. Available at: https://doi.org/10.4000/artefact. 6882.

Marchand, P. (2005). L'enseignement technique et professionnel en France 1800-1919. *Techniques et Culture. Revue semestrielle d'anthropologie des techniques*, 45 [Online]. Available at: https://doi.org/10.4000/tc.1343.

Méa, S. (1884). Le Musée de Marine. *Le Journal des Arts*, 1.

Méa, S. (1893). Le Musée de Marine au Louvre. *Le Journal des Arts*, 1.

Musée naval (1828). *Annales maritimes et coloniales, partie non officielle*, Volume 1. Imprimerie Royale, Paris.

Pâris, E. (1872). Le Musée de marine. *Revue maritime et coloniale*, 34, 974–983.

Pâris, E. (1881). Note sur le musée de marine au Louvre. *Bulletin de la Société d'encouragement pour l'industrie nationale*, VIII(90), 2nd series, 266–269.

The Musée de la Corse and the Citadelle de Corte, Experimentation of Museum Mediation in the Service of a Shared Future

5.1. Museum geography in Central Corsica

The Musée de la Corse, also known as the Musée régional d'anthropologie (Regional Museum of Anthropology), opened its doors in Corte on June 21, 1997, in a stimulating intellectual context, benefiting from a strong political support aiming at consolidating this new cultural establishment structuring the scale of the Corsican territory. The quality of the exhibitions and publications produced, as well as the dynamism of its mediation policy, quickly positioned it as a museological reference and patrimonial site within an architecture that is still appreciated today.

As a museum with the "Musée de France" designation, its main mission, since its opening and still today, is the collection, preservation and knowledge of Corsican cultural patrimony. Its contract of objective, renewed in 2019, specifies that it must contribute to "the affirmation of an original culture […] and the enhancement of a patrimony with a strong expectation of authenticity claimed by the public [...] be one of the instruments of overcoming the dialectic 'center/periphery's dialectic".

The base funds that presided over its creation are the pure product of the ethnographic look at the island in the middle of the 20th century in the approach of arts and popular traditions. The museum then enriched its collection by diversifying the types of objects kept: handwritten and printed geography maps, various

Chapter written by Marion TRANNOY VOISIN.

iconographies and ethnomusicological recordings. Today, these make the Musée de la Corse the resource institution in terms of ethnography of Corsica between the end of the 19th century and the 1970s.

Figure 5.1. *Entrance of the Musée de la Corse (© CdC, Musée de la Corse/P. Pierangeli). For a color version of this figure, see www.iste.co.uk/balmon/cultural.zip*

After 25 years of existence, the assessment shows a technical and technological obsolescence of the permanent courses in which are proposed, on the one hand, a glance centered on a rural and mountainous Corsica, far from the contemporary Corsica and its plurality; and on the other hand, a series of trailers of temporary exhibitions "to come", remained in place well after the production of the aforementioned exhibitions.

Moreover, the disciplinary field (anthropology) that presided over the creation of the institution does not always favor a comprehensive response to contemporary issues, or at least an open-ended questioning that would be facilitated by a "societal" approach (Drouguet 2015).

In light of this observation, the museum's scientific and cultural project needs to evolve once again by taking the time to ask the fundamental questions: who are we? What is the purpose of this institution and for whom? These questions are all the more salutary in view of the renewal of museums in general, of the Musée de la Corse landscape, in particular, and more widely in the Mediterranean. It appears very clearly that the current stake of the Musée de la Corse is to be a tool of visibility and recognition of the Corsican society on the Mediterranean, national and international scale, a cultural institution not limited to the patrimony in the classic sense of the term, but opened on the immaterial patrimonies and on the contemporary creation; a place of debate and reflection questioning the porosities of its territory within the world of today; a place where the modalities of construction of knowledge and its diffusion are a subject of reflection to envisage new relations of governance of the establishment.

Moreover, the link to its location – the Citadelle de Corte – becomes significant in this questioning, beyond the simple physical installation of the museum in one of the military barracks of this fortified place. For this reinvention of the museum, the integration of the history of the place in the museography and the weaving of a coherent link between the interior spaces of the museum and the exterior spaces of the citadel are today imperative to find a synergy of site.

5.2. Landscape inscription

So, let us change scale and look at this military construction that houses the Musée de la Corse.

Figure 5.2. *Aerial view of the Citadelle de Corte (© CdC, Musée de la Corse/Hugo Lalisse, studio de l'éphémère). For a color version of this figure, see www.iste.co.uk/balmon/cultural.zip*

The first sight of travelers, whether they come from Bastia, Aléria or Ajaccio, the Citadelle de Corte stands out from the rest of the city and characterizes the landscape and geographical horizon. But it was also, for the French army of the 18th century, an ultimate goal, a utopia to be achieved: to build an impregnable citadel in the center of Corsica, the only one of the seven citadels of the island inland. Christian Corvisier, historian of architecture and fortification, describes it as "the greatest architectural project of French military engineering in Corsica" (Corvisier 2008, p. 41) for this period.

Its construction, a true technical feat, took 350 years, and the citadel, as it exists today, is based on a pre-existing construction: a 15th-century medieval castle, built by a Corsican nobleman, Vincentello d'Istria, proclaimed viceroy of Corsica by the King of Aragon. The Château de Corte – *u Castellu* – was installed in 1419 to dominate the Center Corsica and, with it, the entire island.

Figure 5.3. *Model of the house of Polidoro, Pietro Salvago Della Chiesa, 1541; pen and ink drawing, sepia ink, watercolor, reproduction (inv.169, © Archivio di stato del comune di Genova, Cancellieri di San Giorgio, Gênes). For a color version of this figure, see www.iste.co.uk/balmon/cultural.zip*

Between the 16th and 18th centuries, this castle was taken and retaken by the Genoese, the French and the Corsicans. Then, in 1768, the "provisional" cession of the island of Corsica to France by the Genoese and the defeat of the Corsican patriots at Ponte Novu in 1769 triggered a new transformation for Corte. As soon as they arrived, under the command of the Earl of Vaux (Comte de Vaux), the French troops planned to build, as an extension of the castle, a citadel according to the principles of the bastioned fortification defined by Vauban, the great general commissioner of fortifications under the reign of Louis XIV. The site remained a quasi-permanent construction site from 1769 until 1860, when the citadel took on its final form.

The French army saw Corte as a strategic place. Symbolically, it also allowed it to take power in the Paoline capital. In addition to the construction of the enclosure, a new fortified city of gigantic dimensions was envisaged.

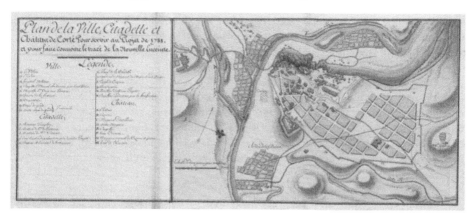

Figure 5.4. *Anonymous, map of the city, citadel, and castle of Corte, to serve the project of 1781 and to make known the layout of the new enclosure – watercolor paper, 1781 (inv.GR 1VH 672 27, © Service historique de la Défense, Vincennes). For a color version of this figure, see www.iste.co.uk/balmon/cultural.zip*

Too expensive and oversized, it was quickly abandoned, and the French Revolution of 1789 put an end to this dream of a new city: Corte had to make do with the fortified upper town, which kept the name of "Citadelle".

No doubt it was utopian to think that a siege army could bring its cannons to Corte. In reality, the citadel was never attacked, and its beautiful defenses were never used. Excessive, the result of the blindness of the military engineers and a technocratic administration, it is still standing, solid and marks the territory, the minds and the hearts. Grandiose in its appearance and its ambition, it is unique in France and in Europe. The Caserne Cervoni of the castle and the entrance gate of the citadel were classified as a site in the national patrimony inventory in 1950–1951. The castle and the ramparts were then classified as Historic Monuments in 1977.

5.3. Change of destination

In 1990, seven years after the departure of the Foreign Legion, Corte ceded the Caserne Serurier (a former military hospital, then a prison) and the adjoining land to the territorial collectivity of Corsica. An international architectural competition was launched in November of the same year to build this new cultural facility in the heart of the historic site. With the installation in 1997 of the Musée de la Corse, in these renovated and enlarged spaces, the cultural dimension and the influence of the site in the city were further reinforced.

The entrance ticket to the museum also allows access to the citadel: a fruitful strategy for the establishment with regard to the landscape attraction of the site which allows it to position itself as the second most visited museum on the island, after the Maison Bonaparte in Ajaccio. But what about its autonomy?

Another building, the Caserne Padoue, which was the center of gravity of the military life of the citadel in the 18th century, has also been the subject of redevelopment projects and progressive occupations since the 1980s: the Fonds régional d'art contemporain (Frac) (Regional Fund for Contemporary Art), the tourist office, and more recently the university, as well as an association, have set up more or less permanent activities there, but without an overall project and without defined governance.

Overall, apart from the buildings dedicated to the museum and the Frac, the citadel suffers from a lack of maintenance and encounters real operating difficulties. The castle, the highest part of the site, has benefited from seven restoration campaigns, undertaken between 1984 and 2009, without the work program being finalized, the vegetation is gaining ground and invading the walls. This feeling of abandonment is strongly criticized by visitors and is coupled with a lack of understanding of the site where the signage is almost absent and where the mediation is limited. Until the end of 2019, an audio guide dating back from the 1990s was used on the sole path to the castle at the exit of the permanent galleries of the museum. "Very beautiful scenery, but no explanation", the museum's guestbook regularly points out.

These gaps between a visitable and metaphorical summit of a complex that is 80% closed to the public, between a place with a very strong symbolic charge for the inhabitants of Corte and the elected officials and this state of architectural wasteland, between the historical defensive function of the citadel and its patrimony attractiveness, led the local authority of Corsica to reflect, in 2019, on a global requalification project for the citadelle de Corte: "Citadella XXI".

Figure 5.5. *Graphic identity Citadella XXI (© CdC, direction du patrimoine/Gaétan Laroche). For a color version of this figure, see www.iste.co.uk/balmon/cultural.zip*

Several pitfalls had to be taken into account immediately in order to reverse the way in which this space was understood: no longer a museum, a Frac, or an office in a citadel, but a citadel including them, on the scale of an urban district. It was thus a question of:

– making decision-makers and citizens aware of the development potential of the site and the economic role that this patrimony area and its visitors could play;

– assuming the economic weight of such a project;

– thinking about a new way of working and to create a viable ecosystem between the different users of the citadel.

It is at this stage of the project that the museum's cultural space will become a mediator in the service of this ambition.

5.4. Patrimonial territory

The year 2019 was favorable to the launch of this requalification program for several reasons. On the one hand, Corte celebrated the 600th anniversary of the castle; it was a question of celebrating the identity of the commune by celebrating its past. On the other hand, the museum had the main lines of its scientific and cultural pre-project validated by the Corsican assembly, which proposed to include the establishment in the dynamics of contemporary museums and to work towards a greater inclusion and involvement of the public in the conception of cultural productions.

That same year, a feasibility study was commissioned from ABCD to outline the new development of the site. These principles and their descriptions are grouped together in a master plan established over 12 years.

This ambitious, evolving and modular project, which aims to welcome as many people as possible and responds to a variety of uses, proposes five operations to enhance the overall value of the site in its geographical, historical and landscape dimensions.

This concomitance will give an unexpected opportunity to share these orientations with the public by making the initial political order of an exhibition retracing the history of the castle and the citadel evolve towards an exhibition exploring the possibilities of its future: *A Citadella di Corti, une citadelle pour horizon* (A Citadella di Corti, a citadel for horizon).

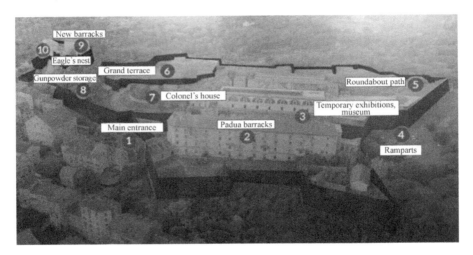

Figure 5.6. *Master Plan Display Panel (© CdC, direction du patrimoine/DR). For a color version of this figure, see www.iste.co.uk/balmon/cultural.zip*

The museographic form chosen for this exhibition is atypical: a digital and graphic show without museum collections, which is combined outdoors with a photographic journey *In terra d'Omi* and a walk through the site of the citadel enriched by augmented reality[1]. An exhibition for young people, *Derrière les murailles* (behind the walls), also enriches the whole by proposing manipulations and short films for schools and families.

---

1 Scenography of Yves Kneusé.

Figure 5.7. *Interior view immersive installation A Citadella di Corti (© CdC, musée de la Corse/DR). For a color version of this figure, see www.iste.co.uk/balmon/cultural.zip*

Figure 5.8. *Exhibition for young people, Derrière les murailles (© CdC, musée de la Corse/DR). For a color version of this figure, see www.iste.co.uk/balmon/cultural.zip*

If these characteristics do not appear to be precisely innovative for contemporary museum models, this project is conceived as a tipping point for the Musée de la Corse and on the island scale. It challenges our classical codes of exhibition design, proposes scenographic or expographic processes that were unusual for us, creates a new relationship with the space and with the site that houses the museum buildings and the various cultural tools present.

This exhibition is to be seen as an operation of restitution of the results of a project in progress. Through it, it is the relationship to the visible, to the direct, and an experience of the body that are favored: the visitor is immersed in grandiose images and a master plan, then is invited to walk the walkway reopened for the occasion, in order to live this experience in reality.

Figure 5.9. *Outdoor photographic installation In terra d'Omi (© CdC, musée de la Corse/DR). For a color version of this figure, see www.iste.co.uk/balmon/cultural.zip*

The collection object is no longer chosen to illustrate a discourse; it is the architectural and landscape patrimony object that builds the expographic discourse.

5.5. Impacts

The objectives, which were pursued through the production of this exhibition, were for the most part achieved: the actual geometry of the citadel and its development potential became clearer to visitors, and also to decision-makers, committing them to put into action the speeches and intentions presented publicly in the exhibition.

This strategic act allowed to go beyond the political colors or a tempting electoral instrumentalization and to put forward a programmatic vision in the service of a territorial strategy for the urban, historical, economic development of the upper town of Corte.

Two years after this presentation – although it has suffered, like many others, from the public health restrictions linked to Covid-19 – the project benefits from a very marked political support and two operations[2] of the five planned in this master plan have already been launched, with the objective of completing these first projects by the end of 2024. These restorations, new facilities and mediation tools should give the citadel the capacity to endure, to create a place for sharing and living where disciplines and views intermingle, a place that will write its future step by step.

Other interventions are currently being discussed[3]. The success of this project should provide guarantees as to the maturity of the overall project. While providing tangible added value to the development of the site, it will constitute a "showcase" for implementing the rest of the plan.

The exhibition, which met the visitors' expectations in terms of the patrimonial presentation of the site that houses the museum, was readapted in mid-2021 in its permanent galleries.

5.6. Example of active and citizen museology

Is this project in line with the evolution of the museum model described in the conclusions of the "Musées du XXIe siècle (Museums of the 21st Century)" mission (Eidelman 2017): an adaptable museum with an inclusive and collaborative vision?

The Citadelle de Corte is not just a museum, but an example of mediation demonstrating that the cultural policy developed there has a museological dimension in which the approaches of conservation, exhibition and dissemination are prevalent. In this respect, this requalification project is in line with citizen museology, which

---

2 The conservation-restoration of the castle; the treatment of the ground of the square to link the elements of the citadel and clarify the reading of the beginning of the visit; the development of the external courses proposing points of interpretation on the history of the place, the landscape, integrating furniture, a new signposting and a development of gardens; the equipment of the large terrace to allow this plateau of the landscape to become a plateau of collective events.

3 In mid-2021, a consultation is underway to create, in the Caserne Padoue, a third place dedicated to bringing together different worlds to carry out actions-projects likely to invite creation, training, mediation and citizen exchanges in which the partners are positioned to "make it together" in the service of the enhancement of the territory and the inhabitants.

consists of ensuring that the social contract structured within it aims to maintain the social link in the city (Meunier and Soulier 2010).

Indeed, this tool for appropriating a project for the territory, which took the form of an exhibition, was aimed at current and future citizens. "Together, we will make this citadel a marvel[4]" to imagine a citadel inhabited and interacting with the city.

The priority audience was therefore the local public rather than an international one, in order to revive a sense of belonging. The challenge was to use patrimony as a development tool and as the subject of a transformation process in which the visitor was positioned as an actor of change alongside the institution and its professionals. The institutional "scientific" discourse had to be able to dialogue with other forms of knowledge that were external to it and had to feed the requalification project and its progress.

The personal experience of visiting the exhibition to discover this indoor/outdoor format allowed a first reappropriation of this patrimony by a more sensitive and personal approach by decentering the reference. The immersive form was surprising in this context and opened the visitors to different possibilities of presentation and approaches of the patrimony. But the visitors were not invited to create and critique the content or its coherence. In the end, the transmission remained rather top-down, and only the reactions on social networks to the communication campaign related to the project were real spaces of expression for our audiences.

So, this project has not yet reached this co-constructed form, but that remains on the horizon. Also, the new steering committees set up for the following operations mix institutions and different territorial actors (university, associations, companies, etc.) to better define their sense of place. To do this, we opt for shared prefigurations on a humble and reduced scale of certain elements of the future work sites (shared gardens, travelling exhibitions, etc.). A "trial and error" methodology to retain what will be efficient, so that this patrimony has a real place in the daily life of all.

The coming years will be devoted to the metamorphosis of this historic site into a laboratory to accompany contemporary Corsican society: *cusì bellu sarà stu locu*[5]! Will the Citadelle de Corte become an agora for the city of Corte and Central Corsica, a historical and cultural place where knowledge and the relationship to patrimony are moved? The movement is underway, the future will tell us.

---

4 Extract from the concluding text of the temporary exhibition *A Citadella di Corti*.

5 "How beautiful this place will be!" the closing words of the exhibition, inviting the visitor to continue the visit to the new outdoor route to (re)discover the citadel.

5.7. References

Corvisier, C. (2008). Histoire naturelle et culturelle de la Corse. *Stantari*, 12, 41–44.

Drouguet, N. (2015). *Le Musée de société : de l'exposition de folklore aux enjeux contemporains*. Armand Colin, Paris.

Eidelman, J. (2017). Inventer des musées pour demain. Report, La Documentation française.

Giorgetti, G. and Trannoy, M. (2019). Extraits de textes, dans le cadre de l'exposition temporaire. In *Exposition : A citadella di Corti – Une citadelle pour horizon*. Musée de la Corse, Corse.

Meunier, A. and Soulier, V. (2010). Préfiguration du concept de muséologie citoyenne. In *Histoire, musées et éducation à la citoyenneté*, Cardin, J.-F., Meunier, A., Éthier, M.-A. (eds). MultiMondes, Montreal.

6

Institutionalization of Passion Instead of Competence

> Stupidity is a structure of thought as such: it is not a way of being wrong, it properly expresses the nonsense in thought. Stupidity is not an error, but a fabric of errors. One knows imbecilic thoughts, imbecilic speeches, which are made entirely of truths; but these truths are low, are those of a low, heavy, and leaden soul (Deleuze 1962, p. 120).

6.1. Introduction: leave your pupils to a guide

6.1.1. *Guides' response to teachers' demands*

The world of patrimony and that of school education have different relationships to knowledge, but they are brought together during school visits. The pupils are then entrusted to a guide who offers a mediation adapted to the museum space. The visitor enters into a relationship with the object through the guide, while the pupil in the classroom receives knowledge from the teacher that they must learn. If the pupils thus escape their teachers during the visit, it is, however, inscribed in the dynamics of the course. The space–time of this visit is not in fact a meeting between the two practices. The guides are the providers of the teachers: they must adapt their practices to meet a particular demand. For freelance guides or a tourist office, building loyalty is essential so that teachers choose to return with other classes in subsequent years: their income depends on it, especially when school visits represent a significant part of their activity. From a business point of view, proof of the quality of their services is given by the loyalty of the teachers.

Chapter written by Nathanaël WADBLED.

The guides and the teachers are therefore not on an equal footing, and are in a neutral space where each can assert their conception of a visit to a historic site. The teachers are in a position of power: their classes are not guests of the museum space who would bend to its rules. The visit remains in school time under the supervision of the history teacher. They do not rely on the way the guides transmit history but expect them to play the school history game. From their point of view, the school space is set in motion to integrate the museum space and the guides' discourse. If the place is qualified by the visitors' experience of it and not just by its physical characteristics, then it is an extracurricular, not a para-patrimonial space–time: the patrimonial space is integrated into the school setting rather than hosting it. It is not a "partnership" (Le Marec 1998), but a schooling of the patrimonial space[1]: the visit is not a tool for knowledge, but an educational outing, because it is integrated into the teachers' pedagogical logic (Zafeirakou 1998; Cohen 2002; Meunier 2008).

This raises the question of the relationship between teachers and coaches. Some guides do not see their role as transmitting historical knowledge; for others, however, it is. They then develop strategies to do so while respecting the figure of the history teacher as the only legitimate person to give a historical word.

6.1.2. *Method and fieldwork: participant observation in a tourist office*

In the continuity of the phenomenological approach that we follow in our research, we seek to make explicit the meaning that the actors give to their experience, independently of an objective description of the situation characterizing a social practice. To do this, however, we do not use the method of formal comprehensive interviews. The data were collected during an "observant participation" (Emerson 2003; Soulé 2007), during which we worked as a guide/lecturer trainee in a tourist office organizing tours on the traces of a battlefield. This method implies living the visit truly among them – rather than observing an activity from the outside and conducting interviews with the actors of a visit in which we did not participate.

The first consequence is legal. Although researchers often present themselves as such to the actors in their field, this was not the case for us. The people concerned have not given their consent to be part of a study and we do not disclose their identity. The institution will be designated as the tourist office of a small town near a World War I battlefield on French soil, one of whose main activities is to show it to schoolchildren who have studied the event in their history classes. It is composed of a director and guides whom we will call Jocasta, Ismene and Tiresias.

---

1 We refer to museums, memorials and historic sites as "patrimonial spaces".

Methodologically, the data collected is therefore the result of non-formal interactions with these people and of our professional experience. Our position as a trainee who had to learn the profession of guiding by modeling it on professionals also allowed us to take the time to observe their practices and to discuss their conception of the profession with them in greater detail, while receiving their advice. Such professional interactions are different from those involved in a formal interview, and the results are therefore different. In particular, this method makes it possible to circumvent an important bias in formal interviews: by revealing themselves, visitors are in effect pushed to assume what they say. Even though the interviewer is non-judgmental and benevolent, the participants are committed to what they say and may tend to recompose their memories according to the experience they would have liked to have had, according to the image they have of themselves or the image they want to give of themselves.

We then report on how we perceived guiding practices by articulating them with contextual observations. They appear to us as the result of interactions with our colleagues. The data are therefore not an objective collection of what they say or do from an external point of view. The account of our own experience is then equivalent to that of an actor participating in a comprehensive interview. We are thus in the tradition of an anthropology whose work claims to be a theoretically expressed testimony (Tedlock 1991; Augé and Colleyn 2009), which is as distinct from an external description based on participant observation as it is from novel writing that provides a subjective account. Observational participation thus imposes the assumption of our own judgments as part of the data – and not as elements that might interfere with our interpretations (Pfefferkorn 2014). The description of the field appears as already being an interpretation.

Epistemologically, then, the observations made only claim to account for this experience. They constitute a qualitative case study. The case is defined not only objectively in relation to the extension of the field, but also by the particular commitment of the researcher. Its value is that of an "exceptional normal" (Ginzburg and Poni 1991): a singular journey that shows a type of possible experience that is neither typical nor representative. It is, on the contrary, valid as a theoretical proposition within the framework of an analytical generalization (Wadbled 2016b): The generalization is not assumed but proposed as a hypothesis. The definition of pupil's guidance on a battlefield is then possible from the way it is constituted on a multitude of sites – not a social practice that actors reinvest.

These methodological and epistemological choices have an impact on the form of the writing. Rather than systematically analyzing the characteristics of this practice, we will seek to describe the context in which each guide finds themself in the case observed. The practice of each guide is a possibility opened by this context. Each element of this context constitutes a tensor, which has its own stakes, and which is transformed by entering into interaction with the next. Nodes of a network of interaction are thus formed, in which each guide positions themself (Latour 2006). Each one functions as a reference point offering "instructions" (Garfinkel 2001, p. 131) or "directions for use" (Yin 2013) that social actors use to orient themselves. They construct their practice according to the way they understand them and the meaning they give them. We are trying to transcribe this unstable equilibrium where each actor does as they can according to their convictions and that all seek to solidify by displaying a certainty of doing well. Organizing this study thematically would have meant giving up on giving an account of this movement and acting as if the actors were caught up in institutions or in social fields characterizing distinct and well-established spheres of activity. It would then have been possible to identify them and to characterize the way they interact, by integrating the actors into their functioning through various modes of socialization. However, this is not the experiment in which we participated.

We therefore reproduce the journey that we took in these complex spaces: the successive constitution of the different nodes organizing the space of this guided tour according to the tensions that are applied to it. This writing gives an account of the reflexive movement of observant participation where the researcher has no general point of view on the situation and discovers it like the actors. It is a question of transcribing as best as possible the questions, expectations, surprises and resolutions. In the first section, we will describe the expectations of teachers who have requirements that school the historical place and how a certain guiding practice based on the relationship to the place can respond to them. In the second section, we will show how guides who care to convey historical information do so by producing a non-historical discourse about history. In the third section, we will present the way in which the guides legitimize their posture epistemologically and construct the legitimacy of non-scientific knowledge. They thus participate, without being aware of it, in a practice of devaluation of the scientific method and encourage credulity.

6.2. Competence of the guides in addition to that of the historians

6.2.1. *Extracurricular practice of a patrimonial space*

The teachers who use the services of the tourist office guides to accompany their day see the visit as a complement to the course. They use the services of the tourist office with a view to schooling of the historic site. It is a matter of giving something concrete and embodying something that the pupils know. On the spot, they perceive the authentic traces. The visit should develop the pupils' interest in history by presenting them with anecdotes that make the events learned in class real. If the visit contributes to the intellectual and visual training of the pupils, it is because they must relate what they perceive to the knowledge they have received in class.

Historical information is illustrated or associated with a concrete experience (Wadbled 2016a, 2018a). The visit then appears similar to document work done in class (Borne 2004; Granier and Picot 2004; Tutiaux-Guillon 2008).

The function of the visit is therefore not to transmit historical knowledge, which is the prerogative of classroom teachers. The teachers do not attribute to the visit any specific pedagogical vocation. They do not deny that a patrimonial space can transmit a representation of history; however, this is not what they expect from a school visit. The museum space is not a substitute or redundant device for the classroom. Visitors arrive with the necessary knowledge and make sense of their experience through the course.

This difference between classroom learning and the visit is not, therefore, that between two epistemologically equivalent moments that bring two complementary relationships to history. The school transmission has a greater value marked by the requirement of serious cognitive attention. The school institution shows itself to be the serious space of knowledge: the relationship to historical traces during the visit is sensory and is associated with emotions (Casey 2003). Even though it is not a pure moment of entertainment, in the context of a learning society, this sensory dimension is associated with a recreational space (Wadbled 2015). This idea is reinforced by the fact that pupils do not behave as they do in class and show contentment in going away with their peers for the day.

If the teachers do not express it explicitly, it appears in the way they recognize the emotional dimension of the visit while reminding us that it has no place in the classroom. There is a difference between the teachers' academic transmission and the guides' extracurricular transmission, where what is normally associated with entertainment can be tolerated alongside the seriousness of knowledge transmission (Iborra-Sanchez 1999). Insofar as historical transmission is provided in class, the presence of emotions during the visit does not call into question the seriousness of historical transmission. Emotion is particularly associated with the attestation function of the visit. Authenticity and presence are things that are felt not only physically, but also emotionally. For teachers, this does not trivialize knowledge, because it is a different place from historical learning, the two do not mix and take place in two clearly defined and clearly separate time–spaces: the classroom and the visit. Therefore, the visit cannot be a learning moment, because it is not in the classroom space. Teachers do not mention the possibility of *edutainment* practice (Minty 1994; Colley et al. 2002; Hooper-Greenhill 2007) where learning occurs in a space perceived as playful.

6.2.2. *Guiding to make people see and understand*

The practice of one of the guides, Jocasta, meets the expectations of the teachers. Her visit consists of presenting the traces of the event and the landscapes without having the ambition to transmit historical knowledge. She wants to make it real by being on the spot. Visitors are invited to imagine, from their experience, traces of the war rather than to understand something reflexively (Wadbled 2018b). Imagination then involves transposing what is perceived into the past to picture how it was. Appearance and mood are developed from the given information that both builds a setting from the landscape and places the described soldiers within it. Jocasta thus offers a visit anchored in the site visited. She assumes to show history in a different way, leaving the transmission of information to the teachers during their classes. She herself reminds the pupils that they have learned information in class that they can use in their perception of the landscape and material traces. To do this, she leaves a lot of time where she does not speak and walks slowly between two stopping points of the visit. The visitors can thus be in a sensitive relationship with what surrounds them and be attentive to the effect on them. They are in an environment that they experience without being constantly solicited by information that only addresses their intellect.

Jocasta's visit embodies a conception of guidance that is not to make information explicit. If the cultural mediators deliver knowledge and share their knowledge (Jacobi and Meunier 1999), the guide invites the visitors to perceive (Gellereau 2005). The tour experience thus has an immediately sensitive dimension (Edwards et al. 2006; Auzas and Van Troi 2010; Dudley 2012): rather than what is understood reflexively or intellectually, the focus is then on sensory presence, as well as the emotional and imaginative charge associated with material elements and spaces. There is a continuity between the material form of the patrimonial writing of the offered story and the sensitive form of the message received. The visitors invest in their own subjectivity, instead of receiving knowledge in a reflexive form. They make the sensitive experience of it.

In this way, they can learn something about this war and battle. By perceiving and imagining, visitors can get a sense of how it was (Wadbled 2018c). From their perception, they understand something and develop an idea of what it was like. It is the effect of the experience of the site, not the observation of given information. Thus, the relationship of the traces is just the complement of the course that attests to knowledge. The perception and the reflection feed each other. What has been learned allows the visitors to organize their representation of the site. It is thus homogeneous with the historical knowledge learned in class. The two are superimposed. The visit thus allows an experience of this knowledge. Jocasta's practice is a form of scientific popularization (Schiele 2001; Raichvarg 2008).

Historical information is taken from the scientific field in order to be reformulated in a mass media perspective.

Rather than giving historical information to be remembered, the role of the guide is to accompany and orient the visitors' perception in this sense. They guarantee this homogeneity between their perceptive representation and historical knowledge. The description of the landscapes cannot directly show the ideas that the visitors remember or realize. They are the traces of events, and it is these events that must be described when reading the landscape. The guide designates them and shows how to understand them in the most accurate way. The visit is thus problematized. It follows a narrative that is not that of the battle, but that of the development of a historically accurate representation of the battle. The subject is organized, and these moments are arranged by leaving time to assimilate it, to find it in the landscape, and to reinvest it in the form of mental images.

6.3. Passing an anti-scientific discourse on history

6.3.1. *Replacing the historical discourse with another*

Some guides do not give up telling something of the story. This is the case with Ismene and Tiresias. This is more generally in line with the state of mind transmitted during the guide-lecturer training. The guides perceive themselves as legitimate to teach something to the pupil visitors. They are thus part of the legacy of a claim on patrimonial spaces, because these institutions are no longer recognized as places of knowledge production and teaching (Conn 2000). This claim is apparent in the way guides assert the seriousness of their practice and refuse to see the visit confined to a devalued sensitive experience alongside serious academic learning. If it has the same dignity as school teaching, the visit must demand a similar attention that is not distracted by a sensible experience. Indeed, it cannot accommodate what might be associated with an entertainment practice. If visitors have an emotional response, it must be independent of what these guide companions transmit, and above all, it should not disturb what the teacher has previously taught the pupils.

This claim corresponds in reality to games of power and institutional recognition based on a valorization of the historical approach learned in books in relation to a patrimonial history perceived in places. The guides must accept the institutional domination of the school as the sole holder of historical knowledge in order to keep their clients. At the same time, they want to assert their role as mediators of history. An unstable balance between representatives of two institutions seeking to assert their right is only possible if neither has power over the other. This is not the case when teachers may not return.

To resolve this situation, they need to come up with something that is acceptable to the teachers. Guides need to be adaptable and resilient. Without resisting or accepting the schooling of their space, Ismene and Tiresias give a lot of information. Ismene says she wants to share a knowledge of history and Tiresias says he wants to bring it to life with anecdotes. The essential thing, for them, is thus not the report to the material traces. The tour experience offered by Ismene is above all intellectual. She gives a lot of factual information on the course of the battles from an external point of view, which describes them globally. On his side, Tiresias tells moments of the battle or the aftermath of the war from the point of view of the soldiers as if he were presenting testimonies. He gives many details.

In order to provide this information while respecting the position of teachers as the sole repositories of historical knowledge, the guides do not recognize themselves as historians, although they claim to have knowledge of history. They develop an anti-historian discourse and change the register. It is anti-historian and not non-historian, insofar as it does not place itself next to history, as a non-scientific discourse recognizing the field of science next to its own. This is what Jocasta does, for example: she does not pretend to be a historian and offers another experience that would make it possible to grasp something of an event, while leaving it to history or archaeology to explain it and to determine what really happened. It does something other than science, without replacing it or competing with it.

The representation of the war that Ismene and Tiresias transmit shows that it owes nothing to scientific history, because it is not problematized as in a historical discourse. The teachers therefore do not see themselves as competing with the guides. Their discourse does not take the form of an explanatory narrative of history (Ricoeur 1983, pp. 265–290). The different sites visited are not associated thematically with issues or chronologically with moments that would allow us to understand the issues of this war. The guides describe what happened on each site visited without drawing on a guiding idea that would be what the visitors should retain. This approach is claimed by the director of the tourist office who considers that the guides' job is simply to give information about the battle, and not to problematize it. This situation is reflected in the general level of the visit, which is not composed as a narrative integrating these different moments. If the order of the spaces visited depends on the quickest route to take by bus, none of the guides takes up this imposed situation in order to give it meaning. The passage from one site to another does not mean the passage from one idea or experience to another according to a certain logic. They are not put in perspective with each other as a whole.

In the case of Ismene, the visit is a succession of subjects approached: tactics, uniforms, the missing, without links between them and without their articulation allowing a synthetic vision of the war. It is a juxtaposition of moments that are not articulated between them and do not compose a narrative – neither chronological nor thematic. In the case of Tiresias, the information is given in disorder, and it is not even possible to identify different moments: each place is an opportunity to talk about all the dimensions of the battle. Tiresias gives the impression that he talks about things when he thinks about them without really having organized his tour. This produces the impression that he is giving more information, because he returns several times to the same elements.

6.3.2. Misunderstanding with teachers

Thus, proposing an alternative discourse to history, which presents itself as equally legitimate, goes with its distancing from the site. Ismene and Tiresias offer a tour that could be done in the same way off-site, in a conference room. They take up the opposition between cognitive attention and sensitive experience to focus on the former. The essential thing is not the presence on the site, which makes it possible to understand the event thanks to an interpretation of the guides. They consider things and landscapes as teachers do: from the documents that attest to knowledge transmitted elsewhere, which is the essential thing to retain. The material elements are there only to illustrate their remarks. Moreover, Ismene and Tiresias do not leave the visitors the time to perceive their physical environment. The movements are fast and, as soon as the group is static, the guides speak by giving information more than by showing the site.

The teachers can live with this, as the pupils still walk through the sites. They are, however, not really paying attention to the relationship they are forming. They just make sure that they do not behave inappropriately. So, there is also a misunderstanding here. They are not aware that by accepting that the guides transmit their anti-historical knowledge, the pupils are not invited to perceive the traces. They are diverted from what constitutes for the teachers the essential goal of the visit. This misunderstanding, which allows the teachers to be satisfied with their visit, is made possible by the attitude of the visiting pupils: in reality, they do not really listen to what Ismene and Tiresias are saying and look at where they are. They take advantage of the time when they are talking to look at the traces. They take a position of polite inattention: facing the guides with an attitude of attention, they are attentive to what they see around the guides, not to what they say[2]. The misunderstanding thus seems to be reversed: the guides believe that the visitors are interested in what they say, whereas it is not the case.

---

2 In order to characterize the visitors' experience precisely, it would be necessary to conduct a comprehensive survey among them. This would make it possible to observe their positioning in relation to their companions.

6.4. Institutionalization of passion instead of competence

6.4.1. *Passion as the praxis of history*

Insofar as the director of the tourist office advocates the practices of Ismene and Tiresias, they are the official position of the institution. She even develops an epistemological legitimacy for them, in order to show that this anti-historical way of telling history is superior to that of historians. Ismene and Tiresias share this epistemology, because it supports their practice. It is an existential stake that forms the basis of their profession as guide-lecturer. By opposing the approach of vulgarization, it is thus about a conception that is quite different from that of Jocasta.

Ismene and Tiresias are in fact not satisfied with mobilizing their status of guide-lecturer to assert their right to transmit something of the story, nor with pragmatic legitimacy (Suchman 1995). The quality of the visit is, from this point of view, considered in relation to the interests of the organization. It is relevant if it achieves the objectives of the tourist office. As an organization whose mission is to promote a territory marked by war, it must attract the public and participate in the duty of remembrance. These two missions are perfectly fulfilled. The director notes that, on the one hand, the teachers are loyal, as they come back year after year; and on the other hand, knowledge of the battle is disseminated.

The guides want to add epistemological legitimacy. They claim to produce a discourse that has the same value as that of historians. It is thus the demand for recognition of an alternative discourse to the scientific one. If the writing and the transmission of the history practiced by the historians are based on a scientific praxis and the knowledge of the historiography, those of the guides result from their passion for the history.

The director says that the quality she expects from her guides is a passion for history. She herself sets the example, claiming to have no interest in historiography. She developed the tour without any particular expertise as a historian or science popularizer. She often recalls that she had to lead tours immediately without any training or preparation. She therefore does not recognize any particular competence conferred by history studies, which she considers useless for talking about history. Historical competence is not necessary.

Passion allows us to have a concrete relationship with the event. It is not constrained by reflexivity and all the procedures that make history a science. The guides are thus part of a perspective that is that of natural memory, as opposed to the artificiality of scientific history (Nora 1997). Passion guarantees the authenticity of what is said, as well as historical work, because it signifies an intimate and visceral interest in the event, which is only one subject of study among others for historians.

The guides claim that their distancing from historiography allows them to think critically by engaging in an unmediated personal relationship to history.

As enthusiasts, Ismene and Tiresias are confident that they have the right view. They do not perceive their discourse as a point of view, but as the transmission of historical truth. The director goes in this direction, by insisting on the passionate character of the guides who work with their guts and oppose them with a reflexive conception of the profession, which would take height and would wonder about what there is to transmit.

6.4.2. *Critical thinking as respect for tradition*

The passion is presented as not being able to lead to any other discourse than that of the director. In fact, it is the tour that she had developed that is always carried out. She passed it on to the other guides. Jocasta and Ismene are young and learned the job with her. Tiresias is a retired person who had not guided before doing it for the tourist office. The memory tour was already set up before they arrived, and the director showed them how to do it. The transmission is what allows them to guide.

There is only one possible representation of the battle, because the natural truth of the event appears once the artificiality of historical practice is removed. As passion gives direct, immediate and visceral access to the event, it is not artificialized by the work of the historian. Not only is it not necessary to know the recent works of specialist historians, because it is possible for each passionate person to have a direct relationship with the sources, but also they would bring a complexity and a counterproductive reflection. Compared to tradition, it is an external knowledge and a reflexive approach that constantly introduces new questions or new points of view. Passion allows for a better understanding, in a simple way, of what happened, and this simplicity has the value of evidence.

Passionate guides give factual information that they immediately take from testimonies or repeat well-known things without the need for historiography or the work of criticizing the sources of historians. The event is observed from a direct relationship with the sources rather than produced by a scientific practice as historians do. The guides thus have a historicist conception of their discourse, as opposed to its historicization (Certeau 1975; Koselleck 1990; Hartog 2005). They feel that they are simply stating the truth about what happened. The discourse of the passionate is thus homogeneous. Any other vision is considered to be the result of a lack of passion betrayed by an interest in historiography. The homogeneity of the history of the enthusiasts is thus a sign of its value, although it is also a sign of its anti-scientific nature.

The guides thus have above all a traditional legitimacy that rests on the certainty that one must repeat what is usually done. They therefore do not have to reflect on their practice and possibly make it evolve – unlike historians who have to grapple with an ever-changing historiography that is always asking new questions. To be passionate, then, means to be subservient to tradition (Weber 2002). The practice of critical thinking as a personal experience detached from the mediation imposed by science is resolved in a submission to tradition.

The passionate guides thus hold the coherence of their discourse as a statement of historical reality, as they do not recognize this coherence as being a construction and a form of writing. In so doing, they confuse historical knowledge, the history of memory and memory (Lowenthal 1998). If the information given is not derived from a knowledge of historians' works, it is indeed based on a representation corresponding to a certain tradition. For example, the soldiers are presented as victims, and not as executioners of their adversaries in a battle that makes sense to them. The guides thus offer a retrospective vision, which is the one constructed by the veterans after the war, and which does not reflect their state of mind at the time of the fighting. The difference between the meaning the soldiers gave to the war while they were living it, the meaning they gave to it afterwards and the meaning it has today is not made explicit and even less problematized to highlight its evolution. Tiresias also takes up the ambition of political actors to give memory tourism the vocation of promoting peace rather than transmitting history. The places of history are thus not the occasion to evoke the different meanings given to war and the difference between the perception that the soldiers had of it, that which was elaborated in the immediate post-war period and that which we have today.

6.4.3. *An organization that favors an anti-historical practice*

This epistemology is supported by the institution's organization. It is not simply an assertion, but also both the foundation and the result of a working method. It is inseparable from it, because it supports and reproduces it. The organization is indeed managed in a paternalistic way (Likert 1967). The director assumes both verticality and connivance with her employees and does not pose as an authority figure based on her status or competence as a historian. Her power depends on the recognition of her tour as the only one possible. Management mechanisms ensure this reproduction.

Work habits prohibit any substantive discussion of the tour. There is no joint work or feedback that could encourage reflexivity. Everyone is in a direct vertical relationship with the director. As there is no horizontal communication between the guides, they do not discuss together the differences between their approaches or how to improve their own practice by comparing it with that of others. As for the relationship with the director, it is not established. It does not conduct a professional interview on the objectives and difficulties encountered by the guides. This is not necessary, because everyone can come and talk to her whenever they want. Any challenge would therefore imply a personal commitment, not just a professional one.

The atmosphere is indeed that of a group of friends, which has the effect, paradoxical in appearance, of both a lack of authority and a hold, in the sense that nobody contradicts the director on principle. The guides cannot deviate from what they expect, on pain of losing their affection and consideration. Moreover, as all the guides accept this situation, any deviation is identified as a break in the quasi-family ties. When everyone respects tradition, the director benevolently accompanies the guides who work for her. There is therefore no discussion possible on the latter. To question it would mean excluding oneself from the organization and betraying it. This social and affective pressure leads to the daily distancing of any historiographic claim. It supports the epistemological justification of the passion for history: the conviction of doing the right thing is reinforced by a daily human experience. If guides did otherwise, the consequence would not only be an epistemological critique, but also a degradation of their working conditions. Thus, there can be no settled epistemological controversies in a discussion of what is most relevant. This possibility is neutralized by the functioning of the organization, which poses a constant threat to employees. It is therefore submission, not competence, that justifies the place of guides in the organization.

Because this is not what justifies their positions, there is no possibility for a new guide to put forward their competence and thus to question that of the director and the guides in place. The consequence is that the question of competence never arises: the anti-historical discourse of the enthusiasts cannot be questioned. The guides must constantly show their interest in history and can only say so with the semantic field of passion. Each of them gives themself up and does so with imposed categories. Everyone recognizes themselves and others as passionate. Discussions about history thus play the role of devices of subjectivation, where each one admits to being part of the organization. Almost daily (Foucault 1976), there is a seemingly informal discussion about the relationship to history that plays this role. However, in a paternalistic organization, informal time–spaces are integrated into its functioning, as there are no clearly identified formal time–spaces, insofar as, in a family atmosphere, we are permanently a member of the family. Moreover, the frequency of these moments and the attention paid to them by the actors indicate their importance. Not participating in them excludes as much as not respecting the tradition.

If Jocasta does not take up the anti-historical discourse carried by the institution during her visits, she shows great communicative intelligence. She states her practice in a way that can be understood as a manifestation of passion, although this is not what she means. She then justifies her different position by a different sensibility – not by a respect for historical work. She is not a passionate person, but the other members of the tourist office may believe it, because she does not deny it. She does not emphasize her skills as a guide. If she considers that she is just doing her job and doing it well, she pretends to have an extra investment. At this level too, there is a misunderstanding that allows her to include herself in the group of guides.

6.5. Conclusion: visiting a place of history in an age of mistrust of science

When the guides meet the expectations of the teachers, they respect the scientific discourse. They renounce transmitting historical knowledge and assume to do something else. Links are then established between the academic form of knowledge and a more informal form. They allow an encounter, if not always a relationship. The two worlds at least overlap. By meeting each other, the actors get to know each other and understand each other's requirements. Although misunderstandings allow this meeting to take place, it does take place. Communication is engaged.

It is what is made impossible by the guides defending an anti-historical discourse that claims to replace the historical one. They elaborate another scientific discourse that they claim to be as legitimate as the historical one and thus cut the links. The guides then participate in a devaluation of science (Bronner 2013). They take up a rhetoric that is that of the negationist discourse and, in a general way, of an attitude of distrust towards science (Ricœur 2000, p. 106; Rousso 2016). In this case, there is no point in basing the content of the visit on knowledge of the work of historians. A scientific discourse and an anti-scientific discourse are put on the same level.

Because the transmission of information in a visit is not the main goal for the teachers, they settle for a discourse on history that does not have a historical form. Moreover, when a teacher considers that the historical information given by the guides during the visit is not relevant, they are satisfied with the visit, because that is not the essential goal. They do not dwell on the lack of problematization and the discrepancies with recent historiography. The issue lies elsewhere: the pupils go through the place and the guides respect the prerogative of the teachers. As they do not really have time to perceive the site, visitors are not likely to learn anything about the battle that they would not have learned in class. Because the guides do not communicate any historical knowledge to them, they also do not learn anything more. The teachers are therefore satisfied. They are loyal to the tourist office and come back regularly, even every year, even though other institutions offer similar programs[3].

They make the mistake of thinking that accepting anti-science discourse is unimportant because the pupils have had a history lesson – especially as what the guides say is not historically false. This is actually trivializing this mode of discourse. The visit takes place as if the history teachers recognize the form and effects of this discourse. They are in the position of a scientist who would let someone say that the Earth is flat or that vaccines are dangerous, while looking down on the other person. But this attitude legitimizes it. The guides say, "I am not a historian, but we know that." This is the very rhetorical form of anti-science. Once an anti-science discourse is legitimized because it does not say anything false, others can use it to say false things. Getting into the habit of accepting this discourse in a historical place has the consequence of blurring the difference between a history based on scientific knowledge and a history based on beliefs and independently of scientific results.

This is what the Creation Museum in Petersburg (Kentucky, USA), for example, is playing with, presenting a creationist history of the Earth in a patrimonial space set up as a science museum. Blurring the difference means that the theory of evolution that we might see in a science museum is equated with the creationist hypothesis (Duncan 2009). The developing habit is also what makes it credible for the French government to say that the Chernobyl cloud stopped at the border (Micoulaut 2006) or that vaccines are more dangerous than smoking cigarettes (Dib et al. 2021). It does not matter that these claims are historically and biologically false from a scientific point of view. They are asserted by tradition, which everyone believes they can directly observe, through a confirmation bias that makes people interpret events from a prior, unquestioned representation that seems obvious to common sense (Bronner 2013). While it may be legitimate for non-scientific institutions to propose a discourse on history alongside the scientific discourse, credulity is characterized when it claims to replace it.

6.6. References

Augé, M. and Colleyn, J.-P. (2009). Le terrain. *Anthropologie*. Presses universitaires de France, Paris.

Auzas, V. and Van Troi, T. (2010). *Patrimoines sensible : mots, espaces, pratiques*. Presses de l'université de Laval, Quebec.

---

3 Their historical relevance should be assessed to observe the relative importance of this dimension for teachers.

Borne, D. (2002). Apprendre l'histoire et la géographie, inventaire critique. *Actes du colloque*, Paris, 12–14 December.

Bronner, G. (2013). *La Démocratie des crédules*. Presses universitaires de France, Paris.

Casey, V. (2003). The museum effect: Gazing from objects to performance. The Contemporary Cultural-History Museums, Archives and Museum Informatics, Europe: Cultural Institutions and Digital Technologies. École du Louvre, Paris, September.

de Certeau, M. (1975). *L'écriture de l'histoire*. Gallimard, Paris.

Cohen, C. (2002). *Quand l'enfant devient visiteur : une nouvelle approche du partenariat école/musée*. L'Harmattan, Paris.

Colley, H., Hodkinson, P., Malcom, J. (2002). Non-formal learning: Mapping the conceptual terrain. Report, Infed, 1–62.

Conn, S. (2000). *Museums and American Intellectual Life, 1876–1926*. University of Chicago Press, Chicago.

Deleuze, G. (1962). *Nietzsche et la Philosophie*. Presses universitaires de France, Paris.

Dib, F., Mayaud, P., Chauvin, P., Launay, O. (2021). Online mis/disinformation and vaccine hesitancy in the era of COVID-19: Why we need an eHealth literacy revolution. *Human Vaccines & Immunotherapeutics*, 18(1), 1–3.

Dudley, S. (2012). *Museum Objects. Experiencing the Properties of Things*. Routledge, London.

Duncan, J.A. (2009). Faith displayed as science: The role of the "creation museum" in the modern American creationist movement. PhD Thesis, Harvard University, Cambridge.

Edwards, E., Gosden, C., Phillips, B., Ruth, B. (eds) (2006). *Sensible Objects. Colonialism, Museums and Material Culture*. Berg, Oxford.

Emerson, R. (2003). Le travail de terrain comme activité d'observation. Perspectives ethnométhodologistes et interactionnistes. In *L'enquête de terrain*, Céfaï, D. (ed.). La Découverte/MAUSS, Paris.

Foucault, M. (1976). *La volonté de savoir*. Gallimard, Paris.

Garfinkel, H. (2001). Le programme de l'ethnométhodologie. In *L'Ethnométhodologie. Une sociologie radicale*, Ogien, R., Quéré, L., de Fornel, M. (eds). La Découverte, Paris.

Gellereau, M. (2005). *Les mises en scènes de la visite guidée, communication et médiation*. L'Harmattan, Paris.

Ginzburg, C. and Poni, C. (1981). La micro-histoire. *Le Débat*, 17, 133–136.

Granier, G. and Picot, F. (2004). La place des documents dans l'enseignement de l'histoire et de la géographie. In *Apprendre l'histoire et la géographie à l'école*, Hagnerelle, M. (ed.). Canopé-CRDP de Versailles, Versailles.

Hartog, F. (2005). *Régimes d'historicité. Présentisme et expériences du temps*. Gallimard, Paris.

Hooper-Greenhill, E. (2007). *Museums and Education. Purpose, Pedagogy, Performance.* Routledge, London.

Iborra-Sanchez, C. (1999). Le partenariat culturel dans la format on : évidence ou défi. In *Entre écoles et musée. Le partenariat culturel d'éducation*, Buffet, F. (ed.). Presses universitaires de Lyon, Lyon.

Jacobi, D. and Meunier, A. (1999). L'interprétation : variations sur le thème du patrimoine. *La Lettre de l'OCIM*, 61.

Koselleck, R. (1990). *Le Futur passé.* École des hautes études en sciences sociales, Paris.

Latour, B. (2006). *Changer de société, refaire de la sociologie.* La Découverte, Paris.

Le Marec, J. (1998). Repenser la relation du musée à son public. In *La Révolution de la muséologie des sciences*, Schiele, B. (ed.). Presses universitaires de Lyon, Lyon.

Likert, R. (1967). *The Human Organization: Its Management and Value.* McGraw-Hill, New York.

Löwenthal, D. (1998). *Possessed by the Past. The Patrimony Crusade and the Spoils of History.* Cambridge University Press, Cambridge.

Meunier, A. (2008). *La recherche en éducation muséale : actions et perspectives.* Éditions MultiMondes, Quebec.

Micoulaut, R. (2006). *Tchernobyl : l'histoire d'une désinformation.* L'Harmattan, Paris.

Miles, M. and Huberman, M. (1991). *Analyse des données qualitatives.* De Boeck, Louvain-la-Neuve.

Minty, A. (1994). That's edutainment. *Museum News*, 73(6), 33–36.

Nora, P. (ed.) (1997). Entre mémoire et histoire. la problématique des lieux. In *Les lieux de mémoire*, volume 1. Gallimard, Paris,.

Pfefferkorn, R. (2014). L'impossible neutralité axiologique *Wertfreiheit* et engagement dans les sciences sociales. *Raison présente*, 191, 85–96.

Raichvarg, D. (2008). La vulgarisation des sciences, espace critique du scientisme. In *Valeurs des sciences*, Chazal, G. (ed.). Éditions universitaires de Dijon, Dijon.

Ricœur, P. (1983). *Temps et récit*, volume 1. Le Seuil, Paris.

Ricœur, P. (2000). *La mémoire, l'histoire et l'oubli.* Le Seuil, Paris.

Rousso, H. (2016). *Face au passé. Essais sur la mémoire contemporaine.* Belin, Paris.

Schiele, B. (2001). *Le musée de sciences. Montée du modèle communicationnel et recomposition du champ muséal.* L'Harmattan, Paris.

Soulé, B. (2007). Observation participante ou participation observante ? Usages et justifications de la notion de participation observante en sciences sociales. *Recherches qualitatives, Association pour la Recherche Qualitative*, 27, 127–140.

Suchman, M. (1995). Managing legitimacy: Strategic and institutional approaches. *The Academy of Management Review*, 20(3), 571–610.

Tedlock, B. (1991). From participant observation to the observation of participation: The emergence of narrative ethnography. *Journal of Anthropological Research*, 47, 59–94.

Tutiaux-Guillon, N. (2008). Histoire et mémoire, questions à l'histoire scolaire ordinaire. In *Quand les mémoires déstabilisent l'école. Mémoire de la Shoah et enseignement*, Ernst, S. (ed.). Institut National de Recherche Pédagogique, Paris.

Wadbled, N. (2015). La sensation d'être au musée : une expérience éducative, sensorielle et récréative. In *Patrimoine, création, culture. À l'intersection des dispositifs et des publics*, Bogdan, C., Fleury, B., Walter, J. (eds). L'Harmattan, Paris.

Wadbled, N. (2016a). L'expérience scolaire de la culture matérielle : spécificité et fonction de l'usage pédagogique des visites de musée. In *De l'école au musée. Interroger les modes de transmission des savoirs*, Barratault, M. and Delassus, J. (eds). HAL-SHS, 101–113.

Wadbled, N. (2016b). Produire des propositions théoriques. Épistémologie de l'usage des études de cas. *Recherches Qualitatives*, Special edition (20), 383–394.

Wadbled, N. (2018a). Apprendre l'histoire à Auschwitz ? Enjeux et fonctions éducatives des voyages scolaires du point de vue des accompagnateurs. *Carrefours de l'éducation*, 45(June), 55–66.

Wadbled, N. (2018b). Apprendre l'histoire à Auschwitz : l'expérience d'une histoire écrite avec des objets. *Médiation et Information*, 42/43, 253–262.

Wadbled, N. (2018c). Un lieu pour se rendre compte. L'activité réflexive des visiteurs au Musée-Mémorial Auschwitz-Birkenau. In *Des lieux pour penser : musées, bibliothèques, théâtres*, Garcin-Marrou, F., Mairesse, F., Mouton-Rezzouk, A. (eds). ICOM-ICOFOM, Paris.

Weber, M. (2002). *Le Savant et le politique*. Livre de poche, Paris.

Yin, R. (2013). *Case Study Research: Design and Methods*, 5th edition. Sage Publications, Thousand Oaks.

Zafeirakou, A. (1998). Comment le musée voit l'école ? In *Entre écoles et musée. Le partenariat culturel d'éducation*, Buffet, F. (ed.). Presses universitaires de Lyon, Lyon.

7

The Contribution of Museums in Non-formal Education and Cultural Transmission

The school, seized and re-seized by the school form (Vincent 1994; Séguy 2018), is an emblematic institution of democratic modernity (Gauchet 1985), particularly in the sense that it embodies in a paradigmatic way the implementation of what Dubet calls the institutional program (2002). The latter carries a strongly normative and integrating socializing conception driven by a "work on others [conceived as a vocation before being conceived as a profession and conceived as] mediation between universal values and particular individuals" (pp. 13–14). This conception gives special importance to formal and institutional education; clearly isolates this part of citizen training from what is considered outside of it (family education, popular education, etc.) as part of what can be called the "school compromise" (Blais et al. 2016, pp. 20–26) or the "social sharing of knowledge" (Meunier and Luckerhoff 2012); is based, *in fine*, on a traditional conception of mediation, transmission and authority; has affected more or less all institutions of cultural transmission through what can be called, after Illich (2004, pp. 203–378), the schooling of modern industrial societies (Blais et al. 2016, pp. 32–48).

It is this that has been centrally questioned from top to bottom – and the scholastic conception of culture that it carries (Jacquet-Francillon and Kambouchner 2005) – in recent decades by the advent of a society of individuals (Blais et al. 2008) and the centrality that the principle of modern legitimacy of individual rights and the generalized attribution of a status of autonomous individual in law occupy in it, that

Chapter written by Anik MEUNIER and Camille ROELENS.

it is a question of a process of becoming autonomous that involves twists and turns and itself needs to be supported (Foray 2016). This, it will be understood, does not concern museum education any less than school education, even though these processes may manifest themselves differently there.

If museums can rightly be understood as reflections of the configurations of knowledge in the societies in which they are inserted (Meunier 2012, pp. 104–109), they are undoubtedly no less likely to be reflections of the conceptions that are considered legitimate of mediation and of the relationships between the individual and the collective which are in use there. Constituted as entities defining their fields of reference and their relationship to knowledge (Charlot 2017) across societies and eras within the institutions they have represented, and which have represented them, museums share this domain of legitimacy with other institutions and social structures. The various institutions of training do share this part; the school is one of them. Thus, within the museums themselves, services have progressively been structured and organized whose intention is to disseminate and share the various forms of knowledge for the benefit of the greatest number of people and not only for experts. This is how a disciplinary field commonly referred to as museum education developed, which

> [...] remains an often vague notion, with contours that are still poorly defined. This term is used in French but is derived directly from the translation of the English term. It covers the notions of education and museums. We know from the outset that these are two broad and complex notions to define. Education can be understood as training, initiation, instruction, or pedagogy, but it can also concern the implementation of different means aiming to ensure the training and development of a human being (Meunier 2008, p. 103).

With the aim of cultural democratization, at the intersection of the individual and the collective, cultural frameworks have been formed with a view to offering access to culture to the greatest number (Blais et al. 2013; Zask 2016). Indeed, these structures have given rise to different formats and forms of public programs, exhibitions and a variety of mediation proposals. In an effort to justify the various actions of cultural mediation, or more specifically of this field called museum education, these approaches are seen as subsidiary, if not necessary to complement those of the school.

To question the interactions of museums and the school form today, as it is the object of the present part, it is thus *in fine* to wonder: how the conditions of the very possibilities of education, training and mediation have been globally disrupted by the hypermodern access of individual autonomy to the status of dedicated goal of all these activities; and how museums have tried – and, if applicable, succeeded – to face this requirement of disengagement of the "active principle [of cultural transmission] of the historical expressions in which it had sunk, in order to put it in the service of another philosophy of the individual and the society" (Blais et al. 2016, p. 252).

In the first section, we will therefore have to make conceptually intelligible the part occupied by non-formal education in the life course of individuals towards their autonomy, as well as what the contemporary system of transmission and mediation may be that supports these twists and turns of becoming autonomous (Foray 2016) and supplying it with cultural resources.

In the second section, we will practically show how, from a diachronic perspective and in response to the social demands linked to this centrality of becoming autonomous, museum institutions have evolved and diversified. This will apply, among other illustrations, to the "paradoxes" underlying museum education, therefore, non-formal, in a certain sense, with regard to formal and school education.

> This movement, which stems from a desire to provide conditions for educational success to as many people as possible and to extend the period of life during which an individual is likely to learn, clearly shows how the term non-formal education will have paved the way for the establishment of notions such as lifelong learning and educational diversity (Rogers 2005, p. 71).

Indeed, by "defining itself in terms of exteriority [in relation to non-formal education] (Rogers 2005, p. 150), it will have pointed to a salutary elsewhere to which museum institutions indeed belong" (cited in Meunier 2018, p. 30). The analysis of the interactions between non-formal education and cultural transmission through the prism of the reception of museum mediation devices used to establish the patrimonial value of objects or practices in order to communicate with contemporary audiences is enlightening here, as well as two case studies of museological training that we will discuss here show this clearly. The adoption of the cultural approach in teaching pedagogical practices and the role of cultural transmitter adopted therein are concerned.

7.1. Places of autonomy and hypermodern mediations

As Lipovetsky (Roelens 2021) and others have shown, the hypermodern world is thus characterized by the exponential multiplication of both the type of mediations necessary to construct ourselves as a human subject in a world of culture, and the diversity of the proposals of mediations that an individual can be led to encounter and to grasp. In other words, when individual autonomy becomes the keystone of the functioning of societies, it affects both the matter and the way of mediation understood as an essential activity of the human being as a cultural being. It affects *in fine* the way in which authority, which "represents a constitutive and irreducible dimension of the human-social space" (Blais et al. 2008, p. 138), can be exercised, certainly in the professions of cultural mediation, in the school or in the museum, in particular, as well as more broadly throughout the whole of the wide spectrum of formal and non-formal education today[1].

7.1.1. *Resources of individual autonomy, or matter of mediation*

Indeed, authority is a very condition of possibility for the establishment of mediation, which is why we can speak of "mediating authority" (Blais et al. 2013, p. 45) between the individual and the world of culture in which they move, the mediator[2], whatever its institutional anchoring or not, playing here a "role of intercessor" (p. 46) human and the ally for the dialogue with these intercessors of another type (that we can say symbolic) that are the cultural works themselves. The stake is here, for the hypermodern individuals, the access "to the reflected mastery of the culture where they have anyway to enter – mastery that includes the freedom to judge it with the ease to move in it". In Charlot's terms, we could say that authority as mediation here consists of helping "subjectivity to construct itself with its contradictions" (2017, p. 250) notably those between the relationship to knowledge of cultural immersion and direct experience of empirical self and the more distanced and reflexive one of epistemic self (p. 236), as all of them participate in becoming autonomous. As Foray (2016) makes clear, individual autonomy is at once complex, composite, singular, vulnerable and multilocalized. School certainly has its part to play in young people becoming autonomous, but no less so than the framework of family or associative activities, visits to cultural places and socialization among peers around the same cultural or sporting activity, or even solitary physical or intellectual experience. In short, it is a question of thinking here about the way in which the education that society gives to individuals through its dedicated institutions is mixed with the education that individuals give to themselves or that they receive from the socio-cultural environment in which they evolve. In the same way, autonomy is not something that is acquired once and for all, but rather a never-ending path that involves twists and turns. Intellectual autonomy, in particular, depends on an ability to understand the world around us, that is, to have

---

1 For reasons of text space, we reduce here to the bare bones a subject whose architecture is deployed elsewhere with the necessary precision (Roelens 2023).

2 It should be noted in particular that since 2020, the Quebec teaching competency framework officially describes these professionals as "mediators of elements of culture". As an indication of comparison, we may note that the French reference system (https://www.education.gouv.fr/le-referentiel-de-competences-des-metiers-du-professorat-et-de-l-education-5753) rather emphasizes this dimension in the context of documentalist teachers and retains semantics that draw more on the lexical fields of mastery and transmission for the other teaching professions.

as many points of orientation and vectors of meaning as possible to direct ourselves in life. As such, it can be said that, on the one hand, the school is required to enable everyone to progress towards the status of an autonomous cultural being, and that, on the other hand, it is structurally (and not through the fault of its agents) incapable of achieving this alone. In the same way, an early education during the years of childhood certainly contributes in an important way to the autonomous becoming on this point, but, as good as it is, it would not know how to exempt from a reflection as for the way in which this type of training of ourselves must be prolonged throughout the life. No one is ever erudite enough, in the hypermodern world, to be able to stop cultivating themself – nor to pretend to do so from now on without any support – without making our own autonomy vulnerable in the long run; the challenge can only be to conceive the forms of mediating authority capable of sustainably providing for increased and diversified needs in this matter.

7.1.2. Benevolent authority, or the way of mediation

To make the individual autonomy of the persons accompanied in one way or another (Paul 2021) the goal that must henceforth guide and regulate all educational and mediation activity, and to think of groups and institutions – including all cultural training spaces – as means placed at the service of persons to achieve this goal (Foray 2016, p. 20), nevertheless implies in return a profound recomposition of what a posture of authority can be. If there is more than ever a matter of mediation of the different relationships of individuals to culture in today's world, the way in which such mediation can be authoritative – that is, recognized as legitimate without constraint and in full co-construction of an intersubjective relationship of support – must now be thought of in democracy, and no longer by mobilizing remnants and memories of form of traditional social organizations.

We have proposed (Roelens 2023) to speak of benevolent authority to describe this capacity to formulate today mediation proposals between individuals or between an individual and a world of culture, implying the influence of an individual on another, being able to participate in making them the author of their individuality and autonomy in the long-term. In this perspective, it is in particular a question of taking good care to contribute to allow others the singular and critical appropriation of the cultural means of their becoming subject, by taking into account for this purpose the singularity of each cultural environment and each particular subjective context of reception. Any cultural mediator, whether a teacher or not, is not conceived as being in the service of a culture itself to which a superior value is attributed, but in the service of other individuals caught up in the hypermodern challenge of generalized individual autonomy, and who are in search of support and resources to find their way.

We could say here that thinking of culture as a means, far from devaluing it, only makes it more indispensable. In the same way, seeing those who exercise it slip from a posture of command to a posture of service, it is possible to think that authority gains in quantitative and qualitative importance of its register of action what it perhaps loses in hierarchical majesty.

7.2. Teachers: mediators in search of appropriate mediations?

A fruitful perspective to contribute to thinking about this contemporary challenge is to take an interest in the way in which these particular individuals can be a companion to the museum – because teachers are also companions by profession – that is, they are people who exercise social functions traditionally understood as places of authority, and therefore are responsible in terms of mastery and cultural transmission.

The school form, in fact, is schematically built around the idea that teachers, by status as much as by vocation, are an authority in matters of culture, and that from the moment they find themselves in professional responsibility, they have to transmit much more than to learn. What precedes suggests rather that, like any other hypermodern individual, the teacher will never cease to become autonomous, and therefore to need mediation. The museum can be, in this register, the place where teachers' autonomy, torn between their theoretical versatility and statutory omnicompetence and the reality of their strengths and shortcomings as cultural beings, go in search of the mediations that should allow them to perfect and update their own mediation capacities in order to assume their role in this register.

Let us note, before looking at the panorama, that we should rather say museums, so much the concern of adaptation to the public, the prevalence of communication and a will of impermanence have given rise today to a great variety of museum models. These major transformations within cultural facilities, as well as the creation of new structures (permanent or temporary) to exhibit content (artistic, scientific, socio-historical) and to raise awareness of current issues (or socially relevant issues), cross several fields and disciplines.

What are the impacts of interactions with teaching audiences on the production and dissemination of discourses and the functioning of mediation devices? What are the explicit or latent effects of a certain scholarization of the modalities and the scope of cultural transmission defined as a transfer of preserved objects, knowledge and values? How do these interactions, increasingly asserted and desired between publics and institutions, influence the effects of mediations and educational intentions in a non-formal context? All these questions converge towards a paradigm that moves away from scholarly education circumscribed in an instituted framework, in a given time and a defined geographical space, and towards hybrid forms of education – notably supported by technological pedagogical tools – inspired by lifelong education models.

It is possible to propose answers to the questions thus raised based on the study[3] of two museological training projects set up at the Musée des beaux-arts de Montréal (MMFA) (Montreal Museum of Fine Arts) and initially announced – entitled "L'école au musée et Formation à l'appréciation esthétique" (School to Museum and Aesthetic Appreciation Training) – with a view to promoting the cultural approach[4] in teaching for which the Groupe de recherche sur l'éducation et les musées (GREM) (Research Group on Education and Museums) of the UQAM was mandated, by focusing on the teachers' relationship with the museum and by analyzing elements that reflect their sense of competence in the role of cultural mediator. Starting with the observation that the initial training of professionals in this field is relatively weak, the survey reveals first of all, on the part of the teachers, a feeling of incompetence, linked in particular to the question of meaning. However, the role of cultural mediator, when considered meaningless, also appears to be an additional burden on the shoulders of teachers who are already overloaded, and, consequently, the question arises as to the type of support that can help them to bear this burden.

In order to compensate for this lack of initial and ongoing training in teaching, some museum institutions are seeking to set up specific training to better support teachers in this role. Bélanger and Meunier (2012) have proposed a typology of training for teachers by museums. They identify four types of training: disciplinary training, didactic training, training in the pedagogical use of the museum and museological training. This last type of training aims to familiarize teachers with the museum, so that they feel more comfortable, both professionally and personally, in using this resource and bringing their pupils to it. The aim is to make the museum known and to enable teachers to assume their role as cultural mediators more easily, which is of particular interest to us. This type of training aims at changing the relationship with the museum, which can be defined as the practices of visiting museums and the interest in the museum and artistic universe.

An inductive research approach was used for both case studies. Individual and group interviews, as well as questionnaires, were designed and used in each project.

---

3 The following builds on an unpublished report *Musée et approche culturelle. Deux études de cas. L'école au musée et formation à l'appréciation esthétique*, delivered in November 2020 by Meunier and Bédard Daneau; see the works cited in the bibliographical references for the complete reference.

4 It can be defined as "the pupil's relationship to culture, understood as a set of dynamic relationships of a situated subject with cultural actors, practices, knowledge, and objects" (Falardeau and Simard 2007, p. 3).

Thus, a mixed methodology, based on qualitative and quantitative data, is used to report the results. Two salient points seem to emerge in particular from the results obtained, which we wish to outline here.

The first is the importance of developing a self-reflexive posture among the trainees in relation to their individual appropriation of the dual status of cultural being in constant evolution and of cultural mediator in responsibility. In this respect, we note that a strong condition put forward by the participants in the survey for the development of a greater sense of competence is an increased autonomy in this area. Thus, in order to be better cultural mediators, they declare that they want to develop a vocabulary linked to the works, or they affirm: "I have an even greater desire to go out [...] If the project stopped, I would do it differently"; "Personally, I would feel more at ease if I took more time and left less to the [museum] mediators. A person who does this project for several years becomes an expert and at the end doesn't need mediators anymore. She is able to facilitate everything." To be autonomous means less, in fact, to realize more things than to have the substantial and concrete freedom, the ability[5], to choose to realize, or not, the greatest variety of them.

For all that, the possibility of having recourse to mediators in case of need, and of then finding offers of mediation adapted enough to be authoritative for each singular individual in demand, constitutes the second salient point that we retain. One participant in the survey states significantly, "I think it's not the museum itself that attracts us, but the intervention of the actors of the museum." The importance of the mediator's presence would be implicit here in the attendance, at least with their group of pupils. To put it differently, the individual relationship to the work and allowed by the mediator, as well as the inter-individual relation between the individual and the mediator provoked by the meeting of the work would be here the two nodal points of the fine comprehension of any device conceived in the perspective of these cultural approaches.

In its most basic definition and in the school context, the cultural approach is concerned with the relationship between the pupil and culture. This relationship seems most of the time to be envisaged – or sometimes thwarted – by teachers who will consider themselves – or not – as a cultural being and passer-by. This relationship to culture is therefore guaranteed by the teacher on the spot, in the museum, during the school trip, or can even be brought back, or postponed, in class. In the end, the question may be more about whether or not the pupil will have contact with an individual who can mediate these elements of culture, whether that individual is a professional cultural mediator in a museum or a teacher mediator of elements of culture within a classroom.

---

5 We will have recognized here the lexicon of Sen and Nussbaum, which Foray (2016, p. 181) mobilizes extensively to describe individual autonomy.

We will add that this idea, according to which the plurality of the works of mediation to direct ourselves in a world of culture today would be vectors of open choices, therefore of more freedom and resources to take up the same challenge – that of individual autonomy today in its cultural dimension – is found when the participants in the survey insist on the difference, and therefore the possible complementarity between a more dynamic experience in the museum and a more abstract and theoretical school teaching. We are perhaps still at the heart of the mission – if not one of the missions – of the function of museum education, by referring "[...] to the complementary character of the museum place in order to encourage a sensitive approach through the 'real things'[6] that the school cannot offer, or to the originality and renewal of the forms that the educational offer adopts in a museum context" (Meunier 2008, p. 104).

Whatever the cultural approach adopted, the school has long favored universal educational and cultural values, attempting to provide everyone with equal opportunities. Thus, the approach to cultural democratization in the school context aims to "emphasize the development, creation, and funding of cultural institutions, the promotion of the arts, the training of professional creators, and the education of the population in the arts and letters, among other things, in the school, in order to promote access by the greatest number to subsidized cultural products" (Côté et al. 2017, p. 83). Cultural democracy is considered less elitist than the previous approach. It relies more on "[...] amateur practices[7]", the decompartmentalization of various cultural disciplines and aims to "[...] promote the community interest of a project rather than artistic excellence. In this perspective, citizens are thought of less as consumers than as producers" (Côté et al. 2017, p. 84). While school remains the primary means of acquiring knowledge and culture today, it is impossible not to recognize the role of non-school forms of acculturation, which determines "the possibility for everyone to learn new knowledge and cultivate themselves without school or outside of school" (Jacobi 2018, p. XV).

7.3. Conclusion

The first section of this chapter has allowed us to show that the occupation of the postures of mediation and transmission has become conceptually democratized, in the double sense that they must justify their contribution to the pursuit of the democratic ideal of individual autonomy in order to be judged legitimate, and that

---

6 The term "real things" was used over 50 years ago by Duncan F. Cameron (1968) in "Un point de vue: le musée considéré comme système de communication et les implications de ce système dans les programmes éducatifs muséaux," see the work cited in the bibliographical references for the full reference.

7 On this point, it is worth referring to the work of Flichy (2010).

more people and places can claim to be the support and the theater of their assumption. This affects museums as much as the school form, but it seizes them in different states and thus produces distinct effects of adaptation. We retain here in particular the double principle according to which: we cannot be adequately and durably a cultural mediator if we are not ourselves a cultural being constantly becoming and conscious of being it; we cannot become and remain such a being without benefiting ourselves, throughout our life and our professional and cultural pathway, from plural and singular mediations.

The second section of this chapter – by identifying and working on the analytical node that we believe constitutes the appropriation by contemporary teachers of their role as cultural mediators, who are themselves in search of appropriate museum mediations from this perspective – has enabled us to specify and further embody this general proposition in a specific and revealing case. Several factors are at play in the promotion of the cultural approach in teaching, and among these, we have noted the absence of school cultural policies that allow the teachers' work to be oriented towards culture. The level of preparation of teachers for their cultural responsibilities is uneven, or sometimes non-existent. Thus, teachers do not necessarily have the tools to assume their role as cultural mediators or facilitators. The integration of the cultural dimension in the classroom therefore depends on the teacher's prior interest in culture or on their own cultural dispositions. As a teacher, we met in a study prior to the two case studies in this text explains: "[...] we teach a little with what we are" (Meunier and Bédard Daneau 2019, p. 15). Moreover, in the Quebec context, individual teachers' attendance at cultural settings is low. According to a study conducted more than 20 years ago (Matias et al. 2001) among many teachers, only 47% had been to a museum in the last five years and, of those, 12% had been only once. This rate is much lower than what can be observed in the United States or France for the same period (pp. 99–100). Finally, many teachers, while very interested in culture, simply lament the lack of time and the pressure of departmental exams, which are based solely on disciplinary skills and content. "The near majority of respondents [teachers] agree that there is pressure to improve pupil achievement. [...] For other respondents, this pressure created insecurity, if not induced a lack of confidence" (Tchimou 2011, p. 113). Field trips are thus perceived as an additional burden on top of an already heavy workload.

We have taken the gamble here of a dialogue between the political philosophy of education (notably school education) and museology (especially museum education) for the understanding of the new relationships to knowledge in cultural training spaces today. We can only hope that similar dialogues will multiply in order to conceive and practice cultural mediation in these fields. In particular, this could give rise to work not so much on the formal accessibility of museums to teachers (which is necessary, but not sufficient) as on the "quality of support for mediators", an emerging and converging element of the analyses carried out in the framework of the two studies conducted. Moreover, because the initial training of teachers appears to be inadequate, if not incomplete (Meunier and Bédard Danneau 2021), training of a museological nature for teachers would seem to be worthwhile. This would be likely to contribute to making teachers autonomous and able to exercise their role as cultural facilitators, as we have noted. Finally, it would be difficult to ignore interdisciplinarity, as it is an approach that is at the heart of all the practices that have been identified, as reported in our observations. Indeed, it appears that all the teachers who have had a more or less long and profound relationship with the museum in a school context have claimed interdisciplinary approaches. These approaches are induced in particular by the diversity of themes and disciplines addressed by the works themselves. They have also manifested themselves in the classroom and have been reported in the school context as a result of teaching experiments in the museum.

Using this logic, each individual, whether pupil, teacher or museum professional, would be primarily understood as a cultural being, having to subjectively construct themself in a problematic hypermodern world (Fabre 2011). It is from this point of reference that the respective contributions of formal and non-formal education and of school or museum institutions to their life journey could be adequately thought out and designed.

7.4. References

Baillargeon, N. (2011). *Liliane est au lycée. Est-il indispensable d'être cultivé ?* Flammarion, Paris.

Bélanger, C. and Meunier, A. (2012). Partenariat université-musée : une proposition dans la formation initiale des maîtres. In *Le musée : entre la recherche et l'enseignement – The Museum: Between Research and Education*, Émond, A.-M. (ed.). Éditions MultiMondes, Quebec.

Blais, M.-C., Gauchet, M., Ottavi, D. (2008). *Conditions de l'éducation.* Stock, Paris.

Blais, M.-C., Gauchet, M., Ottavi, D. (2013). *Pour une philosophie politique de l'éducation.* Arthème Fayard/Pluriel, Paris.

Blais, M.-C., Gauchet, M., Ottavi, D. (2016). *Transmettre, apprendre.* Arthème Fayard/Pluriel, Paris.

Cameron, D.F. (1968). Un point de vue : le musée considéré comme système de communication et les implications de ce système dans les programmes éducatifs muséaux. *Vagues : une anthologie de la nouvelle muséologie*, volume 1. Presses universitaires de Lyon, Lyon.

Charlot, B. (2017). Rapport au savoir et contradictions de l'apprendre à l'école. *Le Sujet dans la Cité*, 2(8), 239–250.

Côté, H., Simard, D., Larouche, M.-C. (2017). Le discours officiel sur les relations entre les ministères de la culture et de l'éducation du Québec de 1961 à 2007. In *Regards interdisciplinaires sur les publics de la culture*, Larouche, M.-C., Luckerhoff, J., Labbé, S. (eds). Presses de l'université du Québec, Quebec.

Dubet, F. (2002). *Le déclin de l'institution*. Le Seuil, Paris.

Fabre, M. (2011). *Éduquer pour un monde problématique. La carte et la boussole*. Presses universitaires de France, Paris.

Falardeau, É. and Simard, D. (2007). Rapport à la culture et approche culturelle de l'enseignement. *Canadian Journal of Education*, 30(1), 1–24.

Flichy, P. (2010). *Le sacre de l'amateur. Sociologie des passions ordinaires à l'ère du numérique*. Le Seuil/La République des Idées, Paris.

Foray, P. (2016). *Devenir autonome. Apprendre à se diriger soi-même*. ESF Éditeur, Paris.

Gauchet, M. (1985). L'école à l'école d'elle-même. Contraintes et contradictions de l'individualisme démocratique. *Le Débat*, 37, 55–86.

Illich, I. (2004). *Oeuvres complètes*, volume 1. Fayard, Paris.

Jacobi, D. (2018). Avant-propos. In *Culture et éducation non formelle*, Jacobi, D. (ed.). Presses de l'université du Québec, Quebec.

Jacquet-Francillon, F. and Kambouchner, D. (2005). *La crise de la culture scolaire*. Presses universitaires de France, Paris.

Matias, V., Lemerise, T., Lussier-Desrochers, D. (2001). Le partenariat entre les écoles secondaires et les musées : points de vue d'enseignants de la région de Montréal. *Revue des sciences de l'éducation*, 21(1), 85–104.

Meunier, A. (2008). L'éducation muséale, un rapport au savoir. *Recherches en communication*, 29, 101–124.

Meunier, A. (2012). L'éducation muséale, fragment d'une muséologie inachevée. In *La muséologie, champ de théories et de pratiques*, Meunier, A. (ed.). Presses de l'université du Québec, Quebec.

Meunier, A. (2018). L'éducation dans les musées. Une forme d'éducation non formelle. In *Culture et éducation non formelle*, Jacobi, D. (ed.). Presses de l'Université du Québec, Quebec.

Meunier, A. and Bédard Daneau, F. (2019). *Le projet pilote Musée-école du Musée des beaux-arts de Montréal*. Université du Québec à Montréal, Montreal.

Meunier, A. and Bédard Daneau, F. (2020). *Musée et approche culturelle : deux études de cas*. Université du Québec à Montréal, Montreal.

Meunier, A. and Luckerhoff, J. (2012). Introduction. Le musée et le partage social du savoir. In *La muséologie, champ de théories et de pratiques*, Meunier, A. (ed.). Presses de l'université du Québec, Quebec.

Paul, M. (2021). *Une société d'accompagnement. Guides, mentors, conseillers, coaches : comment en est-on arrivés là ?* Raison et Passions, Dijon.

Roelens, C. (2021). Penser l'éducation avec Gilles Lipovetsky. *Penser l'éducation*, 49, 77–104.

Roelens, C. (2023). *Quelle autorité dans une société des individus ?* Presses universitaires de Rouen et du Havre, Mont-Saint-Aignan.

Rogers, A. (2005). *Non-Formal Education. Flexible Schooling or Participatory Education?* University of Hong Kong/Kluwer Academic, Hong Kong/New York.

Seguy, J.-Y. (ed.) (2018). *Variations autour de la "forme scolaire". Mélanges offerts à André D. Robert.* Presses universitaires de Lorraine, Nancy.

Tchimou, M. (2011). Nouvelle régulation de l'éducation et transformation du travail enseignant : une analyse des expériences des enseignants de Vancouver, Toronto et Montréal. *Éducation canadienne et internationale*, 40(1), 97–120.

Vincent, G. (ed.) (1994). *L'Éducation prisonnière de la forme scolaire. Scolarisation et socialisation dans les sociétés industrielles.* Presses universitaires de Lyon, Lyon.

Zask, J. (2016). De la démocratisation à la démocratie culturelle. *Nectart*, 3, 40–47.

8

Cultural Space, Digitization and Training in the Museum

The missions attributed to the museum today overturn the traditional conception of access to cultural knowledge. The exhibition spaces are orienting visitors' practices towards the search for a global understanding of the works in a context of modernization. Do physical journeys (approaching, moving away, scanning) and digital journeys (recognizing works) invent new relationships to cultural knowledge? How can the digital museum be a training space for teachers? What does the museum reveal about their pedagogical practices?

Methodological aspect: a case study, written for the option of the external *agrégation* (preparation of four hours, duration of the test of one hour), concerns the presentation of a lesson in relation to the school programs – the agrégation is a French competitive examination for the recruitment of teachers destined to teach in high schools, in preparatory classes, in universities and in the *grandes écoles* (prestigious schools). It is the only example in the world of a body that is present in both secondary and higher education.

In a given high school and post-baccalaureate teaching context, the candidate presents a progression of a teaching sequence. The presentation is followed by an interview with the jury, during which the candidate is invited to justify their didactic and pedagogical choices.

The topic related to museums includes several questions on innovative digital initiatives that are multiplying in museums. Future teachers must conduct an argued reflection on the impacts in terms of management, modeling and digital competence, and reflect on the relationship with pedagogical practices in cultural training spaces.

Chapter written by Corinne BAUJARD.

The jury also asks questions of the future agent of the public service of education, who will have to take into account, within the framework of their teaching, the construction of pupil learning and their needs, the diversity of the conditions in which the profession is practiced, the thoughtful knowledge of the context, the different dimensions and values that support it, including that of the Republic (see the jury's report[1], the order of August 4, 2020, the order of July 1, 2013[2]).

8.1. Context of the case study

Museums around the world are developing new means of communication in order to modernize their image at the international level. The diversification of digital devices in exhibition spaces is modifying visiting practices and affecting the cultural challenges of museums for visitors and teachers. From the Guggenheim in Bilbao to MoMA in New York, from the Metropolitan Museum to the Museum Lab in Tokyo and the Tate Gallery, all the major museums are enhancing their cultural patrimony by offering visitors, teachers and pupils broader access to their uses (Baujard 2019).

In the digital museum, many websites present collections and digitized works. In the in situ museum, interactive and multimedia terminals in the exhibition spaces accompany the digital assistants to applications on cell phones, social networks and Twitter. According to Article 1 of Law No. 2002-5 of January 4, 2002, the museum is defined as "any permanent collection composed of goods whose conservation and presentation are of public interest, and organized for the knowledge, education, and enjoyment of the public. The recommendation of the Council of the European Union of May 22, 2018, defines the principle of a European core of social rights that are "necessary for everyone's personal fulfilment and personal development, employability, access to a sustainable lifestyle, success in a peaceful society, healthy life management, and active citizenship". Thus, the museum appears as a new form of education outside the school institution (Garnier and Kahn 2016).

A major museum in France (which we will refer to as the "Musée des Arts") has been deploying digital devices in the exhibition halls and on the Web for some time. These new museum practices enrich visitors' real or virtual visits while considering their expectations. This development model in culture requires differentiation in terms of content. This is the reason why the museum wishes to improve its attendance by attracting new visitors, and more particularly the school public.

---

1 www.devenirenseignant.gouv.fr.
2 Order of July 1, 2013.

The digital project aims to facilitate access to the exhibition spaces for pupils and teachers. Cultural mediation tools are offered through touch tables equipped with adapted applications that allow pupils to listen to the description of the painting during the visit, and to learn about the history of the painter through video films. Tactile terminals bring scientific knowledge to life. Each visitor can discover through augmented reality the most famous paintings of the museum. The geolocation allows for the receipt of information when the visitor is in front of the painting. They receive the artist as they are painting or a commentary on the painter's life.

Attendance is not only in the physical museum. The museum wants to use social networks to build loyalty and diversify its visitors. Facebook and Twitter present the programs of conferences on restoration and loans of works. Numerous blogs provide a tool for monitoring museum news. In view of the increasing number of visitors (10 million by 2021), this "Musée des Arts" wishes to encourage school visits as part of the preparation of a new experimental project called "Museum artLab."

8.2. Presentation of the experimental project at the museum

The museum asks itself several questions about the complementarity of the relationship to knowledge between in situ and off-site spaces. The off-site cultural space constitutes an essential element of the educational relationship of the school visitor. We wonder how it is possible to improve relations with pupils while taking into account the particularities of communication with the works in the different exhibition spaces. For several years now, the museum has been developing a number of innovations within its departments and services.

8.2.1. *First report: enriching the museum's relationship with its school audience*

Today, the museum is confronted with new visitor behaviors within the museum in situ and the digital museum. The access to information, in order to enlarge its school public, leads it to structure the information of the collections to integrate them into a knowledge process. But it is increasingly obliged to update it to make it accessible to the general public. To carry out this important evolution, the museum wishes to accompany this major change in its realization phase. The aim is to provide curators, managers and documentalists with a database for the scientific description of the collections. The database, which conforms to the recommendations for the museum inventory defined in the decree of May 25, 2004, sets the technical standards for keeping the inventory and the register of goods deposited in a museum in France, but it also presents a playful aspect in the presentation of the collections.

The playful version of eMuseumPlus transforms the way we look at patrimonial objects by multiplying the approaches to the museum and the interactions with the school public. Nevertheless, the museum remains a cultural place to be discovered physically, which allows knowledge to be made accessible from the immediate physical environment. The collection set, in the form of personalized web pages, is undoubtedly a way to make the collections, information about the artists and upcoming exhibitions accessible and understandable online through a secure server.

Based on the candidates' knowledge, the jury wonders what educational resources could be offered to pupils. At the research level, pupils with secure authentication can access patrimonial objects more quickly through the search engine. In order to establish their cultural identity, they can create a personal portfolio of their favorite works during the visit. This interaction between works, pupils and the museum encourages the emergence of a new way of thinking about museum practice. The traditional mission of conservation is called into question by new exhibitions, tours and access mechanisms to public collections. Within the museum in situ, spaces of knowledge mediation put patrimony on stage (Meunier and Luckerhoff 2012). The traditional forms of displaying works offer an unexpected visibility of the objects on display. However, the pathways for pupils to visit are complex. To address the educational design, museums are offering an expanded consultation of the collections on display on the Internet, involving pupils in the enhancement of cultural exhibitions. Various digital tools are already reinventing the museum tour experience: virtual reality, augmented reality, mobile applications and artificial intelligence.

8.2.2. Second report: preparing the school visit with the teachers

The presence of the museum on its website gives information to prepare for the visit with the class. The address, access map, opening hours, prices, information on offer and current exhibitions are available. The visitor buys an electronic entrance ticket, can order catalogs, subscribe to the newsletter and access files. Then, progressively, content is added to discover the patrimony on display. Links open video images and audio commentaries. The digital museum becomes a relational mode with the public that creates personalized support among the digitized works. The "Musée des Arts" site thus seeks to develop a true interaction with pupils (Chabanne et al. 2012, p. 297) going from the website to the public. It asks what impact the site can play on attendance. Access to museum content must lead to knowledge and to appropriation by visitors.

The jury asks the candidate what methodology they propose to analyze the success of the visit in terms of quality, communication and pleasure of the museum visit. What elements should be taken into account to evaluate the relationship with cultural knowledge? The candidate proposes to carry out a survey among the pupils, in order to ensure that ergonomics encourage attendance. The idea is not to recreate the experience of the physical museum, as the site should be used to enhance the pupil's experience. Obvious navigational aids should be available on all pages, so that the pupil can easily move through the site from a hyperlink attached to the home page. The pupil's personal interest has an impact on the relationship to cultural knowledge.

In order to complete the pedagogical attendance, the museum wishes to encourage the passage of the pupils in the various exhibition spaces. The jury asks how the relationship between the two spaces, physical and virtual, can be achieved. Several solutions are possible in the classroom. For example, reserving time on the Internet to avoid waiting in the museum, freely choosing the time of the visit and offering interactive tools. Satisfaction during the navigation responds to the affective and cognitive dimension, influences satisfaction with the website and the intentions of visiting the museum. Commitment is essential, and the satisfaction of a virtual visit encourages frequentation. The jury's recommendations for a complementary physical and virtual space to help pupils find their way around the museum were widely emphasized. A high level of web traffic is likely to develop a high level of attendance at the museum. Also, maintaining a site tour experience avoids the gap between the virtual site and the physical museum. It allows for the development of an important interactivity, rich thanks to the sound, the word, the skills offered by the video, in order not to exceed the visitation capacities of the museum.

The "Musée des Arts" has chosen to transform the pupil into a content producer. Recently, it has invited them on its blog to suggest themes for future exhibitions. After the visit, the pupil has the option to write about their tour experience, to post photographs to prolong the physical visit and to see the works again or to relive the highlights of the visit. Many educational interactions are offered.

After the visit, the museum can send SMS messages to get feedback on the visit or offer activities to build loyalty. Interactive markers (or virtual tags) can be viewed on cell phones or mobile devices. RFID (Radio Frequency Identification) is a geolocation technology that allows the reconstruction of the visitor's route and time during an exhibition. Each visitor receives a card containing an RFID chip with a unique identifier. During their visit, if they show an interest in a work or a space, they indicate it by passing their smart card in front of the appropriate readers. The system records their choices at home. The pupil accesses a website that offers additional resources on the works they like. Digital technology represents a change for the museum, which must take into account new technologies to communicate with the public, establish a more active contact allowing to "go outside the walls" and build knowledge in a different way in a cultural diversity perspective. An ethnographic approach is an opportunity to identify the practices and uses of pupils on the Internet through a concrete practice of immersion of the researcher in the social environment. The knowledge of the context is rooted in their own involvement in the museum. Observations are analyzed as the data collected emerges. Emphasis is placed on the digitized content that is likely to build the relationship to the work of art. The exhibition visit is requested when the school public follows a specific itinerary or when they discover a painter or a historical period. In such a context, the museum approach aims to understand how mediation is constructed in exhibition spaces, how the practices, behaviors and uses of pupils are disrupted by the digitization of patrimony (Vidal 2012), and how the museum institution seizes it. It is a matter of building knowledge in relation to the thematic knowledge of the different courses.

8.2.3. *Third report: art education and aesthetic relationships to art training with digital devices offered to pupils in the exhibition space*

The introduction of multimedia and interactivity aims to blur the boundaries between the visit in the museum's rooms and the virtual consultation at home. The museum seeks a balance between technology and educational content to transmit knowledge. It is a question of knowing more about the practices of visits, in order to consider the stakes involved in the development of new mediation environments. Young people who download works on their mobile devices have become more demanding. It is therefore necessary to train all teachers in the various services of the museum, as well as in the new expectations of the public. But the museum is wondering about the possibility of deploying, thanks to the new tools, the interactivity and the immersion that allow us to appropriate the exhibition space. The jury therefore questions the candidate on the learning that pupils can experience in the aesthetic relationship to art within the museum.

The multiplication of immersive exhibitions, constructed as environments physically involving the pupil in the scenographic treatment of an exhibition space in situ, puts the pupil in the dispositions of a virtual space rather than as an interaction of a multimedia application. The experience of visiting the public in the real environment of the exhibition is taken in a context of interactions that depends on the exhibition space. The presentation of the works varies the way the public considers it. The perception depends on space, time, social environment and emotion. With its immersion in the virtual universe, we transpose the status of visitor from the real exhibition.

With this type of device, the museum becomes the place of a cultural experience and a sensory transmission of knowledge to the young. To encourage learning, the interactive terminals help the intuitive navigation of the pupils' visit. A click on an interactive object gives access to a description of the work, and another click allows the work to be viewed.

The images and the movement on the screen intrigue the pupils. The motivations are contextual and related to the exhibition. The moving image, its history and the image projection device convey the values behind visual devices. The navigation must be playful in the discovery of the works. The reading will increase the time of visit. It is a way to have a real cultural experience. The young person is not only an actor in a multimedia application. They take into account the behavior of other pupils in their class during the exhibition. The advent of Wi-Fi and mobile computing makes it possible to evolve audio guide support during the visit: data can be downloaded remotely on audiovisual sequences that are integrated into the visit, on the visitor's phone or laptop. Personal digital assistants, interactive kiosks and augmented virtual reality on tablets can illustrate certain themes. Permanent sensors make the content reactive to the context or situation defined by the visitor, who changes color or sound ambiance according to the interaction on luminous video tiles that facilitate the acquisition of knowledge.

If today, museums tend to immerse young visitors in spaces using video screens; interactive terminals are pleasant and accessible. The risk is to end up with entertainment that would negatively modify the exchange between public and museum. The jury asks the candidate how to find a balance between technologies and contents to transmit knowledge. The museum is a place of education, as well as a place of knowledge exchange. If fun and practical applications are increasingly successful, the risk is that schoolchildren will desert public visits to museums in favor of consultation outside the walls. Culture and entertainment within exhibitions and displays mix objects from the collections and scientific content in spectacular settings, as in some shopping malls. By letting us believe that it is equivalent to seeing the works in a museum or in virtual reality, a scientific current is developing that alerts us to our different aesthetic approaches. Museums are adopting different interpretations in which pupils' behaviors become "predictors" of success or failure, based on different types of knowledge about the objects and technologies present in or outside the museum. But if some museums adapt their pedagogical approach, others do not take the risk of modifying their scientific project in order to give priority to tools and attendance. They still prefer to emphasize the conservation of public collections. In any case, most museums are now experimenting with new cultural spaces to meet pupils' expectations.

8.2.4. Fourth report: the museum's organization

The concern raised by the museum is the disaffection of the museum to the benefit of the site outside the walls. There is always a risk of competition between the two forms of mediation. The site positioning must be in line with the expectations of young visitors, as experience, knowledge and information are directly sought (Baujard 2013). To accompany the change, the modalities of digital initiatives must adapt to the digitization of the museum offer, in order to accommodate the school public. Accompanying change in the context of digital evolution is to understand upstream how to anticipate and organize knowledge (Cifali 2018) and information to make it accessible to young audiences. It is a question of understanding the museum from the perspective of its organizational dimension, which is being transformed. This implies an institutional mutation, whether it be in terms of activities, professions or organization.

The museum is changing its organization by offering new services. The renovation of spaces redefines the patrimony vocation of museums. The development of temporary exhibitions encourages the creation of new services and new functions: events and programs, reception services, and cultural objects produced, distributed or sold. Organizational arrangements are being developed inside and outside the museum with a multiplicity of participants.

In reality, the practices of access to cultural knowledge through museums are based on pedagogical conceptions that favor patrimonial knowledge. They are no longer only a space of patrimonial conservation; they diversify the cultural mediation by redefining the temporality of the visit with the educational actors who can dialogue, discuss, react or train. During temporary exhibitions, the social networks develop the loyalty of their school public by offering educational guides to teachers.

Beyond the pleasure provided by leisure activities, sports and games, the pupil learns without any educational intention, while being attentive to what they are doing, and without being aware at the time of having learned something (Brougère 2016, p. 52). Experience, the set of situations to which the young person is or will be exposed, gives meaning to what they are experiencing or has experienced: learning from experience implies reflexivity (Schön 1994). Learning by experimentation, as a means of adapting to our environment, bears witness to making sense of experienced situations. It is a reflection on action. Learning that forges the pupil's identity through what they have achieved integrates emotions, feelings, intuitions and experiences. In this context, the project represents an important social, economic and political challenge. Its recognition allows pupils to gradually adapt to the university, to "succeed in their affiliation" (Dubet 2010). Such a system should make it possible to identify the skills acquired and to rethink the transition between high school and university based on research conducted on school and university dropouts.

Different approaches lead pupils to question not only the actual content of their social visiting activities, but also the set of situations that give them meaning, their personal involvement, the cognitive and behavioral effects in return. The approach is part of a process of self-transformation and constitutes formative feedback of skills. Bringing the cultural spaces of training closer to school knowledge is formative. Thinking about our experience is to engage in a process of self-training, in order to develop our cultural path. However, there are still some challenges that tend to promote one type of knowledge over another, recognizing that it is as important to learn from social life as it is to follow school knowledge on action knowledge; we learn from others by multiplying learning experiences within new educational spaces.

An educational model is progressively constructed, both as a means of acquiring new cultural knowledge and as the result of a formative activity that depends on the pupils' interactions with the cultural environment. The main instruments dedicated to cultural expression are art education and cultural education, two aspects essential to the development of the pupils' personality and citizenship. Education, centered on a logic of transmission of knowledge and learning, approaches the relationship to the museum in a logic of artistic training "as the appreciation of the importance of the creative expression of ideas, experiences, and emotions in various forms including music, performing arts, literature, and visual arts". This competence, defined by the European Parliament and then by the Council of the European Union on December 18, 2006, for lifelong learning, is a set of knowledge, skills, and attitudes necessary for personal fulfilment and development, social inclusion, citizenship and employment[3]. This ambition implies an awareness of the local, national and European cultural patrimony and its place in the world, while seeking to maintain the quality of arts education in formal and non-formal learning environments. The fifth part of decree No. 2006-830, relating to the common base of knowledge and skills, envisages the attitudes of the humanistic culture provided in school to give a personal cultural life through the frequentation of museums, in order to develop "the awareness that human experiences have something universal".

The cultural space of training gives place to observation, imagination, games, restitution, according to a scheme of knowledge, allowing cognitive activities that give ideas of route to the museum, in order to obtain a knowledge of ourselves by the human experience. The museum is increasingly involved because of its

---

3 Full text of the report: http://ec.europa.eu/culture/library/index_en.htm.

importance in the school program. The emergence of digital networks has had an impact on the museum, as it has to deal with the development of devices, both in the production and in the reception of cultural training. Thus, young people and teachers are no longer receivers, as they are led to play a role in cultural training, allowing the development of numerous learning activities in exhibition spaces. The mediation function of this "third space" upsets the relationship to knowledge between the school and the museum.

Therefore, how can we not rethink the cultural spaces of education? Observing pupils looking at paintings, reading labels or screens, strolling around, communicating with each other, invites us to interpret triggers specific to their understanding of the world. All awareness of the world comes from immediate, sensitive experience (Dewey 1915, p. 46). But this is not enough. This intention presents a particular form, allowing us to concretely convey humanistic culture, which invites research in education sciences and training to focus on new pedagogies in interaction with the museums of the cultural environment. Around a unique research object, the museum transforms the relationship to ourselves and to others. It is the encounter between new pedagogical situations that offer varied experiences of visit. The academic vocation must therefore be combined with the discovery of ethical imperatives.

8.3. References

Baujard, C. (2013). *Du musée conservateur au musée virtuel*. Hermes-Lavoisier, Paris.

Baujard, C. (ed.) (2019). Environnement numérique et musées. *Les Cahiers du Numérique*, 15(1/2), 9–19.

Brougère, G. (2016). De l'apprentissage diffus ou informel à l'éducation diffuse ou informelle. *Le Télémaque*, 49(May), 51–63.

Chabanne, J.-C., Parayre, M., Villagordo, E. (eds) (2012). *La rencontre avec l'œuvre. Éprouver, pratiquer, enseigner les arts et la culture*. L'Harmattan, Paris.

Cifali, M. (2018). *S'engager pour accompagner, valeurs des métiers de formation*. Presses universitaires de France, Paris.

Dewey, J. (1915). *L'art comme expérience*. Folio Essais, Paris.

Dubet, F. (2010). *Les places et les chances, repenser la justice sociale*. Le Seuil, Paris.

Garnier, B. and Kahn, P. (eds) (2016). *Éduquer dans et hors de l'école. Lieux et milieux de formation*. Presses universitaires de Rennes, Rennes.

Le Louvre (2021). Oser le Louvre, mode d'emploi. Groupes scolaires et périscolaires. Enseignants préparer votre visite. Se former et trouver des ressources [Online]. Available at: https://www.louvre.fr/visiter/venir-en-groupe#groupes-scolaires-et-periscolaires.

Meunier, A. and Luckerhoff, J. (2012). Le musée et le partage des savoirs. In *La muséologie, champ de théories et de pratiques*, Meunier, A. (ed.). Presses de l'université du Québec, Quebec.

Schön, D.-A. (1994). *Le praticien réflexif.* Les Éditions Logiques, Montreal.

Vidal, G. (2012). *La sociologie des usages. Continuités et transformations.* Hermes-Lavoisier, Paris.

PART 3

Reading and Cultural Mediation

Introduction to Part 3

Reading induces an appeal to several senses in the educational context. Without wishing to devalue sight, which ultimately makes us think of the act of reading, touch, and hearing are senses to be used in our contexts when we understand the language–culture. Smell and taste are not treated as a priority here, but we have no doubt about the need to read in preschools through these senses, either when children start devouring plastic or cloth books, or when they get lost in them, through the smells of materials offered and carefully prepared for this discovery. For Passos (2008), a specialist in Freirean theory, the word "reading" means reading with the body conscious and flooded by an experienced story of a real world. The real world is that complex space where all kinds of meanings, ideas, images, contradictions, and contexts are intertwined.

But the pleasure of having reading at hand is not known to all teachers and learners. Touching a book and flipping through it is like unveiling a world filled with words and meaning. Passos (2008) states that "reading the world and the word is, for Freire, a subjective right, as through understanding signs and meanings we become human, we access mediations of power and citizenship" (p. 240, loose translation[1]).

There is a growing trend to get books out of the hands of our teachers. We can access them virtually, but having access to reading via the screen is still a distant reality for many teachers and learners. The reading that we experience at home, that

---

Introduction written by Denise Gisele DE BRITTO DAMASCO.

1 The Paulo Freire dictionary presents the term reading, which was defined by Luiz Augusto Passos, from the Portuguese: "A leitura do mundo e da palavra é, em Freire, direito subjetctivo, pois, dominando signos e sentidos, nos humanizamos, acesasando mediações de poder e cidadania" (Passos 2008, p. 240).

can become an extension of our arms and fingers, the reading that can be our alter ego, may never happen for some.

If we do not feel satisfaction in the act of reading, how can we transmit it to our learners? This is the question that Nathalie Bertrand, a certified teacher of literature and field trainer in French for primary and secondary schools, has been asking herself since 2009 at the Institut national supérieur du professorat et de l'éducation at the Université de Strasbourg. How many experiences in the field did Nathalie Bertrand have to go through in order to send us her reflections on the importance of the cultural practices of reading and writing? She presents us with the chapter entitled, "Developing New Teaching Practices for Reading and Writing in French Elementary Schools Involving Book Mediators." As she is responsible for the initial training of students in the master's program in teaching, education, and training, she is particularly interested in the links between schools and cultural partners in order to develop solid acculturative practices that reflect a commitment to the act of reading and writing.

Nathalie Bertrand highlights training that promotes reading and writing to combat illiteracy based on the cultural practices of those who pass on reading, who collaborate in order to help each other against a weakening of the written word, knowledge of texts and the relationship with books. Spreading training devices that favor the interaction of educational actors and the spaces of book mediation, such as libraries, authors, and associations for the promotion of reading, plays a crucial role in the development of professional gestures related to the acquisition and transmission of culture.

We can define the term *culture* as "a way of living in a society, which includes the arts, religions, customs, ways of life, technologies, language, and knowledge that structure it […]" (Gustsack 2008, p. 237). The choice to engage in the deepening of acculturating professional gestures makes us value either touch or sight in our training of trainers.

Hearing, as an element that triggers reading, can also be present in our daily teaching life. Pascale Gossin and Isabelle Lebrat present us the chapter entitled "Making Books Resonate: A Cultural Mediation Exercise Offered to Trainee Schoolteachers." The authors highlight a practice of cultural mediation offered to trainee teachers, based on books read aloud. Pascale Gossin, lecturer in information and communication sciences at the Université de Lorraine and the Université de Strasbourg, and Isabelle Lebrat, associate professor of literature and doctor of French literature at the Université de Strasbourg, make us reflect on reading aloud.

The authors assert that we can access an active literary culture when we listen to each other, because there is a specific rhythm in an oral language, and the emotions that flow from it. The act of hearing is a "pedagogical virtue", according to Freire, when we learn to listen (Fischer and Lousada 2008, p. 301). From this virtue comes dialogue, as a result of this humble action of listening to the other. Knowing how to listen is not simply an auditory capacity, nor is it politeness. We open doors and windows, we build bridges, we build our identities in this collective educational space. The teacher and learners listen to each other and decide to enjoy each other's sounds. Everyone learns by listening to each other. In Freirean theory, knowing how to listen, according to Saul (2008), "is a condition for the development of a democratic educational practice. When we understand that we must learn to listen to the learner, patiently and critically, according to Freire, we can speak with them and not for them, as if the truth belonged only to us" (p. 171, loose translation[2]).

Passos (2008) highlights the fact of rereading the world. To reread it, there is room for silence, for exchanged words, for shared writings. There is a symbiosis between reading a word and reading the world, as "three realities, in space and in historical time, are welded together in an undeniable way: the world, us, and the others" (p. 240, loose translation[3]). To us to begin this action of reading and rereading of the world that induces all cultural mediation from the personal devices, our body and spirit, and the professionals that we have in our educational contexts.

References

Fischer, N.B. and Lousada, V.L. (2008). In *Dicionário Paulo Freire*, Streck, D.R., Redin, E., Zitkoski, J.J. (eds). Autêntica, Belo Horizonte.

Gustsack, F. (2008). Invasão cultural. In *Dicionário Paulo Freire*, Streck, D.R., Redin, E., Zitkoski, J.J. (eds). Autêntica, Belo Horizonte.

Klein, R. (2008). Ler/Leitura. In *Dicionário Paulo Freire*, Streck, D.R., Redin, E., Zitkoski, J.J. (eds). Autêntica, Belo Horizonte.

Passos, L.A. (2008). Leitura do Mundo. In *Dicionário Paulo Freire*, Streck, D.R., Redin, E., Zitkoski, J.J. (eds). Autêntica, Belo Horizonte.

Saul, A.-M. (2008). Escutar. In *Dicionário Paulo Freire*, Streck, D.R., Redin, E., Zitkoski, J.J. (eds). Autêntica, Belo Horizonte.

---

2 Translated from the Portuguese: "Saber escutar é condição para o desenvolvimento de uma prática éducativa democrática. Na medida em que aprendemos a escutar, paciente e criticamente, o educando, afirma Freire, podemos passar a falar com ele e não falar para ele, como se fôssemos detentores da verdade a ser transmitida."

3 Translated from the Portuguese: "Três realidades, no espaço e no tempo da história, encontram-se soldadas, indiscriminavelmente: o mundo, nós e os outros" (Passos 2008, p. 240).

9

Developing New Teaching Practices for Reading and Writing in French Elementary Schools Involving Book Mediators

This chapter's subject is to discuss two training programs implemented at the Institut national supérieur du professorat et de l'éducation de l'académie de Strasbourg, designed to develop the reading and writing skills and knowledge of future elementary school teachers in France, thanks to a partnership with book mediators inside and outside the school.

9.1. What professional skills are expected?

At the Institut national supérieur du professorat et de l'éducation (INSPE), we train our students, teachers and trainee teachers for the master's degree in teaching and 1st degree training in French. This means that we prepare them for the competitive examination, as well as, and above all, for the profession of schoolteacher. In particular, we help them to develop the professional skills mentioned in the reference framework for teaching and education professions[1] under the heading: "Teachers, professionals who carry knowledge and a common culture," around the mastery of disciplinary and didactic knowledge, as well as of pedagogical practices on the study of written and oral language and the study of texts and statements in all their diversity, including children's literature.

Chapter written by Nathalie BERTRAND.

1 Bulletin officiel no. 30 du 25 juillet 2013 NOR : MENE1315928A. Arrêté du 1-7-2013 – J.O. du 18-7-2013. MEN – DGESCO A3-3. ©

The mastery of reading–writing skills by future schoolteachers is a legitimate implicit expectation in initial training. If we are interested more specifically in literacy skills, we should be able to consider that our students have developed skills in this area at least during their school years, as well as within certain university courses. Thus, if we retain the definition of the notion established by Lafontaine and Pharand (2015), they are supposed to be familiar with the variety of textual materials, to have a multidimensional vision of statements, to know what their academic and extracurricular uses are and of course to have personal, professional and sociocultural practices. And why not, have some knowledge of children's literature production, or even a form of appetence for reading these texts.

9.2. State of the art in initial training

However, it is clear that this assumption has not been true for several years now within the cohorts that we accompany and that the gap between our training expectations, the needs of the profession and the reality of the field continues to grow. A large number of our students entering the master's program, for example, have difficulty defining a fable as anything other than a poetic form (which is often a text to be recited by heart). They do not situate La Fontaine in his time, do not make the connection with Aesop's texts, have forgotten the names of the classical playwrights they studied in high school, have difficulty analyzing an excerpt from a contemporary novel, or, to abandon the register of classical and patrimonial literature, cannot name several great authors of children's literature, not even the Alsatian-born writer Tomi Ungerer. What is even more alarming is that they do not feel attracted to or even concerned by children's literature, which they will have to promote in their classes.

We do not want to blame them: there are extenuating circumstances, there are several reasons for this decline in competence. First of all, in general, this decline can be seen in the cultural practices of the French, and our students are no exception to societal evolution. According to the latest results of the "Cultural Practices" survey[2], conducted by the French Ministry of Culture in 2018 on 9,200 individuals, and which is the main instrument for monitoring the behaviors of the French in the field of culture and media, we note, for the age group of our students, the lasting decrease in the practice of reading books and, to a lesser extent, of visiting libraries. This trend, observed since the beginning of the 1990s, is a counterpoint to the rise of video games and digital practices.

---

2 https://www.culture.gouv.fr/Sites-thematiques/Etudes-et-statistiques/Publications/Collections-de-synthese/Culture-etudes-2007-2021/Cinquante-ans-de-pratiques-culturelles-en-France-CE-2020-2.

Secondly, the very nature of the recruitment exam has partly modified the training that students have been able to benefit from until 2014: an oral option, the children's literature option, which had been introduced in 2006, disappeared at that time. At the time, it was overwhelmingly chosen by candidates, which made it possible to ensure a first literary culture, as well as the means to initiate the study of it and to develop a taste for it in children.

The third reason is that the universalization of the course has increased students' commitment to the development of other skills and in various fields, such as research, neuroscience or education sciences, for example. As the time frame of the training models is not infinitely expandable, the amount of time devoted to disciplinary training has been considerably reduced, and the part devoted to the teaching of texts and children's literature is shrinking.

To assess this trend of deculturation in our student body on our own scale, and to try to get a better sense of their shortcomings, in order to figure out how to fill them, we have launched declarative surveys of our first-year students in 2019 about their personal reading and writing practices. This involves, each year, a cohort of about 100 individuals, mostly born in the late 1990s. We present here a few main lines from the results of one of these surveys conducted in September 2020, at the beginning of the master's program (M1), among 58 students, without presenting the entire questionnaire or going into the details of its use.

To the question: "Do you like to read?" five students answered in the negative, 44 in the affirmative, which is at first sight rather reassuring. However, 10 more students said that they only liked to read in moderation, depending on the subject or the time, and one student "learned to like it".

When asked about the number of books they read in their personal practice (not related to their studies), 20 students said they read between one and three books per month, 17 from one to five per year (more often two or three); five were avid readers, with one to three books per week. Many of them do not feel legitimate in this respect in their future teaching practice. Most of them consider themselves to be irregular or occasional readers (regardless of the number of books they read) and tend to read in the summer or during the vacations, because they do not read more because of a severe lack of time.

When we ask them to formulate needs to develop their skills and offer them our help, we get 19 non-responses, which we interpret as an admission of their own responsibility for not engaging in the activity, and the awareness of having to get started by finding an intrinsic motivation. Others, more numerous, would like to have time: to have a free mind, not to be preoccupied by studies, to be free of screens, to organize themselves better, in order to free up time dedicated to reading.

Some of them wish to find an impulse, a motivation that they express by a request for access to "simple" books (which we interpret as not too long, not too literary, easy to read and if possible with pleasant subjects; in other words: leave the classical literature of another age). Others, finally, want recommendations, reading advice, as well as input on literature, and mention a possible contact with mediators, in the library, for example.

This survey confirms the impression of growing deculturation among our cohorts. If we take into account the ministerial will affirmed by the operation "Mobilisation en faveur du livre et de la lecture" (Mobilization in favor of books and reading) launched in August 2019 by the French Ministry of National Education, placing reading and writing at the rank of fundamental teaching in schools as a crucial factor in the success of students; we understand all the more the crucial importance of developing these same skills in the adults responsible for educating them.

9.3. Cultural mediation practices in the master's program

We trainers therefore find ourselves obliged to rethink the way in which we transmit classroom practices aimed at developing a taste for reading in children, by first working to develop the enthusiasm of their next teachers. We therefore postulate that by training future teachers in a better understanding of the world of books and reading practices, by putting them in contact with other readers[3], we will promote both a better teaching of texts in all their varieties in the classroom and the development of reading pleasure for all. But how can we allow this meeting between two worlds when we are trainers in INSPE?

For several years, we have chosen to turn to non-formal education, by associating book mediators with a training module, in order to teach future teachers how to become intermediaries with their students, in actions between the school and other places of reading and book promotion. A teaching unit entitled "Interdisciplinarité. Initier à la pédagogie de projet dans les classes" (Interdisciplinarity. Initiating project-based teaching in the classroom) has as its theme "Développer des projets culturels avec des partenaires pour faire lire et écrire en classe" (Developing cultural projects with partners to promote reading and writing in the classroom). We have 30 hours to demonstrate how to use cultural objects, places and resource persons to build a project for the class, to help find a partnership and to be supported in the implementation of the class project (even though it is modest) through meetings with cultural partners in the school. These

---

3 Frier, C. (2006). *Les Passeurs de lecture : lire ensemble à la maison et à l'école.* Éditions Retz, Paris.

partners can be virtual within the framework of national actions, such as the Press and media week in schools, organized in March by the CLEMI[4], the Printemps des poètes[5] or the Bibliothèque nationale de France (National Library of France) and its partners, who offer an annual writing contest[6]. However, we are particularly interested in fostering relationships with regional or local partners. We therefore begin by giving the group of students the opportunity to experience the benefits of pedagogical projects and even project-based learning.

The first meeting presented, through the departmental language and reading–writing officer, the Printemps de l'écriture (springtime of writing) competition which, since 1987, in Alsace, has proposed, around a theme renewed each year, subjects of written and artistic expression from kindergarten to high school, in connection with the museum structures of the region. Languages, texts, images, sounds and works are associated in a multidimensional and transdisciplinary approach. Students are invited to compete with their class and regularly produce excellent works, which are awarded by the jury.

The director of the Wittenheim youth and cultural center then proposes to discover the Ramdam festival[7], festival of books and youth, which it organizes every year and which programs activities with and for classes. It is therefore always accompanied by another partner, a member of the association Lire et faire lire[8] (read and make read) or librarian in the neighborhood, for example, that the director puts forward methods of promoting reading to children outside the classroom, in a mediation entirely focused on the notion of shared reading, aiming to develop the "desire to read" by encouraging a happy and intimate experience with the practice of reading to facilitate the appropriation of the written or iconographic language and to contribute to giving meaning to the learning of reading skills. Inspired by the methods of popular education, its team favors an interactive approach that associates numerous cultural, educational and associative partners, and encourages the public – as broad as possible – to appropriate the festival by being an actor and by participating in its creation.

Last important meetings for our students: those of the active and retired members of the l'Éducation nationale de l'association colmarienne l'aBéCéDaire (National Education of the Colmar Association aBéCéDaire)[9] who, in conjunction with the

4 Centre pour l'éducation aux médias et à l'information: https://www.clemi.fr/.

5 https://www.printempsdespoetes.com/Le-Printemps-des-Poetes.

6 http://classes.bnf.fr/concours.htm.

7 https://www.ramdamwittenheim.fr/.

8 https://www.lireetfairelire.org/.

9 http://www.crdp-strasbourg.fr/main2/ecole_elementaire/abecedaire/.

youth team of the Festival du livre de Colmar[10] (Colmar Book Festival), solicits the students in the preparation and the operation of a booth during the weekend of the festival, to welcome children from 3 to 11 years old around workshops related to the annual theme. This same association also runs a reading challenge from cycle 1 to cycle 3. The student volunteers are involved in the carrying out of games for the partner classes of the department. Finally, each year, this double partnership allows us to welcome a recognized author of children's literature at INSPE (J. Dalrymple, E. Jadoul, V. Cuvellier, S. Morgenstern, etc.). A small team of students is in charge of the reception, the internal communication, and together with the author, the constitution of their bibliography, which they are in charge of reading in its entirety in order to prepare an exhibition intended to highlight their work within our institute; they also have to build the meeting space (other than by a game of questions–answers, with a real staging) and finally, they are in charge of the animation of the meeting, which is done in front of the public of the site users. These encounters are always different, but impressive for our students, and they allow us to make the presence of children's literature more concrete, and to think of other ways to share it with others, adults or children.

9.4. Looking back on the experience: the students' point of view

Each year, at the end of the "Interdisciplinarity" teaching unit, an assessment allows us to take stock of the students' experiences, the transformations in their emerging practices, as well as their own way of understanding reading and writing activities, thanks to other mediators, outside of school, in interaction with other educational environments. The project was adopted unanimously (opinions were collected anonymously, so that everyone could express themselves freely), and more than a hundred students spoke[11] of the pleasure they had in learning in a different way and how this particular teaching unit nourished their desire to discover, learn, make and exchange. Many of them write that they were initially frightened by the magnitude of the task to be accomplished, made even more complex by the fact that they had to manage the tasks independently in small groups of students who did not necessarily belong to the same training groups, as there was a mix of multi-skilled students (teaching in French) and bilingual students (teaching linguistic disciplines in German), as well as students preparing for the competitive examination to become a schoolteacher and others who were already in training. Among them, some are finishing their master's degree, while others are enrolled in a university degree. Finally, some of these students are undergoing professional retraining and come from sectors as different as the tertiary sector, craft trades, technical or technological training, etc. The feedback from these students speaks of "luck"

---

10 https://festivaldulivre.colmar.fr/.

11 Extracts from these reports are attached to this text.

(having had the opportunity to experience these moments within a university training program), as well as of motivation, pleasure and even passion. Some of them had never attended a literature festival and took a liking to it, looking forward to the next editions. The transposition with classroom practices is done naturally, and barriers are lifted: they see that children are interested in these activities and are happy to participate, whether in class, during the festivals, or in the other dedicated reading spaces. One student writes that she learned "how to open the book to children in the classroom".

Each of the mediators we met provides structure and support for the beginning experiences of our teacher trainees, as well as helps, through non-formal learning, to develop their necessary acculturation to writing. After having heard, seen and practiced with us in these various contexts, like journeymen, our students launch into their classes in a form they imagine after appropriation. And the results are not long in coming. Often dubious about the estimated burden of this implementation and the really time-consuming aspect of carrying out a project, they measure in a few sessions the benefits they have to draw from this other way of teaching with their students.

As an illustration, here is the eloquent testimony of a student who was doing an internship during three periods of her project with a host teacher in a class made up of pupils who were struggling with the act of reading, and who decided to apply the reading methods presented during the meetings. She was then writing her master's research paper on the subject of triggering the desire to read in the classroom, which contributed to her reflexivity about her practices.

– Early March:

> I have felt all along that there is that little something missing to develop pleasure in all students. I invested, on the advice of Ms. X^{12}, in two booklets[13] with headphones. The special needs students choose the books they want to read, I record the stories beforehand, then they place the storyteller on the sticker of the book and they can discover it while benefiting from listening to facilitate understanding.
>
> I thought I would suggest that they create a plastic composition from a shoebox, representing a scene, a passage from a book that they loved the most. Each creation would be accompanied by a piece of writing (title of the work and a text illustrating their box and indicating their

12 Director of the MJC of Wittenheim, Ramdam festival.
13 https://www.mybookinou.com/la-conteuse-bookinou/81-bookinou-3770013172069.html?gclid=CjwKCAjwhuCKBhADEiwA1HegOQ42Cr0FmApaORRCqsA4olazQI10BRYzngEwo UJfCPFPm1pDPWz6X xoCUF4QAvD_BwE.

source of inspiration, to make others who do not know the book want to borrow it). They could then be displayed in a library.

I feel like this is that little something I've been missing all along: building self-esteem, a sense of competence, creativity, and the joy of sharing personal reading. I hope that their reading habits will be impacted […].

– Mid-April:

The involvement of the students exceeded my expectations. There was such a sense of excitement. In retrospect, I think it was the lack of competition. The goal was to have fun reading and to share that fun. The project included all pupils, regardless of their level, and no one felt excluded. X is a non-reader because he has not mastered graphophonic correspondence, but he has a good command of oral language (syntax and lexical stock). He trained with the bookinous (followed reading with audio listening, then alone), he borrowed eight books. XX does not speak French well (allophone parents). For him, I did things differently. I first explained the story orally, then I made the recording, starting with the explanation of the complicated words and then the audio story. He borrowed six books. He admitted to me that he did not have any books at home […] Different kids, but not incompetent, just needed to be given the opportunity to participate […].

– June:

The students loved the animations. In Ms. Y's class, out of 22 students present, I recorded 57 loans. Thank you so much for giving us the children's literature bug… We are over the moon!

We can easily imagine that the transmitted literature virus will be contagious for years, but for the good of all, in this case.

9.5. New innovative pedagogical device to be tested: Fabulathèque

In order to continue and complete this experience, which has lasted for more than 10 years, we decided to go further in the experimentation of an innovative training, on the occasion of the reconstruction of our university library. We have integrated a children's area into the library that will allow us to welcome classes from cycle 1 to cycle 3, in a sort of "application library", on the model of the old French annex schools. The teachers of the department classes and their students will be invited to the Fabulathèque (this is the name we have chosen for this third place), accompanied upstream in their approach by a team of trainers, INSPE teachers, librarians, other mediators of reading, according to the project which will be built with and for them. Various courses will be offered, in German, in regional languages and in French, in a training catalog: from the library, the "cultural lung" of the school, to the knowledge of the book subject, from school reading practices to work with other "readers", from literary texts to other forms of writing, from books without text to texts without images, etc.

Our first- and second-year students will be trained in these pathways, linked to traditional teaching units, and will also be able to volunteer in their own time to work with pupils and teachers. They will thus benefit from in vivo training in the supervision of children, according to a pedagogical approach carried out outside the walls of the school, but on the university training site. The Fabulathèque is thus thought of as a laboratory combining training, teaching and research, in order to develop acculturating professional gestures[14] to writing and lead students and pupils in their care towards literacy. The first meeting scheduled at this location in May 2021 was with Nathalie Brisac, author of children's literature and director of communications for the children's publishing house L'école des loisirs[15]. This is another opportunity for our students to "open up" the reading spaces in the classroom, to expand their network of mediators of reading and literature, while appropriating the many tools and materials they make available to teachers.

Through this program, students, teacher trainees and primary school teachers will continue to learn about and become familiar with written culture, its works, linguistic codes and social practices. They will then be able to question their future or current classroom practices around texts, books and reading, to make them more attractive and effective and to achieve the objectives of their mission, which is to "train competent readers, but also active readers who have a taste for and interest in reading in all its forms and who have acquired a culture of the written word[16]".

9.6. Appendix

Excerpts from the anonymized individual assessments made by second-year (M2) master's students who participated in the theme "Developing cultural projects with partners to bring reading and writing into the classroom":

> It has motivated me to implement such projects when I am in the field,
> I was very apprehensive that it would not work.

---

14 *Rapport de recherche Lire-écrire au CP*, edited by R. Goigoux 2015, pp. 365–369. Available on the Ifé website: http://ife.ens-lyon.fr/ife/recherche/lire-ecrire.

15 https://www.ecoledesloisirs.fr/.

16 https://eduscol.education.fr/576/mobilisation-en-faveur-du-livre-et-de-la-lecture.

This new way of working was not common to me in my studies. All in all, it was a bubble of oxygen for me within this semester.

We started from nothing and ended up creating something beautiful.

It was a great and unique opportunity.

I loved seeing the kids involved in the workshops, attentive to the story.

I enjoyed reading the story to the children and seeing them interested in it.

The kids were happy, some came back [to the booth], enjoyed doing multiple workshops, and that to me is the greatest reward.

Desire to carry out projects in our classes.

Positive cultural opening with the possibility of meeting authors, big names in children's literature.

It's worth it for the purpose.

This option is something to do at least once in your life; you discover beautiful people, beautiful books, and all that in a joyful way.

We were able, through teamwork, to cooperate all together. In our university career, it is not often that we can work with such cohesion. Indeed, we realized the plot all together, and even if we were then in small groups for the workshops, we always had an eye on the whole, to know the progress of each one, to exchange new ideas [...] Moreover, this experience awoke passions. We had a real pleasure to implement everything, and it seems to me that during a project with a class, the students feel the same way. Also, seeing INSPE involved in this type of project is heartwarming. I have really grown.

This teaching unit was an opportunity for me to discover the cultural partners we can call upon for our class. It was very enriching to learn about a multitude of writing projects that have been done in class, which gave me ideas and the desire to do some myself. As for the design of our booth for the book festival, it showed that a lot could be done with a team of committed people and little means. All in all, it reinforced my belief that it is important to embark on projects, even if they are small in scale.

I was able to observe, while practicing the research, the method, the setting up of the booth, and thus I was able to project myself by imagining a similar project with students. This gave me the desire to look for a learning process behind each creation by having an objective and by allowing a cultural opening. The school also has this role.

As I expected, a great experience, enriching, with interesting encounters, many new discoveries [the festival itself, the aBéCéDaire[17]] I had a lot of fun throughout the project, it was motivating to work all together for the same goal. It was really good to be able to blossom in a project that interested me, motivated me, to work differently, despite the work, rather a breath of fresh air in the daily life of a student at INSPE. As a matter of fact, when you have fun, the work goes more easily! Thank you to all the people who made this experience possible.

I think all future teachers should have this knowledge and could explore the project of writing a story or participating in events like the Book Festival.

This teaching unit was very rewarding and informative, as it allowed me to discover how a cultural project is organized with a class, as well as with a cultural partner, such as the Colmar Book Festival. I had a lot of satisfaction to be part of the communication team to promote the work of INSPE at the Festival, as well as the author's visit. During the Festival weekend, the activities at the INSPE booth were very fun, and I had a lot of fun guiding the visiting children through the different activities.

I was able to learn a lot of things with pleasure, and doing cultural or artistic projects with a class is no longer "scary".

9.7. References

Frier, C. (2006). *Les passeurs de lecture : lire ensemble à la maison et à l'école*. Éditions Retz, Paris.

Goigoux, R. (ed.) (2015). Rapport de recherche Lire-écrire au CP. Institut français de l'éducation (ifé), 365–369 [Online]. Available at: http://ife.ens-lyon.fr/ife/recherche/lire-ecrire.

---

17 Events organized within the framework of the master 2 theme "Developing cultural projects with partners to promote reading and writing in the classroom."

Lafontaine, L. and Pharand, J. (2015). *Littératie : vers une maîtrise des compétences dans divers environnements*. Presses de l'Université du Québec, Quebec.

Lombardo, P. and Wolff, L. (2020). Cinquante ans de pratiques culturelles en France. Report, Ministère de la culture, Paris.

10

Making Books Resonate: A Cultural Mediation Exercise Offered to Trainee Schoolteachers

Here, we report on an experiment in the resonance of books, conducted by a dozen schoolteachers. They placed themselves at the service of the media library of the city where they study: we are in the south of Alsace, in Colmar, France. They turned into sound two books, which they read to the children at the Festival du livre de Colmar (Colmar Book Festival). How did the trainee teachers feel about this assignment? How did they relate this experience to their professional practice? To answer these questions, we will begin by giving the floor to authors of French literature who describe oral reading situations. We will then look at the place that this reading modality has in school practices, by looking at school programs from the 18th century to the present. We will present the module followed by the trainee teachers and will conclude by indicating how they experienced what one teacher called "an adventure".

10.1. Reading aloud in literature

Since the reading aloud of texts in Antiquity, through the practice of the Flaubertian "gueuloir" (the practice of reading prose as loudly as possible), the passage through the voice has always been felt as a sensitive mode of appropriation of the literature by writers. We have chosen three extracts from works belonging to the literary patrimony to enter the subject.

Chapter written by Pascale GOSSIN and Isabelle LEBRAT.

10.1.1. *Jean-Jacques Rousseau and fellowship*

Jean-Jacques Rousseau testifies to the paternal fellowship experienced in the context of family readings. "We began to read them after supper, my father and me. At first, it was only a question of exercising myself in reading by means of amusing books; but soon, the interest became so lively that we took turns reading without respite and spent the nights in this occupation" (Rousseau 2006).

10.1.2. *Émile Zola and the social gaze*

Émile Zola, in his novel *La Terre*, describes peasants in the context of a vigil:

> Let's see," said Fouan, "who's going to read this to us, to finish the vigil? [...] Jean had taken the book, and, immediately, without being asked, he began to read, in the white, stammering voice of a schoolboy who does not take punctuation into account, and we listened to him religiously [...] All had heavy hearts, this reading weighed little by little on their shoulders (Zola 2006, pp. 77–78).

10.1.3. *Jean-Paul Sartre and the entrance into reading*

In *Les Mots,* Sartre evokes the magical and anguishing effects of oral reading. The mother disappears to let the book speak. This brutal access to the symbolic can be read like a metaphor of the entry in the literature:

> Anne-Marie made me sit opposite her, on my little chair: She bent over, lowered her eyelids, and fell asleep. From this statue-like face came a voice of plaster. I lost my head: Who was telling? What? And to whom? My mother was absent: not a smile, not a sign of connivance, I was in exile. And then I didn't recognize her language. Where did she get her confidence? After a moment, I understood. It was the book that spoke (Sartre 2010).

These three strong messages, which we could have multiplied by continuing to go through existing literary works, show the effects of oral reading.

Today, cultural centers welcome storytellers, slam poets, actors, in order to allow their audiences to benefit from oral reading. The school is not left out.

10.2. School practice

10.2.1. *Past school practice*

In 1840, oral reading was applied to written work; the regulation of August 29, 1840 specified: "The writing lesson will begin with the reading aloud of a few copies; then the teacher will read the subject for the following lesson; he will end by reading the model of the one that has been corrected" (Chervel 1992, p. 140). On August 20, 1857, the Minister Rouland gave the following instruction: "The aim is to ensure, first of all, that the reading is done with ease and naturalness, and in general, in a conversational tone; then, that the children get into the habit of understanding all the words and thoughts" (Dessaw 2021). The institutional concerns of the time remain close to those advocated today: not teaching fluent reading as a technique limited to the oral reproduction of text, but reaching meaning, making comprehension the goal of reading. From 1850 to 1972, reading aloud was mentioned in various school programs. The primary school certificate includes a reading test: "It is an expressive reading, that is, a text read with the expression it contains. The aim is for the examiner to be sure that the candidate understands what they are reading and feels its beauty. Naturally, reading and recitation require a clear and sharp delivery in order to verify an intelligent and accented reading" (Lebucheur 1918, p. VII). In 1905, a decree concerning teacher training colleges stipulated the need for third grade teachers to be trained in public evening readings to instruct in "popular lectures on beautiful and edifying texts". The circular of May 3, 1935, for the 50th anniversary of Victor Hugo's death, states: "The reading aloud, which teachers often do on Saturday afternoons to reward students for the good work of the week, should preferably be borrowed from Victor Hugo." The official instructions of 1941, 1944 and 1947 specify that reading aloud represents the culmination of learning to read. For a hundred years (1850–1950), oral reading was considered the culmination of the process of learning to read. It made the link between the act of writing and reading (1840), revealed access to meaning (1898), and gave teachers a role as cultural facilitators (1935). From 1972 on, nuances appear. Deciphering and oralization are perceived as an obstacle to understanding. In 1976, Jean Foucambert puts forward the idea that reading is an ideovisual process, fundamentally and perfectly silent in the expert reader. Evelyne Charmeux (1988) thinks that reading aloud is a separate discipline. In about 20 years, oral reading has become a particular gesture, with specific functions. The 1995 elementary school teaching programs once again consider oral reading by the teacher to be essential. It aims at impregnation and must arouse the taste for reading. In 1998, the National Reading Observatory defended the idea that reading stories to children contributes to the success of learning to read. However, in the cycle 3 programs, dated 2002, it still appears in a very limited way, as it is a matter of "oralizing texts (known, memorized, or read) in front of the class in order to collectively share the pleasure and the interest". It is also mentioned to serve writing activities. "Reading aloud plays an important role when writing a text or revising it. Saying one's own text or the text of a classmate means experiencing its cohesion and effects" (Ministère de l'Éducation nationale 2002). The interests of reading aloud appear in a more marked way in the *Documents d'application des programmes en littérature* of 2004. "If reading aloud is a way of exploring texts, it can also be an end in itself," it states. These official programs call on teachers to use reading aloud through dramatization, as an exercise in interpreting, listening to and remembering texts. In a sign of greater recognition, from 2005 to 2010, one of the tests in the competitive examination for schoolteachers included an option for children's literature, in which the candidate was asked to read a text of about 20 lines.

The 2007 curricula for the three cycles of primary education include indications related to this reading modality. In kindergarten, "each time the teacher reads a text to their students, they do so clearly, with a properly posed voice and without hesitating to mobilize effective means of expression" (Ministère de l'Éducation nationale 2007, p. 22). In cycle 2, "the parallel use of children's literature, facilitated by numerous read-alouds by teachers, is just as necessary and remains the only way to work on understanding complex texts. The abilities expected at the end of the cycle are precise: "In reading aloud a text of five lines already read and studied, correctly restore the accentuation of groups of words, as well as the intonation curve, taking into account punctuation and simple prosodic elements". Cycle 3 is responsible for bringing all students to a fluent reading of texts commonly read at this level. "These encounters with the works include read-alouds (by the teacher or pupils) and silent readings. The pupil must be able to read in front of the class, to share the pleasure and interest, a passage of about ten lines from a known text."

The 2008 programs give less precise indications and retain two types of situations: listening and practice. In kindergarten, the aim is to listen silently and understand a text read by an adult. At the end of cycle 2, pupils must know how to "read aloud alone", respect punctuation and listen to patrimonial texts. In cycle 3, the work of listening is no longer specifically mentioned, but the pupil must be able to "read with ease (aloud, silently), an excerpt of text after preparation of the text" (Ministère de l'Éducation nationale 2008).

The official texts, over time, retain different entries. The reading made by the teacher lived a period of apogee during the first half of the 20th century. This function of cultural mediation continues, but this time within the classroom. The link between reading and writing has also experienced two periods of practice: 1840 and 2002. Reading aloud is seen as a way to check whether the reader is accessing the meaning of the text.

10.2.2. *Current school practice*

The 2020 programs, currently in effect, emphasize the importance of reading aloud. Thus, from cycle 2 (CP to CE2, children aged 6–9), "reading aloud is a central activity for developing reading fluency and ease" (Ministère de l'Éducation nationale 2020). At the end of this cycle, students should be able to read fluently, after preparation, a half-page text (1,400–1,500 characters). They should be able to participate in a dialogue reading, after preparation. The updated edition of the guide entitled *Pour enseigner la lecture et l'écriture au CP* (Teaching reading and writing in the first grade) is an opportunity for the ministère de l'Éducation nationale to reaffirm the value of reading aloud. The statement is justified by research findings:

> Researchers tell us that oral reading fluency is a direct predictor of good reading comprehension (pupils with the lowest fluency scores also have the lowest comprehension scores). It is developed through practice reading aloud from isolated words in early learning and then from prepared texts (Ministère de l'Éducation nationale 2019).

This practice would also be a way to better guarantee access to text comprehension: "Oral reading fluency is a predictor of good reading comprehension" (Ministère de l'Éducation nationale 2019). In cycle 3 (CM1 to 6th), daily practice in silent reading, as well as in reading aloud, is recommended in all subjects.

Reading-aloud experiences undoubtedly help build this active culture. Reading in the space of the class makes it possible to open to the possibility of meaning without imposing it authoritatively, a coherent and non-exclusive grasp of the text, to experience a rhythm and a language, to encourage the emergence of emotion without simplifying the circulation of meaning, but by allowing the enjoyment of the complex. The creation of a community of voices in the classroom makes it possible to awaken a sensual experience of otherness and to activate literary culture as an opening onto the world and onto the other, as an aid to the construction of identity.

Such is the anthropological range of the work of art where the seizure by the experience, conscious or unconscious, of a sound object, thought by a radically other subject and which, however, speaks to us and makes us grow, is played. Taking risks, willingness to go to the end of the attention to language through relationship, towards a new perception of the world, towards a relational ethic, such would be the path that the pupils' listening voice indicates to us when the teacher works on representations. Nathalie Rannou's (2016) work on the reception of poetry shows that hearing the poem leaves more room for rhythmic dynamics and emotional charge, whereas silent reading focuses from the outset on the construction of meaning and its inception. She defends the thesis that oral reception would be part of the devices favorable to the subjective and fertile appropriation of the literature. "A poetic experience of the matter-emotion passes by the word and the voice," affirms the researcher. The read text is carried by evidence, which ensures its legitimacy and frees the reader from deciphering. The mediation of the text by the voice would thus be effectively a bridge towards the constitution of the meaning, even a propaedeutic to the silent reading, as recommended by the new programs.

At school, reading a text aloud would be a way of listening to its sound modulations, its musical material. In this singular experience, the student can then feel truly involved in the accomplishment of the meaning.

10.3. Putting in resonance

Based on these data and on what past and current practices and official texts teach us about the sensitive reception of the literature, we proposed an exercise of putting two books in resonance to eight trainee teachers.

We chose two books by the same author: *Tour de manège* (1995a) and *Le Défilé* (1995b) by Olivier Douzou. Rich in meaning, with a reduced number of words, the two texts give the possibility of creating a sound atmosphere: a funfair for the first and a large popular demonstration for the second. The *Tour de manège* can be understood as the description of the sensations that a child feels when they climb on a merry-go-round, but a deeper reading shows that it is also the story of life. *Le Défilé* is built around a social meeting; we read a wink built around the hierarchy in the political organization.

Two paintings were proposed to the schoolteachers, the eight participated in the two paintings. *Le Défilé* was built musically on a Brazilian rhythm: the *batucada*. For *Tour de manège*, we worked with the sounds of "mechanical toy" pianos and music wheels.

The teachers oralized the texts, which were of course not modified. However, some words were repeated to create a mise en abyme. The books were also put into space by means of movements. The objective was to perform, to put themselves on stage, within the framework of the Festival du livre de Colmar, the city of their studies.

This work was part of a teaching unit called "Interdisciplinary Teaching," for which they could choose between several modules.

At the end of the course, they answered a questionnaire to measure their experience.

10.3.1. *Reasons for choosing the module*

The motivation for the choice of the theme is based on a liking for reading and music, as evoked by the following:

– The desire to work with a music professional. The training was co-taught by a teacher from the Institut national supérieur du professorat et de l'éducation (INSPE) and a teacher from a Centre de formation des musiciens intervenants (CFM).

– The desire to create, offer and share a conviction is mentioned. Only one student indicated a choice made by chance.

10.3.2. *Difference between foresight and reality*

Three students feared that the audience would lose interest, while others said that they were driven by the conviction that the exercise was relevant. All of them emphasize that they were surprised by the strength that the resonance of the texts brings.

10.3.3. *Role of the schoolteacher*

The eight people concerned unanimously affirm with conviction that they were indeed in the performance of their duties when they put themselves on display in this way.

10.3.4. *Professional contributions*

The students say that they gained confidence and changed their professional posture as a result of this experience. They mention that they have measured their function as cultural mediators and the necessary commitment that this implies. They noted the rich emulation inherent in group work. They measured the strength of children's literature and the link that can be woven between it and music.

10.3.5. *Challenges*

For all of them, the most difficult part was to set the rhythm and sound of the texts. They also mentioned the need for tension in order to relate to the audience, to manage their stage fright and to put themselves on stage.

10.4. Conclusion

In *Le Plaisir du texte*, Barthes says that "if it were possible to imagine an aesthetic of textual pleasure, it would have to include: writing aloud. This vocal writing (which is not speech at all), we do not practice it, but it is undoubtedly what Artaud recommended and what Sollers asks for" (Barthes 1973, p. 103). This writing aloud is not expressive; it belongs entirely to the significance, because it is carried not by the dramatic inflections, but by the grain of the voice, which is "an erotic mix of tone and language" (Barthes 1973, p. 103). "What it seeks (in a perspective of enjoyment) are the impulsive incidents, it is the language lined with skin, a text where one can hear the grain of the gullet, the patina of the consonants, the voluptuousness of the vowels, a whole stereophony of the deep flesh: the articulation of the body of language, not that of the sense, of language" (Barthes 1973, p. 103). Later, Barthes will speak about this rustling of the language that he defines as "the noise even of the plural enjoyment" (Barthes 1984, p. 100). This vocal writing would let itself be heard even in a silent reading. It is not certain *in fine* that the voice of a text requires absolutely to be read aloud. The paradox wants the text to be able to be read and said, "to full mouth" (Barthes 1984, p. 89) without there being passage by reading aloud. Undoubtedly, there exists a subvocalic reading[1], a throat voice, an inner diction made of music, breath and tension. This "absent of all mouths of flesh", according to the definition of Julien Gracq, would open an interior ear that the philosopher Philippe Lacoue-Labarthe names "the third ear, the artistic, stylistic ear, suitable to discern in the writing, the speech, the language, a fundamental music, in that it makes sense" (Lacoue-Labarthe 1979, p. 246).

---

1 In *Les Neurones de la lecture*, Stanislas Dehaene states that "today, a consensus is emerging: in adults, both reading pathways exist and are activated simultaneously. We all have a direct way of accessing words, which prevents us from pronouncing them mentally before understanding them. Nevertheless, in the expert reader, the sound of the words continues to be used, even if we are not always aware of it. It is not articulation – we do not need to move our lips or even prepare a mouth movement. But at a deeper level in our brain, information about the pronunciation of words is automatically activated. The two word-processing pathways, the lexical and the phonological pathways, therefore work in parallel, one supporting the other (Dehaene 2007, p. 53).

This vocality, the secret principle of writing, awakens in the shadow of hearing when the reader begins to listen and enters into resonance with this tacit voice. In *Les Paradisiaques*, Pascal Quignard contrasts the voice of the mouth, the sonorous voice, the word that establishes dialogue, that forms society, and the voice of the throat, the inner voice, essentially intimate, "held in silence, lurking near the Adam's apple". He suggests that "the unvoiced language of literature is not addressed to the mouth voice, but to the throat voice. The language of those who read is transported directly from throat to throat, from inside to inside" (Quignard 2005, p. 107). To read a text, it would be to hear someone speaking to us from inside. Is this not one of the most intimate experiences a human being can have?

10.5. References

Agence nationale des pratiques culturelles autour de la littérature jeunesse (2006). *Lire à haute voix des livres aux tout-petits*. Érès, Paris.

Aragon, S. (2004). Les images de lectrices dans les textes de fiction français du milieu du XVIIe siècle au milieu du XIXe siècle. *Cahiers de Narratologie, Figures de la lecture et du lecteur*, 11, 1–11.

Barthes, R. (1973). *Le plaisir du texte*. Le Seuil, Paris.

Barthes, R. (1982). *L'obvie et l'obtus. Essais critiques III*. Le Seuil, Paris.

Barthes, B. (1984). *Le bruissement de la langue. Essais critiques IV*. Le Seuil, Paris.

Barton, D. and Hamilton, M. (2010). La littératie : une pratique sociale. *Langage et société*, 133(3), 45–62.

Char, R. (1965). *Pauvreté et privilège, recherche de la base et du sommet. Œuvres complètes*. Gallimard, Paris.

Charmeux, E. (1988). *La lecture à l'école*. Cedic, Brussels.

Chartier, R. (1985). *Pratiques de la lecture*. Cercles de la librairie, Paris.

Chervel, A. (1992). *L'enseignement du français à l'école primaire – Textes officiels*, volume 1. Institut National de Recherche Pédagogique, Lyon.

Dehaene, S. (2007). *Les neurones de la lecture*. Odile Jacob, Paris.

Dessaw, G. (2021). Le temps des instituteurs [Online]. Available at: http://www.le-temps-des-instituteurs.fr/ens-francais-lecture.html [Accessed 19 November 2021].

Dolz, J. and Schneuwly, B. (2009). *Pour un enseignement de l'oral : initiation aux genres formels à l'école*. ESF, Paris.

Douzou, O. (1995a). *Tour de manège*. Éditions du Rouergue, Paris.

Douzou, O. (1995b). *Le défilé*. Éditions du Rouergue, Paris.

Érard, Y. (2006). Un texte c'est quelque chose qu'on lit. *A contrario*, 4(1), 7–34.

Foucambert, J. (1976). *La manière d'être lecteur*. O.C.D.L, Paris.

Fouché, P. (2005). *Dictionnaire encyclopédique du livre*. Cercle de la librairie, Paris.

Guennoc, C. (2019). Gestes d'écoute : parcours de l'écouter lire dans l'enseignement du cycle 1 au cycle 4. *Le français aujourd'hui*, 2(205), 75–84.

Habert, B. and Lapeyre, C. (2019). Former par corps ? Une expérience du texte et du geste en formation initiale. *Le français aujourd'hui*, 2(205), 13–22.

Haussin, C., Rayna, S., Rubio, M., Séméria, P. (2019). *Petite enfance : art et culture pour inclure*. Érès, Toulouse.

Jean, G. (1999). *Lire à haute voix : histoire, fonctions et pratiques de la "lecture oralisée"*. Les Éditions de L'Atelier, Ivry sur Seine.

Lacoue-Labarthe, P. (ed.) (1979). L'écho du sujet. In *Le sujet de la philosophie*. Flammarion, Paris.

Lebrun, M. (2006). La vive voix : une voie interprétative essentielle. In *Écoute mon papyrus, littérature, oral et oralité*, Clermont, P. and Schneider, A. (eds). Centre régional de documentation pédagogique d'Alsace, Strasbourg.

Lebucheur, P. (1918). *Guide du certificat d'études primaires et secondaires*. Hatier, Paris.

Manguel, A. (1998). *Une histoire de la lecture*. Actes Sud, Arles.

Martin, S. (2006). Non l'expression, mais la relation : avec des poèmes pour l'oralité. In *Ecoute mon papyrus, littérature, oral et oralité*, Clermont, P. and Schneider, A. (eds). Centre Régional de documentation pédagogique d'Alsace, Strasbourg.

Ministère de l'Éducation nationale (2002). Horaires et programmes de l'enseignement primaire. *Bulletin officiel*, Special edition, 1.

Ministère de l'Éducation nationale (2004). *Littérature*, volume 2. Centre national de documentation pédagogique, Paris.

Ministère de l'Éducation nationale (2007). Programmes d'enseignement de l'école primaire. *Bulletin Officiel*, Special edition, 5.

Ministère de l'Éducation nationale (2008). Les nouveaux programmes d'enseignement de l'école primaire. *Bulletin Officiel*, Special edition, 0.

Ministère de l'Éducation nationale (2019). Enseignements primaire et secondaire. Recommandations pédagogiques. *Bulletin Officiel*, 22.

Ministère de l'Éducation nationale (2020). Enseignements primaire et secondaire. Programmes d'enseignement de l'école primaire. *Bulletin Officiel*, 31.

Pennac, D. (1992). *Comme un roman*. Gallimard, Paris.

Pled, B., Roudy, P., Hameau, C. (1997). *Lire à haute voix au cycle 3*. Nathan, Paris.

Ponti, C. (2019). Ce n'est pas en donnant un livre qu'on donne la lecture. *Enfances & Psy*, 2(82), 60–68.

Quignard, P. (2005). *Les Paradisiaques*. Grasset, Paris.

Rannou, N. (2000). *La lecture à haute voix en seconde*. Institut Universitaire de Formation des Maîtres de Bretagne, Saint-Brieuc.

Rannou, N. (2016). Lire et faire lire la poésie : états d'une recherche et perspectives pour une didactique en devenir. In *Être et devenir lecteur(s) de poèmes : de la poésie patrimoniale au numérique*, Brillant-Rannou, N., Boutevin, C., Brunel, M. (eds). Presses universitaires de Namur, Namur [Online]. Available at: http://books.openedition.org/pun/4858.

Rateau, D. (2005). Entrer dans les écrits par la voix d'un autre. *La lettre de l'enfance et de l'adolescence*, 61–69 [Online]. Available at: https://doi.org/10.3917/lett.061.74.

Rateau, D. (2009). Du désir de lire à voix haute des livres d'images…. In *Lire à haute voix des livres aux tout-petits*, Agence nationale des pratiques culturelles (ed.). Érès, Paris.

Ros-Dupont, M. (2004). *La lecture à haute voix : du CP au CM2*. Bordas, Paris.

Rousseau, J.-J. (2006). *Les confessions : livres I à IV : Récit autobiographique*. Petits classiques Larousse, Paris.

Rouxel, A. (2006). Appropriation des œuvres et culture littéraire. *Actes des 7ᵉ Rencontres des chercheurs en didactique de la littérature*. Institut Universitaire de Formation des Maîtres de Montpellier, Montpellier.

Sartre, J.-P. (2010). *Les mots et autres écrits autobiographiques*. Gallimard, Paris.

Svenbro, J. (2008). Grammata et stoikheia. Les scholies à La grammaire de Denys le Thrace. *Kernos*, 21 [Online]. Available at: https://journals.openedition.org/kernos/1616 [Accessed 19 November 2021].

Tabet, C. (2019). *Des petites victoires sur l'illettrisme : portraits en bibliothèques publiques*. Érès, Paris.

Zali, A., Hunziker, H., Held, U. (1999). *L'aventure des écritures, la page*. Bibliothèque Nationale de France, Paris.

Zola, É. (2006). *La terre*. Le Livre de poche, Paris.

Part 4

Informal Learning, Formal Learning, Hybrid Training

Introduction to Part 4

It is generally accepted that the mission of education falls first to the family, insofar as it is the child's first space of socialization. Next comes the school, which, for its part and in parallel with the family, fulfills an educational mission by inculcating in pupils the values intended to promote a peaceful and respectful way of living together, and by dispensing knowledge in the form of varied and adapted teaching that takes into account the age and maturity of the child. In both cases, the objective of transmission is affirmed, intended to promote harmonious personal development and successful social integration. There is also a desire for elevation, for positive growth that ensures the child's promotion to a young person who will gradually become an adult and will then assume the role of an educator themself. Family and school learning are therefore foundational in the child's development; however, learning is not limited to these two types of socialization. Education is also nourished by encounters in other spaces and with other people, and it is enriched by various social interactions, particularly among peers. Learning contents are therefore varied easily combined with one another, or marked by their difference, even their opposition, and it is only gradually that the child will learn to situate themself in relation to all these offers. Rather than an organization of knowledge by simple juxtaposition, a slow and complex process of memorization, selection and incorporation of knowledge takes place in the child, to which is grafted a set of behaviors that they adapt with more or less success to the various situations according to the experience acquired, according to the advice given or the constraints imposed. Bernard Lahire, in *L'Homme pluriel* (The Plural Man), uses the metaphor of "social folding" to account for the plural logics of which the individual, considered as a social actor, is the product. While school plays an undeniable role in

---

Introduction written by Sylvie CONDETTE.

the child's development and in their ability to cope with diverse, complex situations by mobilizing relevant knowledge, it is not the only place for learning and, alongside the formal knowledge it represents, other, more informal knowledge is constantly offered to young people.

What, then, is the status of this "non-academic" knowledge, sometimes called "bushcraft" because of its somewhat diffuse and clandestine nature? Research conducted on *curriculum* development has examined these different types of knowledge and the status they are given. Bruno Garnier in particular questioned the place of knowledge outside the school domain in a dossier he coordinated in 2018 for the journal *Carrefours de l'éducation* (2018), "L'éducation informelle contre la forme scolaire?" (Informal education versus the school form). This question is particularly interesting, in light of the social hierarchy of knowledge that tends to give major importance to school, considered the preferred – and for some, exclusive – place of learning. In this discriminatory logic, the primacy of the school leads to the minimization of, and even contempt for, everything that can be learned outside the school setting.

From this point of view, and to counteract this school-centered perspective, UNESCO has been promoting different forms of knowledge for many years and has invited the multiplication of learning spaces. This institution dedicated to education, culture and science in the service of a better knowledge and recognition of others has produced definitions of "formal", "informal" and "non-formal" education, in relation to aid programs for developing or emerging countries. These definitions, accompanied by recommendations and proposals for action, have made it possible to become aware of the consistency of informal education and have contributed to its structuring and revaluation. The 2012 report, UNESCO Guidelines on the Recognition, Validation and Accreditation of the Outcomes of Non-formal and Informal Learning, clearly highlights both the need for and the benefits of informal education. Informal education is indeed necessary, because it opens a field of possibilities for young people who would not be in proximity to or in connivance with the school culture. It is a way of extending the range of knowledge without limiting it to school. Informal education also brings a certain benefit, because it recognizes other forms of access to knowledge, and even encourages them.

It is therefore necessary to go beyond the sterile opposition that would involve separating formal and informal education, at the risk of producing discrimination and a rejection that would be very harmful for the learners. On the contrary, the objective is to associate these educations by highlighting their complementarity.

With this in mind, 144 delegations from UNESCO Member States adopted mechanisms for the recognition, validation and accreditation (RVA) of non-formal and informal learning at the end of 2009. The adoption of these guidelines was intended to give pride of place to all the learning and competencies that individuals develop throughout their lives.

From this point on, it is easy to see that there are many training spaces, rich in their diversity. This is what the contributors to this part of the book clearly demonstrate. The analyses offered unanimously demonstrate the added value of other forms of education. Far from competing with the school or university form of education, they support and extend it, while at the same time discussing it in order to better understand it and perhaps even make it evolve so that it can accommodate the diversity of pupils and students, and also take into account the singularity that each of them develops in a learning situation.

Chapter 11 examines the place and role of the public library in becoming a "cultural space of learning". Theodora Balmon effectively proposes to link the concepts of school form, popular education and informal learning by showing how they resonate and change the way we learn. If, as the author notes, the configuration of learning is more or less affiliated with the school form, the library does not impose any learning constraint and, on the contrary, leaves each person the possibility of documenting themself and of freely choosing the materials and content that interest them. The library is a place open to all, and going to the library is a matter of choice and undoubtedly also a certain form of motivation. Everyone, at their own pace, and according to their desires, tastes and availability, can take time to listen, observe, read and practice using multimedia tools. The school form finds here a relevant extension that allows access to knowledge according to other modalities.   The library thus becomes a space for cultural training and self-transformation. It participates in the individual's development and fulfillment by offering them a set of resources that they can use as they wish.

Chapter 12 follows the same dynamic of promoting the individual and the collective. Rana Challah and Geneviève Lameul mobilize three concepts – collaborative research, the boundary object and the passer – which are all levers to be activated, as, in a complementary manner, they are placed in the service of student success. Project DESIR (Développement d'un enseignement supérieur innovant à Rennes (Development of Innovative Higher Education in Rennes) (2017–2020) is described in its various stages and is analyzed with regard to the effects it produces, not only at the end of the project, but also throughout the collaborative process that has been set in motion. This project, which aims to transform university pedagogical practices through pedagogical and digital innovation, with support from educational and e-educational research, is based on coordination and co-construction between three poles, the Maison de la pédagogie (The Pedagogy House), the Living Lab and the Data Tank. Starting from the specificity of the contributions of each of the stakeholders, the project studies, through the interactions that are at work, the way in which they manage to identify, understand and agree with each other. Practices are gradually transformed and foster the emergence of informal learning spaces that are likely to change the university form.

In Chapter 13, Régis Malet and Martine Derivry-Plard highlight the development of a master's degree dedicated to the training of trainers in an international and multicultural approach. They explain the initial choices and objectives underlying this specific training offer. This master's program welcomes a varied public from different cultural areas, both French and English speaking. The mobility that students experience and on which they are led to work on in a reflective perspective allows them to acquire intercultural and linguistic skills and to open up to otherness. The pedagogy used is innovative through the use of digital tools and collaborative practices where cooperation is strongly encouraged. The hybrid format is organized through distance learning, face-to-face sessions and independent group work. The methods chosen for this training are based on the strong involvement of students, all of whom already have proven professional experience. In this training, students are considered "intellectuals in action" capable of "creating the conditions necessary for deliberative democracy to flourish in their classrooms, in the hope that it will extend to the societies in which they act". The training rests therefore on innovative methods based on commitment and proactivity, on the collective practice of the values of solidarity and cooperation that they will then pass on to their students or the young people they supervise.

Chapter 14, presented by Salma Itsmaïl, is based on the analysis of a "case study of the Arganeraie Biosphere Reserve in Morocco". This is a project of cultural discovery and openness intended to make a group of pupils better acquainted with the local patrimony. This project, prepared upstream by the teachers, exceeds the initial objectives in that all the participants are confronted with non-school realities. This leads to a reconfiguration of knowledge in which learning distances itself from the traditional school form to integrate a large part of informality. In addition, the authors clearly show the limits of a formal education in patrimony, which is essentially book-based. This is particularly unsuitable for students who are already uncomfortable with the usual functioning of the school system. According to the authors, formal education only reaches a minority of pupils. The experience that young people have in this new setting contributes to a better appropriation of the patrimonial culture and helps build a sense of belonging to this culture. This appropriation is further reinforced by the active participation of the inhabitants who appreciate sharing their knowledge and passing it on to the new generations. The status of the trip or excursion is revisited here, insofar as it does not have a simple recreational purpose but contributes usefully to the appropriation of knowledge.

In all of the chapters, we have just given a few highlights on addressing the ordinary school or university form, not to denounce it by insisting on its imperfections and limitations, but on the contrary to complement and enrich it. Informal education and the various forms of its deployment, as well as the hybridization of training, made possible in particular by the mobilization of new technologies, actually bring an added value to school education. It allows school learning to be enhanced by experiments that touch the learners personally by engaging them in an active process of searching for meaning and appropriation.

11

Informal Adult Learning in Libraries: Between School Form and Popular Education?

Public policies in favor of adult education seem all the more imperative in the context of the knowledge society, where, according to Proulx (2016), knowledge tends to become the main raw material among all production factors.

Beyond the economic field, digital and technological devices have multiplied in all fields of activity, implying a new relationship to knowledge on multiple aspects.

The question also raises social and cultural considerations. On the social level, in fact, a society in which the demand for qualifications tends to rise, in a diversified and intense way, entails an increased risk of "marginalization of workers with few qualifications or little education" (Doray and Bélanger 2005). On the cultural level as well, "insofar as such a project with a standardizing tendency would be opposed to the search for identity and empowerment of people" (Doray and Bélanger 2005, p. 120).

In order to respond to these economic, social and cultural issues, researchers in the field of adult education propose to broaden the sphere not only by addressing different spaces, such as "the school system, businesses, or community associations", but also by considering various forms of formal, non-formal and informal learning (Carré 2005, 2016; Doray and Bélanger 2005; Taylor 2010; Carré and Caspar 2017).

Chapter written by Theodora BALMON.

However, it is clear that, despite the incentive-based public policy frameworks (Doray and Bélanger 2005), progress in the field of adult education is still limited. On the one hand, companies are struggling to meet their employees' training needs, whether on a strictly pragmatic level in relation to current professional activities, or even more so in terms of other professional developments, not to mention non-professional training projects (OECD 2020). It is worth noting, moreover, that since 2012, the Organization for Economic Co-operation and Development (OECD) has begun to collect data on the non-formal field. Although still very partial and patchy, these data are an indicator of the tendency to think about the extension of the educational field beyond the formal alone. On the other hand, it is hardly plausible that the school alone can cope with the missions of education and emancipation throughout the course of an "educational biography", according to Paul Bélanger's vision (2015). Finally, popular education, "a movement towards equality of knowledge and power", according to Morvan's (2011) summary, which traces its genealogy from the French Revolution, followed by the Industrial Revolution, through the Astier Law of 1919, and up to the present day, has seen its missions, as well as its resources, diminish as educational activities have become more specialized by field and by age group.

Also, following the proposed broadening of the field of adult education (Carré 2005, 2014, 2016; Doray and Bélanger 2005; Taylor 2010; Carré and Caspar 2017), we are interested in informal adult learning in the context of public reading libraries.

The reasons for this are related, on the one hand, to the extensive properties that the informal field seems to have, and, on the other hand, to the historical links of public reading libraries with popular education and even with schools (the 1860 law in France supporting the establishment of libraries in elementary school – open to adults after school hours).

Thus, we wonder if the public library can constitute a "cultural space of training", according to the notion of Le Marec (2006), which attempts to weave a link between diverse cultural institutions, notably with regard to a dynamic of informal learning.

In order to test this proposition, we confront, in the first section, the library institution with the prisms of the concepts of the school form, of popular education, and then we try to make explicit the notion of informality. In the light of the particularities identified during this first stage, we proceeded to carry out an exploratory survey of library users, the methodology of which we briefly outline in a second section, and the results in the third section. Finally, we discuss these results and conclude in the last section.

11.1. Library between school form and popular education

11.1.1. *In the filter of the school form*

Guy Vincent's (2019) theory of the school form, a model inherited from "the transmissive conception of the high school classroom and to the Ferry laws at the end of the 19th century, and even to the Christian schools of J.B. de La Salle a century earlier" (Carré 2016, p. 9), can be used as indicative of certain characteristics of libraries.

We recall that the school form implements a system of unity of time, place and action, embodied in a classroom or training room, a syllabus, a program, a progression perspective, a teacher or an instructor. Underlying this operation is a set of principles aimed at abstraction, homogenization and decontextualization. The five essential principles of the school form can be summarized as follows:

– a place separated from other social practices;

– a pedagogization of the social relationships of learning;

– the codification of school knowledge and practices;

– the school also becomes the place where power is exercised, that of the "supra-personal" rule in the first instance – this rule is binding for both the pupil and the teacher, as is also shown by Pierre Kahn[1], in a rather prevalent way, at least in the 19th century and at the beginning of the 20th century;

– the written language is the unavoidable medium of access to the codes, contents and metalanguage promoted by the school. The school form inculcates "a scriptural-scholastic relationship to language and the world".

The school form institutes gaps between family life, daily life and the professional world. Nevertheless, the effectiveness of the school form has conquered many fields, including, for example, the field of adult education – even though today, these school precepts would not be as effective in this context. On the other hand, in France, the public reading library has claimed, especially since the 1970s, a typically cultural mission (Bertrand 2010). But is it so alien to the school form?

Moreover, despite the rise of digital technology, or even because of this rise, according to Bruno Latour (2011), the library would tend to reinforce some of these school functions. Thus, the library would be the space par excellence of the "synthesis that the fragmentation of documents no longer allows". It would even

---

1 Pierre Kahn, "La laïcité dans la formation des maîtres : de Jules Ferry aux ESPE." Lecture given at the ESPE, Ajaccio, December 6, 2017.

merge with classrooms or laboratories, as it is no longer necessary to go through the walls to obtain data. Moreover, "the production, archiving, orientation, consumption, refreshment of data, their visualization, synthesis, and demarcation, have become tasks as new as reading, writing, or calculating" (Latour 2011, p. 36). Thus, the mastery of writing and code reaches a paroxysm here.

Recent statistical statements prove Bruno Latour right. Thus, in 2018, according to figures from the Ministère de la Culture, 9 out of 10 libraries have acquired learning resources. And it is moreover "on this type of digital content that the feedback from users is considered the most satisfactory by libraries. Self-learning resources are thus fully part of the tools that libraries can seize to carry out their educational and social missions" (Synthèse nationale des données d'activité 2018 des bibliothèques municipales et intercommunales (National summary of 2018 activity data for municipal and inter-municipal libraries) 2021, p. 50).

Finally, the school system appears to represent a natural environment. Thus, elementary schools represent the preferred partners of libraries, to the point that the survey conducted in 2018 tends to show that "today's young audiences are much more likely to visit a library than previous generations at these ages" (Synthèse nationale des données d'activité 2018 des bibliothèques municipales et intercommunales (National summary of 2018 activity data for municipal and inter-municipal libraries) 2021, p. 50). Partnerships with middle and high schools are also growing.

11.1.2. *Legacy of popular education*

Among the activities developed in our contemporary libraries, those centered on reading, such as read-alouds and book clubs, as well as more directly on exchanges, such as conversation circles and conferences, could be linked to those that were developed and practiced in 19th-century France with, at the time, a clearly stated intention of popular education.

For those who shared the most open perspectives, the aim was to lay the foundations of a critical spirit, but in accordance with the phenomena of the social and political changes that had begun – and which met with resistance from the old elites; for others, it was a question of providing the people with sufficient instruction to be able to adapt to the necessities of economic progress, but not enough, however, to shake up the social order in place. In any case, it was quite rare to avoid a certain paternalism.

Nevertheless, this diversity of contributors and this rivalry, too, undoubtedly explain the profusion of projects and the imagination that presided over their conception. In this way, a pedagogical authority of the learned and educated classes was established over the others. This began with a form of recuperation of the use of the so-called "popular" vigil to institutionalize and orient it.

Thus, in 1848, the Ministre de l'Instruction publique et des Cultes, Hippolyte Carnot (Ministry of Public Instruction and Cults, Hippolyte Carnot), announced the organization of public evening readings for the people in a communiqué published in the *Moniteur universel* of May 4, 1848. Carnot explains the objective and the form of the readings. They consisted of "reviewing the principal titles of our great writers for the admiration of Europe and posterity", supplementing them with the indispensable historical details about the author and the work. The framework and the schedule are specified. The readings were to take place "in the most populous districts of Paris", twice a week, during one-hour sessions.

These initial approaches paint a succinct picture of learning opportunities within the library between the school form and popular education. The notion of informal learning, broad enough to bring together contradictory tendencies and vague enough to stimulate the imagination, can complete this portrait.

11.1.3. *Informal learning*

The notion of informal learning varies with the authors, sometimes in a complementary way, as well as in a contradictory way. For Allen Tough (1989, 1999), informal learning concerns the practices of adults that are "self-programmed" and intentional, but outside the formal educational sphere. Intentionality is not retained in Abraham Pain's (1990) or Schugurensky's (2007) definition. Marsick and Watkins (1990) consider a two-axis design, one for reflection, the other for action, where the positioning of the cursor would capture the shift from formal to informal. Carré (2016), for his part, in his theory of learning, identifies three processes: intentional learning (voluntary and conscious), incidental learning (involuntary, but conscious) and implicit learning (involuntary and unconscious).

Finally, we have attempted to synthesize in Figure 11.1 the elements contributed by the various authors, in a continuum approach ranging from the formal to the informal. The degree of "formal–informal" composition can be appreciated according to the degree of (conscious) distribution of the "reflection–action" phenomena in the experience.

The "pedagogical guidance" of the individual on themselves makes it possible to define autodidactic and self-learning (Carré 2005). The distinction is made at the level of the environment: informal for autodidactic, "open formal" – not represented here – for self-training. The affective and intersubjective dimensions could also have been added to this diagram.

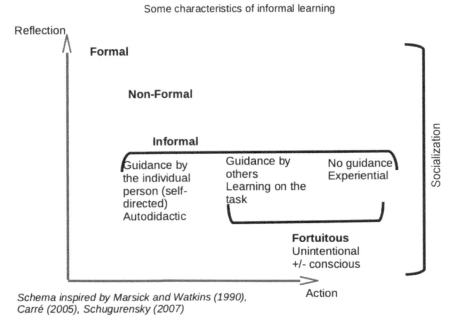

Figure 11.1. *Learning continuum and characteristics of the informal (source: author's diagram)*

While the learning processes may be informal, the outcomes of that learning are formal. Schugurensky (2007) distinguishes two categories of learning outcomes: those of a cumulative nature and/or those of a transformative nature. Cumulative learning reinforces an existing paradigm on a given subject, transformative learning brings about a paradigm shift in relation to the individual's previous knowledge.

This diagram constitutes our reading grid in an attempt to identify the manifestations of the informal learning process in the interviews with readers and visitors to the library.

11.2. Methodology of the narrative survey

To search for the facts supporting these propositions, we used the methodology of narrative inquiry with a small number of people.

11.2.1. *Comprehensive paradigm*

The data we are trying to collect on the manifestations of informal learning are not directly observable and, at this stage, not very quantifiable or measurable. This is because participants do not follow a set curriculum under the authority of a trainer. Therefore, on the one hand, they do not produce any documentation that would allow them to evaluate a pathway based on the trainer's expectations; on the other hand, they are not themselves observable in the process of training under the careful supervision of an educator. Nor would they be observable to the researcher, as this learning experience does not seem to be deducible from the external attitude. Thus, we are in the tradition of comprehensive sociology where facts are collected through the participants' discourses. The aim is to study the meaning that the participants themselves give to their "narratives" and to try to identify categories of learning in them, using the reading grid formalized in Figure 11.1, the main criteria of which are: the notion of experience, phenomena of action and reflection, guidance, socialization, intentionality and consciousness. In order to do this, we have chosen the method of the non-directive interview. Thus, we do not ask any questions of the individuals being observed, in order to leave all the room for the participants to speak. We propose a broad introduction by focusing the initial theme on the role that the library can have in their environment. More specifically, we use Clandinin's narrative inquiry (2007, 2013), which we believe has at least two advantages. On the one hand, it gives a prominent place to the participants, notably with regard to the validation, or invalidation, of the research data. On the other hand, it can be useful to the participants themselves through the formalization and updating of an experience that may result from it.

11.2.2. *Sample and exploratory interviews*

Statistics exist on the populations that frequent libraries and cultural institutions in general. In France, the surveys on cultural practices conducted by sociologist Olivier Donnat, in particular for the Ministère de la Culture, have paved the way since the 1970s. However, in our case, we have opted for a small, non-representative sample, because the purpose of our study is less to survey known practices than to explore in depth the still unknown and certainly diffuse relationship to informal – potential – learning in these practices. This also explains our use of a narrative survey rather than a questionnaire. In addition, there was a major pitfall in drawing a representative or random sample of people. It does not seem possible in a reasonable amount of time and at a sustainable cost to constitute a representative or random sample of people willing to participate in an interview of this type. However, we may be able to mobilize knowledge from previous surveys on cultural practices and, by inference, link people to certain sociological categories. Finally, these exploratory interviews could eventually allow us to develop a relevant questionnaire intended for a larger panel.

11.3. Findings

The analysis of the interviews confirms the potential for learning within the public library. We can see that the configuration of this learning is more or less affiliated with the school form, as well as that the experiential character specific to each person can be projected there and detached from the school form. Finally, the variety of learning processes and their combination sketches the project of an institution , allowing a hybridization between the school form, popular education and the informal field, resulting in new educational forms. The notion of third place, sometimes used to describe this movement (Urrutiaguer 2018), is indicative of these new comprehensions. Here, the concept of Le Marec's (2006) cultural space of training seems to us particularly suitable.

11.3.1. *Profile of survey participants*

The five exploratory interviews presented here were conducted between September 22, 2018 and February 7, 2019, using the narrative inquiry methodology described above. Three female and two male participants agreed to narrate the place of the library in their diverse practices:

– male, 18 years old, Asperger's syndrome, literary baccalaureate, in his first year of graduate studies;

– male, 33 years old, accountant, with an advanced technician's certificate, resuming graduate studies for professional progression, married, one child (infant);

– female, about 45 years old, 1st year of high school, immigrant from a sub-Saharan African country, hairdresser, married, two children (one child in college and one in a technical college);

– female, 23 years old, master's 2 student, law, parents immigrated from China;

– female, about 70 years old, plastic arts diploma and theater diploma, retired, artistic profession, pursues cultural and artistic activities, has children and grandchildren.

The interviews took place in public reading libraries in France, in various medium-sized cities. It has been shown that the size of the city and, consequently, often the size of the library, is not a discriminating factor when it comes to activities, except at the extremes, that is, either very large facilities (e.g. Bibliothèque publique d'information (BPI) du Centre Georges Pompidou à Paris (Public Information

Library at the Georges Pompidou Center in Paris)) or very small facilities (Glorieux et al. 2007).

11.3.2. *Formal/informal duality*

The pathways that emerge in people's stories allow them to see the facts in the context of an experience, not in an isolated manner and disconnected from other facts. Without the narrative exercise, these informal learning experiences, which are all different from one another, would be virtually impossible to capture. Moreover, the individuals themselves do not necessarily conceive of them as learning. The characterization of the place may have an impact on this lack of perception, as specified by Joëlle Le Marec (2006). The school form is very prevalent and normative. It alone seems to legitimize learning and perhaps even prevents it from being discerned outside of the instituted frameworks. However, even though the library does not define itself as a school form, we have seen that it is not hermetic, and even that it shares essential criteria. Observations suggest that informal learning takes place in the library, with the school form as a support, more or less directly linked to the inculcation during the school curriculum or to the incentive of the library environment itself.

Thus, all these elements seem to support the idea of a potential for the intersection of the formal and the informal, of autonomy and mediation.

11.3.3. *Types of learning identified in the interviews*

The five cases include a cumulative learning component, particularly in terms of cultural knowledge, but not exclusively. One of the participants (the second) is precisely in the context of a resumption of studies with the objective of obtaining a diploma, and, consequently, in a very formal perspective. For the five people, transformative learning is also operational, as the actions taken – action appears to be primary in the processes described – have an impact on their personal reflection and evolution.

Thus, the third participant, a woman of about 45 years of age, originally from sub-Saharan Africa, who arrived in France in 2008 and works as a home hairdresser – specializing in so-called "African" hairstyles – is, in her words, "a passionate reader". She says on several occasions: "Whenever I have a free moment, I come here to read." For this person, reading is an experience of discovery, because: "When you read these books, it makes you travel to countries or places that you didn't even think you knew. It makes me travel, discover other ways of life."

This reading activity is also a socially situated act of which she is aware. Thus, she underlines the astonishment that she can arouse by her cultural habitus, which would be in contradiction with the representations of her social and professional status.

But it is also an experience that strengthens her skills: "It makes me discover other words and strengthen my French and all that." She does not mention that she is in a learning process, but it is notable that this activity of discovering other cultures and linguistic enrichment is not a coincidence. Indeed, she states that she lives 500 meters from the library, she could just as easily go home, have other leisure activities, such as watching TV, downloading a movie or even reading. This is a tried and tested approach, as she spent four years in Italy before coming to France. There, she visited libraries and learned Italian.

In the experience of the fifth participant, a woman of about 70 years old, French, retired, trained as a visual artist, having worked in the theatrical field, the library seems to constitute a continuum in her different cultural and artistic activities. Thus, the library provides her with the corpus of works she needs to build the content of animations, including those she has realized in various cultural places and also in elementary school for several years. She also takes part in conversation workshops for foreigners. In view of these activities, she would therefore be more on the side of those with a training role.

In this other case (the fourth participant), a young woman, 23 years old, French, student in her second year of a master's degree, daughter of parents of Chinese origin who immigrated to France, also has a multiple experience of this cultural place. We will note in particular the development of a certain research methodology that she has implemented. Thus, following questions, for example, historical, she read "[…] 4 or 5 novels that talked about it, and it touched my curiosity. So, I did a lot of research on the Internet about this period. I watched a lot of documentaries (found in libraries and online) and in the end, it's always these legends where there are a lot of hypotheses and where we don't have exact answers".

11.3.4. *Exchanges and socialization*

Situations of interaction and socialization were evident in three of the five interviews.

This is the case for the retired artist when she contributes to conversational workshops, or when she participates in other festive and cultural events at the libraries, or when she performs there as an artist. She also often shares her cultural and artistic research with one of her granddaughters.

Seeking interaction is also a goal for the first participant, an 18-year-old male French college student with Asperger's syndrome who wants to make writing his primary activity. He is involved in literary events, meetings and conferences.

Finally, the fourth participant also mentions the library as a place to meet rather than to work: "Actually, at the time, it was more about seeing each other... being together."

Moreover, it is a place that is easily accessible and where we can come without having "really any ideas of what else one could do".

11.4. Discussion and conclusion

From a methodological point of view, this preliminary phase made it possible to begin to verify both the operationality of Clandinin's (2007, 2013) narrative inquiry applied to this specific field and that of the criteria of the reading grid (action, reflection, cumulative and transformative aspects, guidance, intentionality, consciousness, socialization), as well as the typology of conceivable learning outcomes either cumulative and/or transformative.

The narrative survey method favored the exploration of practices without directing the respondents' words. Thus, at no time did we explicitly indicate the objective of the research, in this case the learning practices. Moreover, the reflective activity that the interview gives rise to is also a moment of formalization of an experience, sometimes not yet conscientized, and this can also be a source of learning for the person themself.

The criteria of the reading grid have revealed their interest in the identification and codification of learning through very different narrative flows. As mentioned above, the phenomena of exchange, particularly during collective events, call for other specific observations.

From a conceptual point of view, these results lead to the development of the notion of cultural space of training (Le Marec 2006). Starting with a somewhat hollow definition that invoked the prominence of the informal mode of education as its main characteristic, the concept gained substance in 2010 with the work of researchers in the field of adult education. Thus, the cultural institution in its various modalities (museums, libraries, archives, historical and environmental sites, zoos, botanical gardens, learned societies, etc.) is determined by its missions of selection, preservation and presentation of elements of knowledge and evidence, of past and present reality, from here and elsewhere: manuscripts, artifacts, documents, animals, plants, natural or historical sites, etc. Furthermore, socially and culturally valued and appreciated by a specific community or communities, its impact on the construction of identity is primordial. Finally, the epistemological – and political – elements that are the objects of the cultural institution represent as many factors of cognitive and social change (Taylor and McKinley Parrish 2010). This seems all the more compelling insofar as the knowledge society "still does not seem to have radically transformed the ways in which educational resources are accessed" (Doray and Bélanger 2005).

These results giving clues about the achievements of learning, especially informal learning in the public library space, are in line with both the expansion of the school form and the transformation of the adult education field, as we hypothesized:

> On the other hand, there is an expansion of the adult education universe through the increased emphasis on informal learning. Adult education and training covers not only formal training, carried out in the school system, businesses, or community associations, but also various forms of self-learning and informal learning (Doray and Bélanger 2005, p. 121).

Nevertheless, they are still very partial and insufficient and must be completed by continuing to collect interviews, as well as by participant observation sessions during various events organized in libraries. After this period of discovery, it still seems essential to consider surveys, on the one hand, on a larger scale; and on the other hand, directed towards the actors of these institutions, finally turned towards other cultural institutions, as the concept of cultural spaces of training invites us to do. The consolidated data could then constitute relevant sources for further research and suitable indicators for public policies.

11.5. References

Bélanger, P. (2015). *Parcours éducatifs : construction de soi et transformation sociale*. Presses de l'université de Montréal, Montreal.

Bertrand, A.-M. (2010). *Bibliothèque publique et public library : essai de généalogie comparée*. École Nationale Supérieure Sciences Information et Bibliothèques, Lyon.

Carré, P. (2005). *L'apprenance : vers un nouveau rapport au savoir*. Dunod, Paris.

Carré, P. (2014). L'apprenance : une autre culture de la formation. *Conférence Espés*. Université Paris Ouest Nanterre La Défense, Paris.

Carré, P. (2016). L'apprenance, des dispositions aux situations. Autour de l'apprenance. *Education Permanente*, 2(2), 7–24.

Carré, P. and Caspar, P. (2017). *Traité des sciences et des techniques de la Formation*. Dunod, Paris.

Clandinin, D.J. (ed.) (2007). *Handbook of Narrative Inquiry: Mapping a Methodology*. SAGE Publications, Inc., Thousand Oaks.

Clandinin, D.J. (2013). *Engaging in Narrative Inquiry*. Left Coast Press, Inc., Walnut Creek.

Donnat, O. (2004). Les univers culturels des Français. *Sociologie et sociétés*, 36(1), 87–103 [Online]. Available at: https://doi.org/10.7202/009583ar.

Donnat, O. (2009). Les pratiques culturelles des Français à l'ère numérique. *Culture études*, 5(5), 1–12.

Doray, P. and Bélanger, P. (2005). Société de la connaissance, éducation et formation des adultes. *Éducation et sociétés*, 15(1), 119–135.

Garnier, B. (2018). L'éducation informelle contre la forme scolaire ? *Carrefours de l'éducation*, 45, 67–91 [Online]. Available at: https://doi.org/10.3917/cdle.045.0067.

Garnier, B. and Kahn, P. (2016). *Éduquer dans et hors l'école : lieux et milieux de formation : XVIᵉ–XXᵉ siècle*. Presses Universitaires de Rennes, Rennes.

Glorieux, I., Kuppens, T., Vandebroeck, D. (2007). Mind the gap: Societal limits to public library effectiveness. *Library & Information Science Research*, 29(2), 188–208.

Latour, B. (2011). Plus elles se répandent, plus les bibliothèques deviennent centrales. *Bulletin des bibliothèques de France*, 1(56), 34–36.

Le Marec, J. (2006). Les musées et bibliothèques comme espaces culturels de formation. *Savoirs*, 11(2), 9–38.

Marsick, V.J. and Watkins, K. (1990). *Informal and Incidental Learning in the Workplace*. Routledge, London.

McKinley Parrish, M. (2010). Reflections on adult learning in cultural institutions. *New Directions for Adult and Continuing Education*, 127, 87–95.

Ministère de la Culture (2017). Enquête sur les Publics et les usages des bibliothèques municipales en 2016. Gouvernement de France, Paris [Online]. Available at: https://www.culture.gouv.fr/Sites-thematiques/Livre-et-lecture/Actualites/Enquete-sur-les-Publics-et-les-usages-des-bibliotheques-municipales-en-2016.

Ministère de la Culture (2021). Synthèse nationale des données d'activité 2018 des bibliothèques municipales et intercommunales. Gouvernement de France, Paris [Online]. Available at: https://www.culture.gouv.fr/Sites-thematiques/Livre-et-lecture/Les-bibliothe ques-publiques/Observatoire-de-la-lecture-publique/Syntheses-annuelles/Synthese-des-donnees-d-activite-des-bibliotheques-municipales-et-intercommunales/Synthese-nationale -des-donnees-d-activite-2018-des-bibliotheques-municipales-et-intercommunales-editee-en-2021-par-le-Ministere-de-la-Culture.

Morvan, A. (2011). Pour une éducation populaire politique : à partir d'une recherche-action en Bretagne. PhD Thesis, Université de Paris VIII, Paris.

OECD (2020). *Education at a Glance 2020*. OCDE, Paris.

Pain, A. (1990). *Éducation informelle : les effets formateurs dans le quotidien*. L'Harmattan, Paris.

Proulx, S. (2016). La critique du capitalisme cognitif. In *Perspectives critiques en communication*, Aubin, F. and Rueff, J. (eds). Presses de l'Université du Québec à Montréal, Montreal.

Schugurensky, D. (2007). "Vingt mille lieues sous les mers" : les quatre défis de l'apprentissage informel. *Revue française de pédagogie. Recherches en éducation*, 160, 13–27.

Taylor, E.W. (2010). Cultural institutions and adult education. *New Directions for Adult and Continuing Education*, 127, 5–14.

Tough, A.M. (1989). Self-directed learning: Concepts and practice. In *Lifelong Education for Adults*, Titmus, C.J. (ed.). Pergamon, Oxford.

Tough, A.M. (1999). The iceberg or informal adult learning (Abridged version). Report, The research network for new approaches to lifelong learning/Ontario Institute for Studies in Education of the University of Toronto/University of Toronto, Toronto.

Urrutiaguer, D. (2018). Le modèle du troisième lieu appliqué aux Bibliothèques municipales : quels déplacements de frontières ? In *Bibliothèques en mouvement. Innover, fonder, pratiquer de nouveaux espaces de savoir*, Maury, Y., Kovacs, S., Condette, S. (eds). Septentrion, Villeneuve-d'Ascq.

Vincent, G. (2019). *L'Éducation prisonnière de la forme scolaire ? : Scolarisation et socialisation dans les sociétés industrielles*. Presses universitaires de Lyon, Lyon.

The Construction of Boundary Objects: A Lever for the Transformation of the University Form

12.1. Introduction: higher education at the heart of change

The massification of the student population has disrupted the organization of French universities in recent decades (Lanarès and Poteaux 2013). This has only amplified the evolution of the European university system initiated in the early 2000s (Rege Colet and Romainville 2006). Also, the heterogeneity of the student population and the diversity of students' needs have manifested themselves in varying levels of engagement (Pirot and De Ketele 2000; Romainville and Michaut 2012). Moreover, the digital transition (Albero 2013) accelerated by the health crisis (Lison 2020), as well as various mutations in higher education, question the university form (Albero et al. 2008; Céci 2018). These mutations also question the researcher–practitioner relationship (Perez-Roux 2017). This contribution proposes an analysis of the interaction processes between actors in the context of collaborative research.

As this contribution focuses on the study of collaborative learning spaces, we begin with a presentation of the research context. From a theoretical point of view, we have undertaken to articulate three concepts in order to understand the collaborative processes under study: collaborative research (Desgagné 1997), boundary objects (Star 2010) and the concept of brokers (Wenger 2000). We outline the research questions that will be addressed in this contribution: how does knowledge evolve in the context of collaborative research? At what moments does it

Chapter written by Rana CHALLAH and Geneviève LAMEUL.

evolve? How are the different roles articulated to become collaborative workspaces that turn into informal learning spaces? We present the methodology for collecting and analyzing the corpus under study. Then, we present the results and the salient elements of this study. Finally, we conclude by highlighting the limitations and lessons to be learned from this study.

12.2. Projet DESIR: contextual elements

Projet DESIR (Développement d'un enseignement supérieur innovant à Rennes 2017–2020) aims to promote the transformation of university teaching practices. The **laureate** of the Développement des universités numériques expérimentales (DUNE) (Development of Experimental Digital Universities) calls for projects and is financed by the Agence nationale de la recherche (ANR) (National Research Agency)[1]. Projet DESIR is implementing a collaborative research project that aims to promote the transformation of university teaching practices with a view to strengthening student success through pedagogical and digital innovation supported by research in education and e-education. In order to achieve the objectives of the project, three poles have worked in synergy:

– The Maison de la pédagogie (House of Pedagogy). A network of teaching support services in Rennes' institutions, consisting of a team of pedagogical engineers[2].

– The Living Lab. A team of researchers and research engineers.

– The Data Tank. A team of statisticians.

We propose to analyze the interaction processes between the practitioners and researchers of the three poles constituted within the framework of Projet DESIR.

Because of its nature, Projet DESIR questions the interactions between the university form and other, less formal, even non-formal or informal, educational modalities, which establish (or rather re-establish) the link between the learner and the social, economic, or cultural worlds, through another relationship with knowledge. Thus, the three "poles" constitute "training spaces", notably through the nature and status of the knowledge mobilized, and perhaps also through the recourse to fewer formal modalities of education. Within the framework of Projet DESIR, the

---

1 https://for.univ-rennes.fr/actualites/rennes-laureat-de-lappel-projet-developpement-duniver sites-numeriques-expérimentales-dune.

2 Pedagogical engineers have hybrid skills. They design, implement, manage and evaluate training courses. Their functions "consist mainly in designing, building, implementing, and evaluating training or professionalization actions, systems, and devices" (Carré 2011, p. 351).

three poles are led to jointly construct common standards and to work together. They are also evaluated "by the yardstick of their collaboration" (Baluteau 2017, p. 22).

12.3. Theoretical framework

Collaborative research was born out of a desire to bring two worlds together: that of research and that of practice (Desgagné 1997; Bednarz 2015). Many works (Desgagné 1997; Bednarz 2015) identify collaborative research as a process of co-construction of knowledge that "takes place in an arranged reflective activity, a shared interpretive zone between researchers and practitioners where the arguments and resources of both are mobilized" (Bednarz 2015, p. 174). For Desgagné (1997), the collaborative approach revolves around three processes:

– of "co-construction between the partners involved";

– a "production of knowledge and professional development of practitioners";

– a "rapprochement, even a mediation between the research community and the community of practice" (p. 371).

Often associated with the notion of learning (Vinatier and Morissette 2015), collaborative research would be a space in which actors analyze their practices in order to "produce individually, and especially collectively, original responses to everyday problems" (Paquay 2005, p. 114). They thus become "actors of change and transformations of professionalism" (Feyfant 2013). How do these transformations take place in practice?

Indeed, Desgagné (1998) develops the evolution of collaborative research in three stages:

– Co-situation. At the beginning of the project, all the objectives of the project are made explicit. "The challenge for the researcher is to harmonize the concerns of the community of practitioners involved and those of the community of researchers working in the field of the subject" (Morissette 2013, p. 43).

– Cooperation. The data collection phase is important: "For the researcher who makes it a subject of inquiry, it will be a research activity, and for the practitioners who make it an opportunity for development, it will be a training activity" (Morissette 2013, p. 43).

– Co-production. This is the stage where the data collected is analyzed. This stage of the project reflects the co-production of research deliverables and results that are of interest to both practitioners and researchers.

Di Marco et al. (2012) mobilize the concept of boundary objects to make explicit the emergence of shared knowledge in a project context. Boundary objects are defined as a kind of "arrangement that allows different groups to work together without prior consensus" (Star 2010, p. 19). They constitute "the information and work requirements as perceived locally and by groups who wish to cooperate" (p. 19). Thus, the boundary object "establishes a common syntax or language that allows individuals to represent their knowledge across boundaries" (Carlile 2002, p. 651) and to initiate collaborative work without prior consensus (Star and Griesemer 1989). Mediation, or brokering, is an "active facilitation process to promote the exchange, sharing, and creation of new knowledge" (Jackson 2003, p. 6)[3].

The model of Di Marco et al. (2012) traces the evolution of knowledge in a project context and illustrates this evolution, which consists of four types of knowledge: dispersed knowledge, local knowledge, clarified knowledge and shared knowledge. At the beginning of a project, actors' knowledge is often "dispersed": each actor or group of actors, practitioners or researchers, has their own knowledge of the project. However, the interactions between all the actors involved in the project can lead to "local" knowledge, that is, shared knowledge. More precisely, a presentation of the objectives of a project or a device facilitates the interaction between the actors involved in the project and allows them to focus on particular aspects of the existing dispersed knowledge and to transform it into shared knowledge. This shared knowledge reflects the mutual intelligibility of the actors who become aware of the importance of the project and the stakes of the collaboration. At this stage, the justification of the results favors a negotiation focused on the development of a roadmap and allows the emergence of "clarified" knowledge. When actors begin to work together on the design and agree on clarified knowledge, "shared" knowledge emerges. While there is an abundance of scientific literature regarding the evolution of knowledge (Benhamou et al. 2001; Gagné 2009; Di Marco et al. 2012), we finally mobilize Di Marco et al.'s (2012) model, which illustrates the evolution of knowledge and its articulation with brokering, to present the temporality of the Projet DESIR and to analyze the process of knowledge construction. Figure 12.1 illustrates the temporality of Projet DESIR.

The construction of knowledge that we have described presupposes a work of clarification between the actors involved in the project. This work of explicitation is carried out by brokers who create links between communities (Wenger 2000). Gaussel et al. (2017) identify three specificities. First, the "broker" co-constructs their scientific production with practitioners who, thanks to this work around common research subjects, "develop a scientific perspective on their practices" (p. 37). The "broker" can also have the posture of a trainer who "pragmatically addresses the live questions arising from the field by relying on research to build

---

3 Loose translation.

efficient professional skills" (p. 37). Finally, the "broker" is someone who "develops a generalist approach to the fields of education. They have a global vision, based on different research and a production that is more of an editorial nature. They are able to understand what is at stake in the research, and thus, as far as possible, to build bridges between disparate, even opposing, conceptions of educational practices" (p. 37).

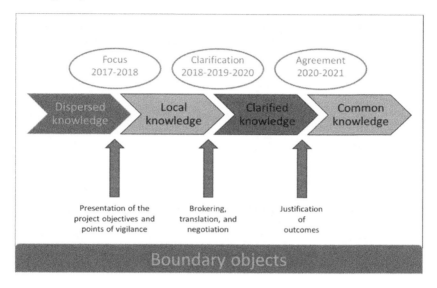

Figure 12.1. *Projet DESIR's temporality (source: figure inspired by Di Marco et al. (2012)). For a color version of this figure, see www.iste.co.uk/balmon/cultural.zip*

The work of brokers "involves processes of translation, coordination, and alignment between perspectives" (Star 2010, p. 602). They must have legitimacy, so they can influence the development of practices and facilitate transactions between actors. Brokers can also be part of the co-collaboration but will have a critical role in introducing partners to each other and maintaining relationships and connections between stakeholders.

The state of the art just presented shows that, by its nature, collaborative research establishes "spaces" or "informal learning settings" that may or may not have objectives, but, by the nature of the interactions that take place in them, they constitute "pedagogical spaces" (Schugurensky and Myers 2003, p. 326) that open up opportunities for individuals to acquire knowledge. Several works highlight the contributions of collaborative research. Some focus on the outcomes, namely the production of "knowledge from experience and knowledge from research" (Vinatier and Morissette 2015), while others focus on the implications of such research and their impacts on researchers and practitioners (Desgagné 1997). The numerous publications on collaborative research reflect its importance, particularly in terms of the mutual enrichment of practitioners and researchers. However, knowledge about how these collaborations unfold remains limited (Marlot et al. 2017; Gredig et al. 2020). Also, little has been written about the processes of translation (Akrich et al. 2006) and knowledge construction that evolve in these informal spaces or what some researchers (Filliettaz and Trébert 2015; Ligozat and Marlot 2016) refer to as "shared interpretive spaces" and which can in turn set in motion a process of transformation of the academic form.

12.4. Methodology

We conduct a qualitative analysis (Huberman et al. 1991) of the corpus of documents shared in this collaborative research. Our work is supported by a content analysis (Bardin 2013) of written documents (intermediary documents: notes taken during the four days of the three poles that took place in 2017, 2018, 2019 and 2020, three slide shows of the presentations of each pole and three final documents: minutes of these days and work meetings).

More specifically, we conduct a thematic content analysis that allows us to "identify the nuclei of meaning that make up the communication" (Bardin 2013) and a directed content analysis that consists of: a definition and categorization of the units of analysis before and during the data analysis; a systematic classification process of themes (Hsieh and Shannon 2005) and based on Desgagné's (1997) models and Di Marco et al. (2012).

12.5. Research findings and highlights

We offer a presentation of results articulating the three stages of collaborative research: co-situation, cooperation and co-production (Desgagné 1998), and Di Marco et al.'s (2012) model, which reflects the evolution of the four levels of knowledge we have presented: dispersed, local, clarified and common knowledge.

12.5.1. *First stage of the project: the co-situation*

The documents shared in 2017–2018 reflect a start that is characterized by many debates around the methodology and around the purposes of the project and those of the data collection. Each pole had specific knowledge related to its own concerns (proposing a training offer, studying a phenomenon, etc.). The knowledge of the three poles was "dispersed" (Di Marco et al. 2012). During this stage, two researchers were brought in to play the role of brokers (broker 1 and broker 2), in order to present the project and its goals, with the aim of joining, harmonizing and showing the intersection of the concerns of the three poles. Projet DESIR was an opportunity for the three poles to set up teams of researchers, pedagogical engineers and statisticians to reflect on the two axes of the project: the transformation of teaching practices and student engagement. The establishment of this framework allowed for the evolution of knowledge towards "local" knowledge (Di Marco et al. 2012). Table 12.1 reflects the boundary objects and the contribution of each broker.

Boundary object	Role of the brokers (B1 = broker 1; B2 = broker 2)
To develop a professional interculture that is essential to create the conditions for of inter-comprehension and trust	B1. Explain the objectives of the project: study of the transformations of practices + student engagement B1. Establish a framework to encourage the actors to scientific and methodological reflection
Articulate cultures (research and engineering, qualitative and quantitative, functional and hierarchical approaches) to approach a serious and in-depth study of the transformations at work	B2. Promote the sharing of information and data (e.g. make resources accessible and and intelligible) B2. Involve stakeholders through the valorization of their contribution B1. Ensure the conditions that allow the achievement of the objective
Understand the goals of the project (to study transformations in teaching practices and student engagement)	B2. Specify the purpose of the data collection: research and/or pedagogical engineering

Table 12.1. *Boundary objects and brokers'*
roles in the co-situation stage

Examination of Table 12.1 illustrates the articulation of the roles of the three brokers whose work was centered on three boundary objects. Indeed, we can see that P1 proposed a framework to "make the objectives explicit", to "establish a framework", in order to allow all the actors involved in Projet DESIR to understand the stakes of the research and to commit themselves. B2 plays the role of the broker by "promoting the sharing of information and resources" and "involving the actors in the project" through the valorization of their contribution.

Boundary object	Role of the brokers (B1 = broker 1; B2 = broker 2; B3 = broker 3)
Define a common methodology for data collection	B1. Reconcile points of view, particularly on on issues of methodology and data collection data collection B2. Identify and propose methodological approaches that allow all actors to come together to facilitate data collection B3. Identify potential methodological problems and propose solutions
Defining the transformations of teaching practices Defining student engagement	B2. Mobilize actors to conduct scientific monitoring B2. Propose indicators to measure transformations in practices B2. Propose indicators to measure student engagement B2. Create collaborative spaces to share measurement tools and data
Understanding the institutional issues	B1. Present the institutional issues B3. Express the institutional and administrative difficulties that could prevent actors from moving forward and finding solutions B3. Explain and understand the timeframes of the three poles and propose a common framework for working together B3. Facilitate workshops and an open forum

Table 12.2. *Boundary objects and brokers' roles in the cooperation stage*

12.5.2. *Second stage of the project: cooperation*

In late 2018–early 2019, the teams identified a methodology for gathering/ harvesting data, but still cannot reach consensus. Knowledge is "local" and methodologically different. Three researchers and a pedagogical engineer acted as brokers to answer many questions: How to collect data? What are the indicators of the transformation of teaching practices? How to define student engagement? What are the indicators that allow us to measure it? We present in Table 12.2 the role of the three brokers who articulated themselves to bring out "clarified" knowledge (Di Marco et al. 2012). The exchanges between the three poles allowed them to identify methodological problems they had not thought of and lead them to reflect on their practices. At the end of the workdays, the researchers and practitioners decided to create shared documents and collaborative spaces to share the data collected.

The reading of the data presented in Table 12.2 illustrates the articulation of the roles of the three brokers and is a continuation of the first stage. Indeed, the co-production stage made it necessary to identify and define the methodology, the axes of transformation of teaching practices and student engagement. We note that the role of the B1 is in line with that of stage 1. Indeed, they facilitate collaboration by "bringing together points of view, particularly on questions of methodology". B2 proposes concrete actions that allow "mobilizing actors around a scientific watch". The B3 identifies the difficulties faced by the actors in order to find solutions.

12.5.3. *Third stage of the project: co-production*

In 2019–2020, several factors, including the project's deadline, coordination between the **brokers** and the frequency of their interventions, are accelerating the mobilization of the teams of the three poles around the project. The teams' knowledge is clarified. At the end of 2019 and in 2020, the project, its goals, its benefits and its impact become more explicit for the three poles, which mobilize around a survey on student engagement. An inter-pole day, organized in January 2020, allowed all the actors, researchers and practitioners to contribute to the development of a questionnaire on student engagement. The exchanges between the three poles around the questionnaire's headings illustrate the "shared" knowledge, the porosity that exists between the world of practitioners and that of researchers and constitute a knowledge base that has favored the project's implication and the implementation of several valorization actions. We present in Table 12.3 the data that reflect the third stage.

The data presented in Table 12.3 reflect the role of B1 and B2, which played a coordinating role between the three poles. Indeed, B1 proposed a framework that allowed the actors, researchers and practitioners to understand the articulation between the deliverables. As in stage 2, B2 proposed concrete actions to enhance the project.

Boundary object	Role of the brokers
Define a strategy for presenting the data collected (deliverables, research report, scientific publication) How do these deliverables interact with each other?	B1. Present the articulation of deliverables: – pedagogical deliverable: how to observe and measure transformations; – methodological deliverable: support methods that could be transferred to the national level; measurement of these methodologies; – scientific deliverable: modeling of the transformation and its formalization B2. Propose actions to valorize the project

Table 12.3. *Boundary objects and the roles of the brokers during the co-production stage*

12.6. Discussion and conclusion

The content analysis of the shared documents, at the end of the work meetings of the three poles involved in Projet DESIR, reflects the articulation of the roles of the four actors who ensured the brokering, thus contributing to the evolution of the knowledge of all actors.

We can see that the quality of the interaction between the three poles depended on the presence of the brokers and the articulation of their interventions. This articulation, which was gradually strengthened in 2019, allowed the three poles to have shared knowledge capable of leading a collective reflection around their concerns. This articulation reflects the stages of co-situation, cooperation and co-production, identified by Desgagné (1998), and recalls Levin's (2013) framework of three overlapping contexts: knowledge production, mediation and mobilization.

Indeed, our results echo the work of Malin and Brown (2020) who believe that the most promising approaches to collaborative research involve: some form of brokering and/or connecting and border-crossing actions undertaken by members of communities of research and practice. Within these broad categories, there is also great diversity. In fact, a whole range of individuals and entities act as "knowledge mobilizers" (p. 3).

Moreover, the proposed analysis methodology and the theoretical frameworks mobilized (Desagné 1998; Di Marco et al. 2012) also allow us to identify brokering tasks in a more refined way and to associate them with the stages of collaborative research. Drawing on Bornbaum et al.'s (2015) classification, we propose to summarize the different knowledge brokering tasks by identifying activity domains and project stages. Table 12.4 illustrates our classification.

A careful reading of Table 12.4 reveals a porosity between the stages and reflects the complexity of the role of the brokers. Indeed, the identification of stakeholders and the mediation work cannot be limited to one stage of the project. Similarly, the identification and sharing of relevant information is a necessary condition for the analysis and production of knowledge. Coordination of work facilitates the emergence of sharing initiatives and networks. Finally, the support provided by the brokers facilitates communication between the stakeholders and strengthens their commitment, which is a lever for the sustainability of the initiatives and the achievement of the targeted transformations.

Classification of knowledge brokering tasks according to business areas	Field of activity		
	Co-situation	Cooperation	Co-production
Identify stakeholders, engage their participation and establish links with them	Stage 1	Stages 1, 2 and 3	/
Facilitate collaboration	Stages 1, 2 and 3	Stages 1, 2 and 3	Stages 1, 2 and 3
Identify and obtain relevant information	Stage 1	Stages 1, 2 and 3	Stages 2 and 3
Facilitate the development of analytical and interpretive competencies	/	Stages 2 and 3	Stages 2 and 3
Create customized knowledge products	/	Stages 2 and 3	Stages 2 and 3
Ensure the coordination of of projects	Stages 1, 2 and 3	Stages 1, 2 and 3	Stages 1, 2 and 3
Support communication and knowledge sharing among stakeholders	Stages 1, 2 and 3	Stages 1, 2 and 3	Stages 1, 2 and 3
Develop a network or community of practice	/	/	Stage 3
Facilitate and evaluate the change	/	/	Stages 2 and 3
Support the sustainability of initiatives	/	/	Stage 3

Table 12.4. *Classification of brokers' tasks (source: table inspired by Bornbaum et al. (2015))*

Our contribution has highlighted the processes of interaction between three poles, which were facilitated by the "brokers", and highlights the articulation and diversity of the roles of the brokers, which, according to Bush (2017), encompass three roles: the creation of resources from research, the creation of partnerships between researchers and practitioners, and the support of practitioners and their encouragement to use empirical data and test their impact. These roles also illustrate the informal learning spaces that form the basis for transforming practices that can drive change in the academic form.

Our research echoes the work of Ward (2017) who proposes a framework that reflects the process of knowledge mobilization via four questions:

– Why and for what purpose is knowledge mobilized (proposing solutions, changing practices, co-producing, etc.)?

– What knowledge is mobilized (scientific knowledge, technical knowledge, etc.)?

– Who mobilizes this knowledge (practitioners, researchers, decision-makers, etc.)?

– How is knowledge mobilized (interacting with stakeholders, linking/brokering, etc.)?

Indeed, it would certainly have been interesting to record the exchanges between the three poles and to analyze the verbatims of all the actors, to propose a finer analysis of the interactions and of the evolution of knowledge.

The results of our study illustrate the potential of collaborative research, which could be a real laboratory for training different actors in higher education to work in a network, in order to equip them to analyze the problems related to their profession.

The emergence of shared knowledge that we have seen shows the possibility of collaboration between different social worlds, which need to have common reference points, and the potential of collaborative research, which contributes to the promotion of intelligibility and to the transformation of the academic form.

12.7. References

Akrich, M., Callon, M., Latour, B. (2013). *Sociologie de la traduction*. Presses des Mines, Paris.

Albero, B. (2013). Quels enjeux pour les recherches sur les usages du numérique dans l'enseignement supérieur ? *Distances et médiations des savoirs*, 4 [Online]. Available at: http://journals.openedition.org/dms/367 and doi:https://doi.org/10.4000/dms.367.

Albero, B., Linard, M., Robin, J.-Y. (2008). *Petite fabrique de l'innovation à l'université. Quatre parcours de pionniers*. L'Harmattan, Paris.

Baluteau, F. (2017). *L'école à l'épreuve du partenariat organisation en réseau et forme scolaire (Thélème 22)*. L'Harmattan, Paris.

Bardin, L. (2013). *L'analyse de contenu*. Presses universitaires de France, Paris.

Barry, S. and Saboya, M. (2015). Un éclairage sur l'étape de co-situation de la recherche collaborative à travers une analyse comparative de deux études en didactique des mathématiques. *Recherches qualitatives*, 34(1), 49–73.

Bednarz, N. (2015). La recherche collaborative. *Carrefours de l'éducation*, 39, 171–184 [Online]. Available at: https://doi-org.distant.bu.univ-rennes2.fr/10.3917/cdle.039.0171.

Benhamou, P., Ermine, J.-L., Taran, J.-P., Tounkara, T., Waeters, A. (2001). Évolution des connaissances et innovation. Application à une technologie laser à l'Onera. *Extraction de connaissances et apprentissage*, 1(1/2), 279–290 [Online]. Available at: https://hal. archives-ouvertes.fr/hal-00984153.

Bornbaum, C.C., Kornas, K., Peirson, L., Rosella, L.C. (2015). Exploring the function and effectiveness of knowledge brokers as facilitators of knowledge translation in health-related settings: A systematic review and thematic analysis. *Implementation Science: IS*, 10, 162 [Online]. Available at: https://doi.org/10.1186/s13012-015-0351-9.

Bowen, S. and Martens, P. (2005). Demystifying knowledge translation: Learning from the community. *Journal of Health Services Research and Policy*, 10(4), 203–211.

Brougère, G. and Bézille, H. (2007). De l'usage de la notion d'informel dans le champ de l'éducation. *Revue française de pédagogie. Recherches en éducation*, 158, 117–160 [Online]. Available at: https://doi.org/10.4000/rfp.516.

Bush, J. (2017). Am I an evidence broker? Reflections on a trip to North America. Evidence for learning [Online]. Available at: https://e4l.org.au/news/am-i-an-evidence-broker-reflections-on-a-trip-to-north-america/.

Carlile, P.R. (2002). A pragmatic view of knowledge and boundaries: Border objects in new product development. *Organization Science*, 13(4), 442–455.

Carré, P. (2011). Pédagogie des adultes et ingénierie pédagogique. In *Traité des Sciences et des techniques de la formation*, Carré, P. and Caspar, P. (eds). Dunod, Paris.

Céci, J.-F. (2018). Les technologies peuvent-elles modifier la forme universitaire ? Certainement ! *Distances et médiations des savoirs*, 22.

Charlot, B. (1997). *Du rapport au savoir éléments pour une théorie*, volume 1. Anthropos, Paris.

Derouet, J.-L. (eds) (2000). *L'école dans plusieurs mondes*. De Boeck, Louvain-la-Neuve.

Deschryver, N. and Lameul, G. (2016). Vers une opérationnalisation de la notion de posture professionnelle en pédagogie universitaire. *Revue internationale de pédagogie de l'enseignement supérieur*, 32(3), 1–15.

Desgagné, S. (1997). Le concept de recherche collaborative : l'idée d'un rapprochement entre chercheurs universitaires et praticiens enseignants. *Revue des sciences de l'éducation*, 23(2), 371–393.

Desgagné, S. (1998). La position du chercheur en recherche collaborative : illustration d'une démarche de médiation entre culture universitaire et culture scolaire. *Recherches qualitatives*, 18, 77–105.

Di Marco, M.K., Alin, P., Taylor, J.E. (2012). Exploring negotiation through border objects in global design project networks. *Project Management Journal*, 43(3), 24–39.

Feyfant, A. (2013). L'établissement scolaire, espace de travail et de formation des enseignants. *Dossier de veille de l'IFÉ*, 87, 1–18 [Online]. Available at: http://ife.ens-lyon.fr/vst/DA-Veille/87-novembre-2013.pdf.

Filliettaz, L. and Trébert, D. (2015). Le travail comme objet d'analyse dans les espaces interprétatifs de l'alternance : le cas de la formation professionnelle en éducation de l'enfance. In *Analyse du travail et formation dans les métiers de l'éducation*, Lussi Borer, V. (ed.). De Boeck Supérieur, Louvain-la-Neuve [Online]. Available at: https://doi.org/10.3917/dbu.lussi.2015.01.0159.

Gagné, M. (2009). A model of knowledge-sharing motivation. *Human Resource Management*, 48(4), 571–589.

Gaussel, M., Gibert, A., Joubaire, C., Rey, O. (2017). Quelles définitions du passeur en éducation ? *Revue française de pédagogie*, 201, 35–39.

Gredig, D., Heinsch, M., Amez-Droz, P., Hüttemann, M., Rotzetter, F., Sommerfeld, P. (2021). Collaborative research and development: A typology of linkages between researchers and practitioners. *European Journal of Social Work*, 24(6), 1066–1082 [Online]. Available at: https://doi.org/10.1080/13691457.2020.1793111.

Hsieh, H. and Shannon, S. (2005). Three approaches to qualitative content analysis. *Qualitative Health Research*, 15(9), 1277–1288.

Huberman, A., Miles, M., De Backer, C., Lamongie, V. (1991). *Analyse des données qualitatives recueil de nouvelles méthodes*. De Boeck, Louvain-la-Neuve.

Jackson, N.J. (ed.) (2003). *Engaging and Changing Higher Education through Brokerage*, 1st edition. Routledge, London [Online]. Available at: https://doi.org/10.4324/9781315194066.

Lanarès, J. and Poteaux, N. (2013). Comment répondre aux défis actuels de l'enseignement supérieur. In *La pédagogie de l'enseignement supérieur : repères théoriques et applications pratiques. Tome 1 : Enseigner au supérieur*, Berthiaume, D. and Rege Colet, N. (eds). Peter Lang, Bern.

Levin, B. (2013). To know is not enough: Research knowledge and its use. *Review of Education*, 1, 2–31.

Ligozat, F. and Marlot, C. (2016). "Un espace interprétatif partagé" entre l'enseignant et le didacticien est-il possible ? Étude de cas à propos du développement de séquences d'enseignement scientifique en France et à Genève. *Raisons Éducatives*, 20, 143–153 [Online]. Available at: https://hal.archives-ouvertes.fr/hal-01346905.

Lison, C. (2020). Une nouvelle ère pour la pédagogie de l'enseignement supérieur ? *Revue internationale de pédagogie de l'enseignement supérieur*, 36(1), 1–3.

Malin, J. and Brown, C. (eds) (2020). *The Role of Knowledge Brokers in Education: Connecting the Dots Between Research and Practice*, 1st edition. Routledge, London.

Marlot, C., Toullec-Théry, M., Daguzon, M. (2017). Processus de co-construction et rôle de l'objet biface en recherche collaborative. *Phronesis*, 6(1/2), 21–34 [Online]. Available at: https://doi.org/10.7202/1040215ar.

Morrissette, J. (2013). Recherche-action et recherche collaborative : quel rapport aux savoirs et à la production de savoirs ? *Nouvelles pratiques sociales*, 25(2), 35–49 [Online]. Available at: https://doi.org/10.7202/1020820ar.

Paquay, L. (2005). Devenir des enseignants et formateurs professionnels dans une "organisation apprenante" ? De l'utopie à la réalité ! *European Journal of Teacher Education*, 28(2), 111–128.

Perez-Roux, T. (2017). Une forme de recherche collaborative impulsée par les praticiens : enjeux, démarche, déplacement(s) des acteurs. *Éducation et Socialisation*, 45(45), 1–15.

Pirot, L. and De Ketele, J. (2000). L'engagement académique de l'étudiant comme facteur de réussite à l'université. Étude exploratoire menée dans deux facultés contrastées. *Revue des sciences de l'éducation*, 26(2), 367–394.

Rege Colet, N. and Romainville, M. (2006). *La pratique enseignante en mutation à l'université*. De Boeck Supérieur, Louvain-la-Neuve.

Romainville, M. and Michaut, C. (2012). *Réussite, échec et abandon dans l'enseignement supérieur*. De Boeck Supérieur, Louvain-la-Neuve.

Schugurensky, D. and Myers, J.-P. (2003). A framework to explore lifelong learning: The case of the civic educaion of civics teachers. *International Journal of Life-Long Education*, 22(4), 352–379.

Star, S.L. (2010). Ceci n'est pas un objet-frontière. *Revue d'anthropologie des connaissances*, 4(1), 18–35.

Star, S.L. and Griesemer, J. (1989). Institutional ecology, "translation" and boundary objects: Amateurs and professionals in Berkeley Museum of Vertabrate Zoology. *Social Studies of Science*, 19(3), 387–420.

Trompette, P. and Vinck, D. (2009). Retour sur la notion d'objet-frontière. *Revue d'anthropologie des connaissances*, 3(1), 5–27. doi:10.3917/rac.006.0005.

Vinatier, I. and Morrissette, J. (2015). Les recherches collaboratives : enjeux et perspectives. *Carrefours de l'éducation*, 39, 137–170.

Ward, V. (2017). Why, whose, what and how? A framework for knowledge mobilisers. *Évidence et Policy*, 13(3), 477–497.

Wenger, E. (2000). Communities of practice and social learning systems. *Organization*, 7(2), 225–246.

Cultural, Curricular and Axiological Challenges of Training for the Education Profession in the Era of Globalization

13.1. Introduction: the challenges of education and training in a globalized world

To support the training and professional development of education and training personnel (Malet et al. 2021), distance or hybrid training is multiplying in education systems: digital platforms making training modules available, offering distance learning education personnel, supported or free consultation; these platforms provide a set of ready-to-use resources or are designed as collaborative spaces, or offer a whole range of hybrid systems. Although these methods are being used today against the backdrop of a global health crisis, they are nevertheless part of a long-term continuum of hybrid training systems that were initiated well before the global health crisis, which accelerated it, by promoting more or less flexible and creative hybrid formats. These schemes are still mostly limited to one-off modules, without there always being any coherence between the tools and modules offered, and without the training of trainers in these tools and schemes being very much invested in on curricular and pedagogical terms.

However, these challenges of digitization and internationalization in the fields of education and training call for a great deal of attention to be paid to social and territorial disparities in terms of learning conditions, accessibility to education, mobility and work. These disparities indeed cover inequalities that fuel a sense of social exclusion and a fragmentation of our societies (Wessels 2007; Brack and Startin 2015; Torres 2017b). Education policies have a central role to play in

Chapter written by Régis MALET and Martine DERIVRY-PLARD.

responding to these challenges, which are linked to those of promoting informed and critical thinking and active and educated citizenship (Malet 2020). To promote this ambition and support democratic challenges, educator mobility still offers a wide range of benefits, including the development of personal and professional competencies and competencies, including increased adaptability to complex and changing environments. However, it is primarily virtual mobility that is being enhanced in the current period. Digital teaching and learning formats may be a relevant option to address current challenges related to cultural awareness, intercultural collaboration and cross-cultural communication competencies (Derivry-Plard et al. 2021; Potolia and Derivry-Plard 2022).

The design of a bi/plurilingual master's degree at the international level[1], which was set up five years ago and which has welcomed nearly 100 students from all continents, is part of a long-term federative reflection within the framework of an Institut de formation des professionnels de l'éducation (INSPE) and is nourished by two major research disciplines, the sciences of education and the sciences of language (in its Anglophone version), and their contributions to education, training and languages. The relationships between languages, education and training, research and intervention, initial and continuing training, local contexts and global issues, face-to-face and distance learning, the construction of knowledge and professional know-how are all key questions for the implementation of a master's degree in teacher training, which is conducive to working on the links between disciplines, spaces, times and languages in training for the education professions in a globalized world.

Hybrid training, provided that it is supported by appropriate mediation, can contribute to providing education professionals with knowledge production tools and reflective tools that support them in their professional development (Malet et al. 2021). If hybrid training systems are to become the norm, then it is important to take into account the growing need to use resources wisely, in order to manage the uncertainties of the present as well as to anticipate future crises (Malet 2020).

13.2. Educating and training in a multilingual and multicultural world

If the world has been multilingual and multicultural since the beginning, the variety of languages was perceived for centuries as a form of divine curse with the myth of Babel. Humans were destined not to understand each other because of the plurality of languages, because they had dared to defy God, and such was their

---

1. Master MEEF de formation de formateurs à l'international: http://pi-learning.inspe-bordeaux. fr/formation-de-formateurs-a-linternational/, becoming a two-year master's degree in September 2022 – Master in International Education and Training (IET).

punishment. We now know that language can indeed generate misunderstandings, but it can also, through translation or change of language, clarify meanings, notions and even discourses. Above all, we know that linguistic understanding between humans is linked to the capacity for language and its development by one or more languages and that it is not purely the linguistics of a language. Two speakers may well understand each other with limited linguistic resources if they communicate in a language other than the one they usually use, and they may well fail to understand an interlocutor with the same language or knowledge of that language. The cultural, socio-cultural and cognitive factors of all human communication are equally important for successful communication in which the interlocutors understand each other, but do not agree. Understanding is part of a socio-linguistic-cultural interpretative order (Liddicoat and Derivry-Plard 2022), in which a whole set of discourses, social and cultural logics, power relations (Bourdieu 2001) and face maintenance (Liddicoat and Derivry-Plard 2022) are at play (Goffman 1967).

13.2.1. *Education, training and languages: a heuristic alliance for the training of educators in a globalized world*

The dual ambition of supporting the mobility of students, teachers and trainers is a democratic issue as much as it is a training issue for teachers and educators. Indeed, the confinement of international mobility to a globalized elite has contributed to the fragmentation of our educational systems and societies. A significant part of our youth – in fact, the most socially and economically disadvantaged – benefits little from this ambition, and this also concerns the teaching world, which was built on a national soil and is, as a whole, still only weakly connected to foreign educational worlds (Ciccheli 2010; Labadie 2012; Malet 2020; Malet and Garnier 2020; Malet and Liu 2021). Numerous studies have shown how mobility accessibility remains socially and occupationally selective, due to persistent determinisms, characterized in particular by unevenly shared "migratory competencies" (Labadie and Talleu 2016). In a context of increasing polarization of youth (Ciccheli 2010), international mobility and intercultural education are at the heart of European strategies (Ballatore 2010; Markovic et al. 2015). A form of de facto devaluation of "native capital" (Retière 2003) (compared to mobility capital nurtured by migratory competencies) tends to widen the gaps between "mobile" and "non-mobile" students and employees (Goastellec 2016; Anquetil and Derivry-Plard 2019). Mobility corresponds to conditions and resources (cultural, social, economic, territorial) or competencies (mobility, project capacity) that cannot be ignored except at the risk of increasing inequalities, which are constructed first and foremost in and through education and training. Therefore, the development of training courses marked by international and multilingual openness, which are accessible to students who are destined for the professions of education and teaching and trainers, constitutes an opportunity to take into account these challenges of democratization of education.

Research has, however, shown the positive contributions of mobility in training, in terms of learning and development of social and civic competencies, as well as personal development, adaptability and social and professional integration (Ballatore and Ferede 2013). These objectives have also been deemed a priority by the European Union in the context of the Europe 2020 strategy, which sets a target of study or training mobility for 20% of students and outlines the contours of a European education area promoting educational policies geared to the development of social, civic and critical competencies (European Commission 2019; Malet 2020).

Plurilingual training and the international mobility of educators and trainers in the making, whether incoming or outgoing, thus respond to many contemporary issues in training for the professions of education, and more broadly for the "professions of the human and of relationships" (Cifali 2012). In addition to improving the employability and adaptation of education professionals to the internationalization of education, such a conception of training contributes to the development of personal, social and professional competencies, as well as an ethic of intercultural relations, an increased adaptability to complex human, social and political environments.

Mobility, whether concrete, virtual or hybrid, can be an effective option to meet the challenges of cultural awareness, intercultural collaboration and transversal competencies in education and training. It allows for the acquisition of intercultural and linguistic competencies, the integration of an international learning experience by multiplying intercultural situations to support open-mindedness and critical thinking.

Finally, it is equally important to recognize plurilingualism in educational spaces, not reinforcing the global trend of exclusively Anglocentric language options. On the contrary, promoting and supporting bilingual programs allows students and teachers – and their students – to practice more than one language as part of their education, and this constitutes an added value in terms of personal development and pluricultural openness and know-how. In this regard, research has shown that qualifying courses and degrees from bilateral joint degree agreements significantly promote the teaching of both partners' languages, opening the door to international projects and initiatives rooted in local realities (Anquetil and Derivry-Plard 2019). Conversely, internationalization on the basis of "all-English" often contributes to a break with at least one of the countries and linguistic cultures, as it functions as a passport for young people to expatriate from their own work environment, solely for the benefit of another culture (Gohard-Radenkovic 2017).

13.2.2. *Dynamics of languages and disciplines contributing to training*

Research in educational sciences and language sciences is conducive to sharing common epistemologies, insofar as, historically, these are crossroads disciplines, sciences whose specific subjects call upon, or even cross, several disciplines and, moreover, are deployed in a close relationship with action. Crossing and working on this intersection between education and languages, in their epistemological and pragmatic dimensions, is therefore particularly fruitful, insofar as education is carried out by means of one or more languages of schooling and that it more or less welcomes, sometimes ignores or even excludes the languages and cultures of its participants (families, learners, teachers and other personnel).

It is from a renewed perspective of languages, language-culture research and practices, and a much more complex and situated perspective of comparative and intercultural education (Malet 2022a, 2022b) that we propose a reflection that is both epistemological and practical of an interdisciplinarity between education and languages. The contributions of sociolinguistics over the past 30 years (Fairclough 2006; Blackledge and Creese 2010; Blommaert 2010; Calvet 2011; Coupland 2013; Calvet and Calvet 2013) have thus reaffirmed the extreme variety of languages in relation to the linguistic policies of countries that organize them according to different statuses on their territories, as well as with the linguistic policies of the major international institutions that use them differently according to their objectives, practices and diplomatic power relations: official language, national language, working language, language of schooling, languages of instruction as a second language or as a foreign language; eventually the foreign language becomes less and less foreign and becomes an additional language.

These contributions of sociolinguistics could not but question the education and training of languages and by languages. Knowing a language was no longer enough to communicate in that language (Hymes 1984). With the development of exchanges and travel for a greater number of students in the 1970s and 1980s, the observation was cruel: a teacher of a foreign language could very well know the language being taught without being able to communicate in this language in a large repertoire of communication situations. The same was true for students who could receive very good grades in a foreign language and still be unable to communicate with a native speaker.

Education and languages have long evolved according to a monolingual paradigm that was gradually built up with the long time frame of nation-states. This paradigm has supported the ideological construction of nation-states, which have equipped themselves with educational systems anchored on the official language or languages that constitute them in order to train, through school education, the future citizens of the nation. In France, for example, other languages were taught through

French, then only according to the doctrine of the target language at the end of the 20th century. Whatever the teaching situation, learning another language exclusively from and through the language of schooling, or only in this same target language while avoiding the source language in an equally exclusive way, the monolingual perspective of language teaching is reproduced in both cases: languages are distanced, separated and compartmentalized according to an ideology of the "pure" language or of the superiority of languages.

This monolingual paradigm remains very powerful and is based on binarities inscribed in the traditional representations of the "native" speaker opposed by the "non-native" speaker, the "native" language teacher opposed by the "non-native" language teacher. Language 1 (mother tongue) is opposed to the second or foreign language, or endolingual communication to exolingual communication. While these oppositions may still retain some operationality, the unified framework of oppositions and binarities of terms and concepts locks up thinking, reduces complexity and limits conceptualization through fixed and fixed categories (Zarate et al. 2008; Kramsch 2009, 2021; Liddicoat and Scarino 2013). It is to overcome this monolingual paradigm, whose domains and effects are not only linguistic but also educational and social, that the design of this hybrid, intercultural and plurilingual training of educators, teachers and trainers at the international level has been worked on, as we will now specify.

13.2.3. *Plurilingual training and promotion of human diversity in education*

The framework of master's degrees in teacher training , which articulate challenges of knowledge, intervention and professional relevance, invites us to be attentive to the challenges of existing territories and expertise, in order to grasp how processes are designed and implemented to articulate training, the profession in contexts and research (Bourdoncle and Malet 2007). The concept of a bi–plurilingual master's degree only makes sense in reference to training objectives in which languages are not simply a tool for transferring knowledge, but both an object and a horizon for learning. The international linguistic market between globalization and globality (Glissant 1997) is crossed by the dominant position of English, the hyperlanguage.

It appears that the policies of internationalization of training encourage the development of master's degrees all in English; this movement is rapid and is part of a certain privatization of the knowledge society, according to a frantic competition to capture the most solvent students, the most "prestigious" teachers, the most "plurilingual" or "monolingual" English speakers, while disregarding human diversity in its languages and cultures. However, the perspective of globality could be more likely to propose bi–plurilingual masters in higher education taking into account the sociolinguistic context of territories and degrees linked to states, but open to this human diversity of languages and cultures, posing the principle of the equal dignity or legitimacy of languages and cultures without falling into reifying culturalism.

It is in the light of these tensions that a bilingual English/French master's degree in international teacher training has been designed (Derivry-Plard and Malet 2019), which is part of this plurilingual conceptual paradigm in which languages and cultures are no longer fixed entities of indissociable rules, but become repertoires: language repertoires, cultural repertoires and pedagogical repertoires. The native/non-native speaker becomes an intercultural or plurilingual/pluricultural speaker. The teaching/learning of languages in training is reconceptualized by developing knowledge and know-how according to institutional objectives and life projects, responding at the same time to academic requirements, to the definition of competencies and to the needs of training and professionalization which concern various professions related to human and socio-educational intervention.

In anticipating that the public of such a master's degree would be plural and composed of subject teachers, language trainers, socio-educational or humanitarian workers and social workers, it was necessary to consider both the content that would allow for an "intercultural and interdisciplinary encounter" between these various users and professionals of the intervention, and also to think of the means that would make this encounter possible and facilitate it between people who are often geographically distant, in addition to being distant because of their professional contexts. The co-construction of the master's degree, in a close dialogue between the language sciences and the educational sciences, has in fact constituted both an opportunity and a real innovation in its training proposal. Indeed, it was not a question of posing the stakes of content independently of their forms of transmission and their trainer character, but rather to consider, from the design phase, the complementarity of these contents, their mutual enrichment and their translation into the very modalities of operation.

In addition to this disciplinary openness, there is an important dimension to the training, which is the plural geographical anchorage of the trainers who teach there. Indeed, the teaching team is made up of researchers and experts who work on all continents. This multi-referentiality of disciplines, combined with the variety of the geographical roots of the contributors, extends the diversity of the public in some way. This is the challenge of the curricular and pedagogical deployment of the program and its protean character: to achieve the ambitious objective of supporting the training of students from diverse professional and cultural-linguistic environments, with clear and coherent training/professionalization objectives, based on a pedagogical team that is itself distant and multidisciplinary.

13.3. Training trainers for democratic education

The hybrid transition in education, both physical and digital, is changing teaching models and the relationship with knowledge and transmission. While not all pedagogical innovations are digital, the notion of digital pedagogical innovation invites us to rethink the learning process, in line with the global transformation of society and the knowledge economy. It challenges the verticality of teaching and promotes horizontality, transversality and cooperation in the production of knowledge, according to the profile and needs of the student. In the education and training professions, virtual mobility cannot replace physical mobility or concrete encounters with otherness, but it is destined to become a complementary and necessary tool, promoting new types of cooperation, through telecollaboration, distance learning, joint facilities and degrees, online seminars, etc. (Derivry-Plard et al. 2021). This is a path that can meet the requirements of internationalization, openness to linguistic and cultural diversity, and social inclusion. Finally, it is part of the education of future European or global citizens (Tarozzi and Torres 2016), an issue that concerns pupils and students, but which by definition includes the training and professional development of future teachers (Malet 2020).

13.3.1. *Content and value challenges for the promotion of intellectuals in action*

In this spirit, the master's degree in international teacher training was designed with the stated objective of welcoming French- and English-speaking students in a hybrid training program – face-to-face and distance learning – that is innovative from a pedagogical standpoint, aimed primarily at supporting the development of the competencies of educators, teachers, socio-educational workers, advisors and trainers involved in international mobility and the training of young people and adults in intercultural contexts (Dervin and Liddicoat 2013). The professional profiles involved are therefore varied in terms of professional and linguistic-cultural roots, but this diversity is channeled by an essential and unifying dimension, that of socio-educational intervention in intercultural and plurilingual contexts, and the concern by students to develop their knowledge and their ability to act on these dimensions of educational action.

The development of the curriculum was made possible on the basis of this ambition and an interdisciplinary consensus on the cardinal objectives and by identifying the key competencies, transversal to the contributing disciplines, which such training was intended to train students in, regardless of their context. These competencies articulate cognitive, ethical, technical, pragmatic, linguistic, axiological, cultural and social dimensions. The training, supported by research, articulates in the training the critical and comparative analysis of educational policies, training systems and the construction/negotiation of professional identities of educators/trainers, considered as "public intellectuals in action" (Torres 2017a; Tarozzi and Mallon 2019) and speaker-actors (Zarate et al. 2008). The comparative case study approach allows for the recognition of semiotic variations in the construction of educational action in contexts (Mjøset 2009) and intends to support the different needs for learning and recognition, developing teachers' transversal competencies. The whole system is nourished by a pluridisciplinary theoretical framework that promotes a conception of training (*bildung*), in the sense of professional and personal development of educators, and oriented towards education for global citizenship, inspired by concerns of justice, equity, recognition and solidarity. In this humanistic and pluralist ecology of education, deliberation and cooperation occupy a central place (Derivry-Plard and Malet 2019), which distinguishes them from an economistic conception centered on human capital and its adaptability.

Thémines (2016) emphasizes the fruitfulness of approaches related to the practice of debate and advocates the promotion of the concept of "spatial actor" as central to understanding the active and situated citizen and to interrogating the "conceptions of justice to which argumentation and decision refer in debates and public action," as well as to facing the challenges related to "individual and collective responsibilities and the necessary solidarity between territories, intra and intergenerational". If becoming a citizen means sharing and committing oneself to certain cardinal values, such as human rights, the recognition of cultural diversity, the quest for justice and equity, then training for the professions of education and training have a vocation to reflect these convictions and values in their design and deployment. This concept of professional training in the service of democratic education is relevant in a period of political instability and rising extremism in various regions of the world, including Europe, torn between a sense of loss of identity and economic globalization. These turbulent times, like the trials generated by the current Covid-19 crisis, are leading to an awareness of the crucial role of education and the promotion and transmission of democratic values in building inclusive societies (Bronner 2022).

This awareness is nourished by an ideal of democratic deliberation and critical and civic vigilance, values for which education and training are essential tools, aiming at the formation of conscious, enlightened, responsible and interdependent citizens. This ambition implies taking into account the advances, as well as the difficulties and regressions, in certain educational and social contexts, in order to better prepare young people and the teachers who support them for controversy, debate, critical citizenship and democratic vigilance, in national contexts where there is a growing attraction, including among the younger generations, for fallback solutions (Malet 2020; Malet and Garnier 2020). Such a program is part of a global solution represented by global citizenship education (GCE), which, as part of the

Sustainable Development Goals (SDGs) for 2015–2030, has been endorsed by 193 nations.

Considering democratic deliberation as a major training objective, taking place in a process of axiologization and humanization that is not decoupled from professionalization objectives, is also linked to an urgent democratic requirement, which is to work to implement the conditions for sharing universal moral values (Burbules 1993). The crises caused by globalization are perceived by many as adding to the ungovernability of democracy, also affecting the role of elites and, consequently, facilitating the challenge to democracy by neopopulisms and their authoritarian tendencies, eroding established democratic virtues and values, systems and institutions, living together and, ultimately, peace. From a scientific point of view, it is appropriate to question the hegemony of a radical authoritarian narrative that is at the center of the threat to the liberal democratic order (Sedgwick 2019).

A democratic alternative consists of defending a social organization of narratives (via individuals or collectives) that question these assumptions and improve public spheres in the service of the common good. Public institutions of education and training obviously have a major role to play in this sense. The role of the teacher, speaking as a social speaker-actor as a public democratic intellectual, is paramount if a commitment to progressive values and action is to be restored (Van Heertum 2008; Torres and Van Heertum 2020).

Education systems thus have a tremendous responsibility to educate and train new generations of educators and trainers in the universal appreciation and implementation of these global commons (Tarozzi and Torres 2016; Torres 2017b; Teodoro 2021) that are expressed in diverse language-cultures. The integration of issues raised by whistleblowers and the consideration of knowledge generated in ecological spheres invite a renewal of co-education, cooperation and eco-education, based on "dissident and radical critiques to create an emancipatory educational project" (Jacqué 2016).

In this context, ethical training is necessary and participates in the development of a critical and reflexive thinking about the situation of the world and the actors who compose it (Darbellay 2019), and of the actors-speakers in all their semiotic expressions (Kramsch 2021). This critical awareness occurs when an individual manages to perceive themself in the world, appropriating its historical reality, which can be transformed and objectified (Kalali 2017). This knowledge does not only come from information or education but also from actively understanding the issues, taking responsibility, making individual and collective decisions about societal challenges and considering these issues not only in principle but also in terms of possibilities for action (Barthes et al. 2017). The stakes are high, because lifelong education and training for critical and active citizenship call into question a development model that has prevailed for nearly two centuries in Western societies, that of a compartmentalized conception of knowledge among themselves on the one hand, and that which separates knowledge from action on the other. Thus, education for sustainable development (ESD), in the wake of the Brundtland Report (United Nations 1987), has been advocated by international bodies (Girault et al. 2014). But this goes far beyond teaching about climate risks or energy production and consumption practices. Linked to social justice issues, it aims at a critical education and contains an essential civic component, consensual in Europe (Meira and González Gaudiano 2016; Naoufal 2017). Indeed, at the heart of global citizenship are these societal issues (DeWaters and Power 2013). Schools and teachers are meant to be at the heart of such an agenda, to ensure the development and learning of proactive behaviors to develop adaptive and engaged citizens.

13.3.2. *Cultural and curricular challenges in the production of transformative knowledge that promotes professional and civic commitment*

This identification of the objectives and competencies targeted by the training program has made it possible to define pluridisciplinary training content, combining the contribution of knowledge on action and for action, and reflective processes of axiologization and semiotization of educational action. The pedagogical variation of these objectives ensures both the relevance of the contributions for students engaged in a return to study or professional exploration for language assistant students in France or the United States, and the cohesive nature of the training allowing for individual and collective mobilization, particularly through group work and coaching for the supporting of dissertations and internships within the framework of a system that is largely distance learning – which, without this group work and coaching, would be conducive, if we are not careful, to a certain amount of student isolation. The hybrid and bilingual training (in a plurilingual perspective) proposed welcomes educators and trainers from various geographical backgrounds and users of English, from the north and the south, grouped within teaching/learning units, in order to respond as closely as possible to the issues, objectives and content of the training without them also being isolated in their interventions. The promotion of concepts of global citizenship education in and through languages aspires to create a new *bildung* that promotes a model of dialogical and deliberative democracy with a view to cooperative professional development, and that does not expose the concept of democracy to the criticism of its "ungovernability" proper to "illiberal democracies" (Zakaria 1997). A model of deliberative democracy can serve as a new "pedagogical social contract" in classrooms, in lifelong learning programs and in society at large, supported by the ethical and legal framework of human rights.

The proposed training combines face-to-face training sessions (one week in Bordeaux per semester), recorded virtual classes, online resources and collaborative work to be done in small groups. The collective dimension of the work expected and the commitment of the students themselves are a driving force of the training, which is only made possible by a particularly valuable technical-pedagogical support, in particular by a work platform (Moodle), interactive virtual classes (Zoom) and synchronized schedules that ensure the feasibility of the theoretical training objectives. The production of a research paper is at the heart of the training process, because it allows students to explore in a theoretical and empirical way, under the guidance of two mentors, a theme that is often at the very origin of their commitment to training. Each student is also supported in their project's progression by a peer, identified as a critical friend, who in turn, has the mission of supporting them in their own project.

The group is also continuously mobilized to advise each person in their research process, so that the objectives of the teacher's training are reflected not only in the content but also in the learning methods, whose formative aim is not reduced to the products of the students' work but extended to their proven capacity to support others in their own training process.

This ethical, deliberative and cooperative dimension of the training system is extended to the teaching units and is based on the composition of different collaborative work groups for each unit. These groups bring together students who, beyond the diversity of their practice contexts or their individual interests, are invited to define a unifying theme for each teaching unit and to co-produce a comparative text, mobilizing a variety of documentary and, if necessary, experiential resources. This collaborative production makes it possible to express, in addition to the ability to produce a consistent and referentially sound piece of writing, a capacity to work, learn and produce knowledge within multicultural groups recomposed according to the teaching units and semesters, in order to multiply these competencies in French and/or English from collective learning to the negotiation of meaning and significance (Liddicoat and Scarino 2013).

The working and presentation languages of the work are English and French according to a circulation of the two languages allowing all participants to gain confidence in their abilities to develop their linguistic and especially communicative repertoires in both languages. Both languages are expressed according to the needs of communication in a space where all speakers (teachers and students) understand both languages and can use one or the other or both in educational exchanges. The circulation of languages is promoted according to a space of benevolent appropriation, open to other languages which could enrich it by a term, an expression coming to question, to supplement the communication and beyond the languages, of the cultural frameworks of thoughts which it is a question in this secured space of exploring and questioning.

The bilingual dimension of the training's working languages is at the very heart of this unifying proposal, both in the transmission of content by the trainers and in the individual and collective productions of the students. Thus, while we ensure a certain balance between the two languages used by the students, they have the choice of languages for their work and the only rule concerns the dissertation, a substantial written document whose oral defense must be done in the language other than the written one.

This curricular composition of the training, from the conception of the contents to their forms of transmission and production, translates a very particular attention to the training objectives of the master's degree, understood not as being subject to a final summative evaluation that would be satisfied by academic productions. In addition to this classic expectation of all university training at master's level, the objectives evaluated are of a formative nature, attesting in acts of a training process attested by the expression of reflective and ethical competencies of support, advice and training in the direction of others, as well as oneself. The master's degree student intends to consider, and in doing so, one of the risks that any training (face-to-face, distance or hybrid) undoubtedly includes, which is isolation and the reduction of the learning and training process to the achievement of individual success.

Since its opening in 2017, the FFI master's degree has welcomed nearly a hundred students, from Canada, the United States, France, Great Britain, Norway, Iraq, Italy, Lebanon, Vietnam, China, the Ivory Coast, Congo, Tunisia, Morocco, etc. These students include future teachers or teachers on assignment in foreign schools or in French schools abroad, at the primary or secondary level, school principals, inspectors, managers in the humanitarian sector, adult educators and intercultural managers. The students' profiles and backgrounds are varied and often very rich. Accustomed to crossing borders, they are also invited to do so within the framework of a training program that opens them up to concepts worked on from different disciplinary and professional perspectives, working collectively on concepts in their semantic and linguistic thickness (back and forth between at least two languages, English and French) and on diverse terrains, as evidenced by the research papers produced and the collective files (Malet and Derivry-Plard 2022).

The humanist tradition of the internationalist ideal in education (Droux and Hofstette 2015, 2020) thus aims to link mobile and non-mobile citizens, initial and continuing education students, and to accompany human experiences at the international level, and not to favor the former by disqualifying the latter (Anquetil and Derivry-Plard 2019). This potential polarization entails a strong risk of more than symbolic separation and, ultimately, the disastrous prospect of a reinforcement of the social inequalities that we have already highlighted, and which are in fact exacerbated by certain forms of internationalization of education that are insufficiently attentive to these social and language issues, which are also democratic issues. If a non-mobile mode of learning can lead to a form of exclusion, it can also result from a desire to preserve a territorial anchorage without giving up quality education or an openness to cultural otherness (Hardouin and Moro 2014). Mobility must remain a right and not become a legal requirement to be fulfilled for social and professional inclusion. Hybrid educational practices, bringing together learners from different countries in telecollaborative spaces (O'Dowd and Lewis 2016; Derivry-Plard 2017) make it possible to take into account the sociolinguistic and cultural realities of the participants, to multiply their experiences, their reflexive competencies, and to capitalize on them by developing their plurilingual competencies of openness to otherness, actualized in different intercultural and international communication situations.

13.4. Conclusion: a plurilingual and pluricultural paradigm in teacher and trainer training to meet the democratic challenges of globalization

The emergence of a plurilingual and pluricultural paradigm is being constructed in parallel with the weakening of nation-states, a recomposition of politics according to the neoliberal hold of the world-economy, and more or less renewed social practices according to the hold of cultural phenomena of homogenization and diversification (the Internet, low-cost travel, migration and the accelerated digitization of social functioning since the Covid-19), which is shaping the whole world or globality (Glissant 1997). Research in the field of languages and cultures made this transition from the monolingual paradigm to the plurilingual paradigm at the turn of the millennium (Coste et al. 2009; Block 2003; Ortega 2013), but the practices of teachers, learners and the general representations of civil society are still largely marked by the monolingual paradigm (Derivry-Plard 2015). The plurilingual and pluricultural paradigm proposes a non-binary perspective, as it is rooted in continua and in the inclusion of differences, of plurality posed as an axiom of reflection on education and training. It is from this perspective that the master's degree in international training for trainers offers training that crosses education and languages, even though we have retained only two working languages, English and French, but from a plurilingual perspective.

This chapter has highlighted the unifying concept at work in the construction of a bi/plurilingual master's degree for the trainers of trainers in international education, based on our respective disciplines and on the epistemological, axiological and democratic challenges at work in its design. This concept of the teaching-learning process in the training of trainers is renewed in languages by the plurilingual paradigm, which no longer only considers language teaching but also language teaching and, ultimately, education in and about languages (Cenoz and Groter 2015). This concept is also renewed in education and more particularly in comparative education by the processes of internationalization, crossed by the questions of inclusion/exclusion (Deyrich and Majhanovic 2017) and of democracy in the face of authoritarianism, totalitarianism and populism (Majhanovich and Malet 2015; Tarozzi and Torres 2016).

An intercultural and intercultural education poses a real challenge to the whole world, because it is not only a matter of conceiving it with contextual limitations, but of putting it into practice according to other contextual constraints and logics, with the aim of preparing for the complex exercise of the profession of educating and teaching in the era of globalization, post-truth and alternative facts. The promotion of hybrid training methods, combining physical and virtual mobility, makes it possible not to give in to the "mandate to move" (Lévy 2011), especially when this mandate produces or adds to social inequalities. From this point of view, the diffusion of digital university campuses constitutes a key element for the democratization of access to higher education, through an internationalization that is nevertheless attached to a territory, but of which neither the students nor the teachers are captive.

One of the challenges in developing this type of training is the revitalization of a form of free and open learning mobility, which is neither directly indexed to questions of efficiency or adaptability, performance and competencies, nor constrained by predefined or prescriptive standards, but which is nevertheless a sound investment in the future of democratic education. Supporting student mobility cannot mean focusing solely on the adaptability of young people (and the future workforce). It must also mean educating young people to be creative, open and to relate positively to others, both during their studies and in their work environment (Cicchelli 2010). In short, it is necessary to prepare and educate young people to make periods of mobility (physical and/or virtual) real opportunities for discovery, learning and capitalization of experiences for personal, ethical and civic development in otherness (Keating 2014; Anquetil and Derivry-Plard 2019), so that they can better engage with cultural, political and ethical issues of understanding the contemporary world, as well as issues of solidarity, brotherhood and peace (Rifkin 2004; Veugelers 2011; Tarozzi and Mallon 2019).

This is a project that wants to contribute to the creation of a new framework for understanding what it means to educate and train and is based on the global commons movement (Tarozzi and Inguaggiato 2019; Derivry-Plard 2020; Malet and Garnier 2020; Torres and Van Heertum 2020). It intends to recognize teachers as intellectuals in action, able to create the conditions necessary for deliberative democracy to flourish in their classrooms, in the hope that it will extend to the societies in which they act.

13.5. References

Anquetil, M. and Derivry-Plard, M. (2019). Reconnaître et valoriser les mobilisés : évolution du management de la "dimension européenne". *Recherches en didactique des langues et des cultures – Les cahiers de l'Acedle*, Special edition, 16(2) [Online]. https://journals.openedition.org/rdlc/6537.

Anquetil, M., Derivry-Plard, M., Gohard-Radenkovic, A. (2017). En finir avec le *Je* contraint et réifié dans l'objet PEL : pour une didactique de la biographie langagière comme processus relationnel. *Revue TDFLE. Travaux de didactique du français langue étrangère*, 70.

Ballatore, M. (2010). Chapitre IV : Des apprentissages de l'international à la fleximobilité. *Éducation et societe*, 133–175.

Ballatore, M. and Ferede, M. (2013). The Erasmus Programme in France, Italy and the United Kingdom: Student mobility as a signal of distinction and privilege. *European Educational Research Journal*, 12(4), 525–533 [Online]. Available at: https://doi.org/10.2304/eerj.2013.12.4.525.

Barthes, A., Lange, J.M., Tutiaux-Guillon, N. (eds) (2017). *Dictionnaire critique des enjeux et concepts des "éducation à"*. L'Harmattan, Paris.

Blackledge, A. and Creese, A. (2010). *Multilingualism. A Critical Perspective*. Continuum, London.

Block, D. (2003). *The Social Turn in Second Language Acquisition*. Edinburgh University Press, Edinburgh.

Blommaert, J. (2010). *The Sociolinguistics of Globalization*. Cambridge University Press, Cambridge.

Bourdieu, P. (2001). *Langage et pouvoir symbolique*. Le Seuil, Paris.

Bourdoncle, R. and Malet, R. (eds) (2007). Nouveaux cursus, nouveaux diplômes. La formation professionnelle des formateurs à l'Université. *Recherche et Formation*, 54.

Brack, N. and Startin, N. (2015). Euroscepticism, from the margins to the mainstream. *International Political Science Review*, 36(3), 239–249.

Bronner, G. (2022). Les lumières à l'ère numérique. Report [Online]. Available at: https://www.vie-publique.fr/sites/default/files/rapport/pdf/283201.pdf.

Burbules, N.C. (1993). *Dialogue in Teaching: Theory and Practice*. Teacher College Press, New York.

Byram, M., Golubeva, I., Hui, H., Wagner, M. (2016). *From Principles to Practice in Education for Intercultural Citizenship*. Multilingual Matters, Clevedon.

Calvet, L.-J. (2011). *Il était une fois 7000 langues.* Fayard, Paris.

Calvet, L.-J. and Calvet, A. (2013). *Les confettis de Babel. Diversité linguistique et politique des langues.* Écriture, Paris.

Cenoz, J. and Gorter, D. (2015). *Multilingual Education. Between Language Learning and Translanguaging.* CUP, Cambridge.

Cicchelli, V. (ed.) (2010). Dispositifs publics et construction de la jeunesse en Europe. *Politiques sociales et familiales*, 102, 103–112.

Cifali, M. (2012). Éthique et éducation : l'enseignement, une profession de l'humain. *Interacções*, 21, 13–27.

Cifali, M. and Myftiu, B. (2006). *Dialogues et récits d'éducation sur la différence.* Les éditions Ovadia, Nice.

Coste, D., Moore, D., Zarate, G. (2009). *Compétence plurilingue et pluriculturelle.* Éditions du Conseil de l'Europe, Strasbourg.

Council of Europe (2016). Compétences pour une culture de la démocratie. Vivre ensemble sur un pied d'égalité dans des sociétés démocratiques et culturellement diverses. Conseil de l'Europe, Strasbourg.

Coupland, N. (ed.) (2013). *The Handbook of Language and Globalisation.* Wiley-Blackwell, Oxford.

Darbellay, F. (2019). From interdisciplinarity to postdisciplinarity: Extending Klein's thinking into the future of the University. *Issues in Interdisciplinary Studies*, 37(2), 90–109.

Derivry-Plard, M. (2015). *Les enseignants de langues dans la mondialisation, la guerre des représentations.* EAC, Paris.

Derivry-Plard, M. (ed.) (2017). La télécollaboration interculturelle. *Les Langues Modernes.* APLV, Paris [Online]. Available at: https://www.aplv-languesmodernes.org/spip.php?article6554.

Derivry-Plard, M. (2020). La citoyenneté interculturelle et les défis de l'enseignement/apprentissage des langues. *Études de linguistique appliquée*, 197, 15–27.

Derivry-Plard, M. and Malet, R. (2019). Concevoir un Master bi/plurilingue à l'international. Le Master FFI de l'ESPE d'Aquitaine. *Cahiers de l'ASDIFLE*, 30, 185–199.

Derivry-Plard, M., Castro-Prieto, P., Biondo Salomão, A.C., Fan, S.-H. (2021). Developing teachers' competencies through intercultural telecollaboration. In *Competency-Based Teacher Education for English as a Foreign Language, Theory, Research, and Practice*, Wang, A.Y. (ed.). Routledge, London.

Dervin, F. and Liddicoat, A.J. (2013). *Linguistics for Intercultural Education.* John Benjamins, Amsterdam.

DeWaters, J. and Powers, S. (2013). Establishing measurement criteria for an energy literacy questionnaire. *The Journal of Environmental Education*, 44(1), 38–55.

Deyrich, M.-C. and Majhanovic, S. (2017). Language learning to support active social Inclusion: Issues and challenges for lifelong learning. *International Review of Education*, 63, 435–452.

Droux, J. and Hofstetter, R. (2015). *Globalisation des mondes de l'éducation : circulations, connexions, réfractions XIX*ᵉ *et XX*ᵉ *siècles*. Presses universitaires de Rennes, Rennes.

Droux, J. and Hofstetter, R. (2020). *Internationalismes éducatifs entre débats et combats*. Peter Lang, Bern.

Erasmus (2016). French national agency report. Report, Agence Erasmus+ Europe Education and Formation, Bordeaux.

European Commission (2019). "Erasmus+": The Union Programme for Education, Training, Youth and Sport. Document, Publications Office of the European Union, Luxembourg.

Eurydice (2017). *Citizenship Education at School in Europe*. European Commission, Luxembourg.

Fabre, M. (2018). Savoir et valeur. Pour une conception émancipatrice des "Éducations à". *Éducation et socialisation, Les Cahiers du CERFEE*, 48.

Fairclough, N. (2006). *Language and Globalisation*. Routledge, London.

Garcia, O. (2009). *Bilingual Education in the 21st Century: A Global Perspective*. Wiley-Blackwell, Oxford.

Garnier, B., Derouet, J.L., Malet, R. (2020). *Sociétés inclusives et reconnaissance des diversités. Le nouveau défi des politiques d'éducation*. Presses Universitaires de Rennes, Rennes.

Girault, Y., Zwang, A., Jeziorski, A. (2014). Finalités et valeurs de différentes politiques d'éducation à la soutenabilité. Éducation relative à l'environnement. *Regards – Recherches – Réflexions*, 11 [Online]. Available at: https://journals.openedition.org/ere/698?lang=en.

Glissant, E. (1997). *Traité du Tout-Monde, Poétique IV*. Gallimard, Paris [Online]. Available at: http://www.edouardglissant.fr/mondialite.html.

Goastellec, G. (2016). La mobilité internationale : une qualité des carrières et des marchés académiques en Europe ? *Journal of International Mobility*, 4, 171–188.

Goffman, E. (1967). *Interaction Ritual*. Anchor Books, New York.

Gohard-Radenkovic, A. (2017). Contre-point. Quand la toute-mobilité peut devenir l'immobilisation des acteurs de la mobilité... et quand sociétés d'accueil et de départ produisent du "brain waste". *Journal of International Mobility*, 5, 157–176.

Hardouin, M. and Moro, B. (2014). Étudiants en ville, étudiants entre les villes. Analyse des mobilités de formation des étudiants et de leurs pratiques spatiales dans la cité. *Norois. Environnement, aménagement, société*, 230, 73–88 [Online]. Available at: https://doi.org/10.4000/norois.5032.

Hymes, D.H. (1984). *Vers la compétence de communication*. Crédif/Hatier, Paris.

Jacqué, M. (2016). L'éducation à l'environnement : entre engagements utopistes et intégration idéologique. *Cahiers de l'Action*, 47(1), 13–19.

Kalali, F. (2017). Accès au(x) savoir(s) et quête du sens. *Questions vives*, 28.

Kaufmann, V. (2008). *Les paradoxes de la mobilité, bouger, s'enraciner*. Presses polytechniques et universitaires romandes, Lausanne.

Keating, A. (2014). *Education for Citizenship in Europe: European Policies, National Adaptations and Young People's Attitudes*. Routledge, London.

Kramsch, C. (2009). *The Multilingual Subject*. OUP, Oxford.

Kramsch, C. (2021). *Language as Symbolic Power*, Cambridge University Press, Cambridge.

Labadie, F. (ed.) (2012). Inégalités entre jeunes sur fond de crise. Report, La Documentation française/INJEP, Paris.

Labadie, F. (2016). Le programme européen "Jeunesse en action" au défi de l'équité. Le cas des jeunes avec moins d'opportunités. *INJEP : Jeunesses : études, synthèses*, 32 [Online]. Available at: https://injep.fr/wp-content/uploads/2018/09/JES32_jamo.pdf.

Labadie, F. and Talleu, C. (2015). Développer la mobilité européenne et internationale des jeunes. Actions et dynamiques d'acteurs dans le cadre non formel. *Cahiers de l'action*, 44, INJEP, Paris.

Labadie, F. and Talleu, C. (2016). Going abroad in order to cope. A "captivating" experience with little support from institutions. In *Learning Mobility, Social Inclusion and Non-formal Education. Access, Processes and Outcomes*, Devlin, M., Kristensen, S., Krzaklewska, E., Nico, M. (eds). Council of Europe Publishing, Strasbourg.

Lelièvre, F., Anquetil, M., Derivry-Plard, M., Fäcke, C., Verstraete-Hansen, L. (eds) (2018). *Langues et cultures dans l'internationalisation de l'enseignement supérieur au 21ᵉ siècle. (Re)penser les politiques linguistiques : anglais et plurilinguisme*. Peter Lang, Bern.

Lévy, J. (2011). La mobilité comme bien public. *Métropolitiques*, 21 September [Online]. Available at: http://www.metropolitiques.eu/La-mobilite-comme-bien-public.html.

Liddicoat, J.A. and Derivry-Plard, M. (eds) (2022). *Intercultural Mediation in Language Learning and Teachning/La Médiation interculturelle dans l'enseignement/apprentissage des langues*. EAC, Paris.

Liddicoat, J.A. and Scarino, A. (2013). *Intercultural Language Teaching and Learning*. Wiley-Blackwell, Oxford.

Majhanovich, S. and Malet, R. (2015). *Building Democracy through Education on Diversity*. Sense Publishers, Rotterdam.

Malet, R. (2008). *La formation des enseignants comparée*. Peter Lang, Bern.

Malet, R. (2020). *Research for CULT Committee – Towards a European Education. Critical Perspectives on Challenges Ahead*. European Parliament, Policy Department for Structural and Cohesion Policies, Brussels.

Malet, R. (2022a). Repères pour une sémiotique comparative de l'éducation. *Éducation Comparée*, 26. 205–242.

Malet, R. (2022b). Comparatisme interculturel. In *Traité des sciences de l'éducation et de la formation*, Albéro, B. and Thievenaz, J. (eds). Raisons et Passions, Dijon.

Malet, R. and Derivry-Plard, M. (2023). Formation des formateurs en contextes interculturels et plurilingue. Questions de savoirs et de valeurs. *Éducation Comparée*, 28.

Malet, R. and Garnier, B. (eds) (2020). *Éducation, mondialisation et citoyenneté. Enjeux démocratiques et pratiques culturelles*. Peter Lang, Bern.

Malet, R. and Liu, B. (eds) (2021). *Politiques éducatives, diversité et justice sociale*. Peter Lang, Berne.

Malet, R., Condette, S., Derivry-Plard, M., Le Coz, A. (2021). De la formation continue au développement professionnel des personnels d'éducation. Situation nationale, comparaisons internationales, état des recherches. Report, Conseil National d'Evaluation des Systèmes Scolaires (CNESCO), Paris.

Mangez, É., Bouhon, M., Delvaux, B., Cattonar, B., Dumay, X., Dupriez, V., Verhoeven, M. (eds) (2017). "Faire société" dans un monde incertain. Quel rôle pour l'école ? *Cahiers de recherche du Girsef*, 110.

Markovic, J., García López, M.A., Dzigurski, S. (2015). Trouver sa place dans une Europe moderne. Report, European Commission/The Council of Europe.

Meira, P. and González Gaudiano, É.J. (2016). Les défis éducatifs du changement climatique : la pertinence de la dimension sociale. Éducation relative à l'environnement. *Regards – Recherches – Réflexions*, 13(2) [Online]. Available at: http://journals.openedition.org/ere/730.

Mjøset, L. (2009). The contextualist approach to social science methodology. In *The SAGE Handbook of Case-Based Methods*, Byrne, D. and Ragin, C.C. (eds). SAGE, London.

Naoufal, N. (2017). Justice environnementale et écocitoyenneté. *Éducation, environnement, écocitoyenneté : repères contemporains*, 101–117.

O'Dowd, R. and Lewis, T. (2016). *Online Intercultural Exchange: Policy, Pedagogy, Practice*. Routledge, London.

Ortega, L. (2013). SLA for the 21st century: Disciplinary progress, transdisciplinary relevance, and the bi/multilingual turn. *Language Learning*, 63(1), 1–24.

Potolia, A. and Derivry-Plard, M. (eds) (2022). *Virtual Exchange for Intercultural Language Learning and Teaching: Fostering Communication for the Digital Age*. Routledge, London.

Retière, J.-N. (2003). Autour de l'autochtonie. Réflexions sur la notion de capital social populaire. *Politix*, 16(63), 121–143.

Rifkin, J. (2004). *The European Dream*. Polity, Cambridge.

Sedgwick, M.J. (ed.) (2019). *Key Thinkers of the Radical Right. Behind the New Threat to Liberal Democracy*. Oxford University Press, New York.

Tarozzi, M. and Inguaggiato, C. (eds) (2019). Teacher education in global citizenship education: Emerging issues in a comparative perspective. Report, Università di Bologna, Bologna.

Tarozzi, M. and Mallon, B. (2019). Educating teachers towards global citizenship: A comparative study in four European countries. *London Review of Education*, 17(2), 112–125.

Tarozzi, M. and Torres C.A. (2016). *Global Citizenship Education and the Crisis of Multiculturalism*. Bloomsbury, London/New York.

Teodoro, A. (2021). *Contesting the Global Development of Sustainable and Inclusive Education: Education Reform and the Challenges of Neoliberal Globalisation*. Routledge, London.

Thémines, J.-F. (2016). La didactique de la géographie. *Revue française de pédagogie*, 197, 99–136.

Torres, C.A. (ed.) (2017a). Why global citizenship? An intervention in search of a theory. In *Theoretical and Empirical Foundations of Critical Global Citizenship Education*. Routledge, London.

Torres, C.A. (2017b). *Theoretical and Empirical Foundations of Critical Global Citizenship Education*, volume 1. Routledge, London.

Torres, C.A. and Van Heertum, R. (2020). UNESCO as the global public intellectual for the twenty-first century. *Humanist Futures: Perspectives from UNESCO Chairs and UNITWIN Networks on the Futures of Education*. UNESCO, Paris.

Tutiaux-Guillon, N. (2015). Questions socialement vives et recomposition disciplinaire de l'histoire-géographie : entre opportunités et résistances. In *Sciences de la nature et de la société dans une école en mutation*, Audigier, F., Sgard, A., Tutiaux-Guillon, N. (eds). De Boeck supérieur, Louvain-la-Neuve.

Tutiaux-Guillon, N. and Lefrançois, D. (2017). Éducation à la paix. In *Dictionnaire critique des enjeux et concepts des "éducation à"*, Barthes, A., Lange, J.-M., Tutiaux-Guillon, N. (eds). L'Harmattan, Paris.

United Nations (1987). Report of the World Commission on environment and development: Our common future (Brundtland Report). Report, United Nations, New York.

Van Heertum, R. (2008). The fate of democracy in a cynical age: Education, media and the evolving public sphere. Report, University of California, Los Angeles.

Veugelers, W. (2011). *Education and Humanism*. Sense Publishers, Rotterdam.

Wessels, B. (2007). Discontent and European identity: Three types of Euroscepticism. *Acta Politica*, 4(22/3), 287–306.

Zakaria, F. (1997). The rise of illiberal democracy. *Foreign Affairs*, 76, 22.

Zarate, G., Lévy, D., Kramsch, C. (2008). *Précis du plurilinguisme et du pluriculturalisme*. E.A.C., Paris.

14

The Emergence of Patrimonial Education in the Arganeraie Biosphere Reserve (ABR) in Morocco

Since the end of the 19th century, the "school form" has seen several phases of evolution, including the introduction of values education. Today, the consideration of values within the school institution is a strongly stated objective. Training in citizenship, creating a sense of belonging among pupils, educating about patrimony, etc., are all missions that the school is now taking on.

Is the traditional school form able to fulfill these new missions?

Our chapter focuses on the emergence of patrimonial education in the Moroccan school system. The objective is to understand how this education implies a modification of the traditional school form, which is diffusing into the formal system to accomplish its missions.

The case study presented is a project developed and launched by a school institution. Interviews with participating teachers, questionnaires distributed to pupils and observations during the project highlight the presence of a new contemporary form of schooling that incorporates what is called "informal learning" or, more accurately, learning in informal situations (Brougère and Bézille 2007).

The results question the effectiveness of formal teaching within the school versus the knowledge and values that pupils have appropriated when a new type of learning is introduced into the school system.

Chater written by Salma ITSMAÏL.

14.1. History of the school form

The school form known so far has been able to inculcate a school image with a number of defined characteristics (Vincent 2019; Monjo 1998), namely a specific space–time, a hierarchical structure in the classrooms (a teacher responsible for a number of children sorted by age), a school content predefined by the state, a division of working hours by a distinct "subject" and "discipline". This form of schooling relies mainly on the absorption of controlled information in the form of examinations for the achievement of results (diplomas, passage to higher grades, etc.); knowledge is supposed to be stable, integrated into textbooks and made known to pupils. During the updating of the school curriculum (1960–1990), the teaching of values was discarded in order to give priority to knowledge. The role of the teacher is limited to teaching without being an educator and is therefore limited by academic legitimacy. The school will therefore be organized around fundamentals determined by age group.

A new change in the school system was to emerge in response to a crisis in the school (Moreau and Joshua 1990). A sudden upsurge in violence, incivility and environmental deterioration led to the integration of values education from an early age.

In the early 20th century, the sociopolitical function of the school[1] is explored by Émile Durkheim (1992) explaining the presence of values in the hidden curriculum (Perrenoud 1993) of education. Thus, the school is designed to both teach and educate. Since the 1990s, we have witnessed the gradual introduction of "educations for" (Audigier and Tutiaux-Guillon 2008) into the school system. This form is not a black box; it corresponds to a specific mode of socialization, which ensures a generation subjected to rules by a personal exercise of reason.

Like all school subjects with a defined curriculum, patrimonial education has come, in turn, to respond to a political project. It is necessary to recall that no discipline in Morocco is taught in the name of "patrimonial education". It takes shape within history, geography or Arabic language courses. The political aim of this integration is to build a memory of the territory in the pupil, a feeling of shared culture, of a common future, in a country that is to be defended and valued. Patrimonial education refers, on the one hand, to making known a collective patrimony, a shared history, in order to develop a sense of belonging and to give the child a narrative identity, and on the other hand, to inculcating in the pupil values that encourage them to preserve their culture. Patrimonial education oscillates

---

1 Notion defined by Prost in 1992. Chapoulie, J. and Prost, A. (ed.) (1992). Éducation, société et politiques : une histoire des enseignements en France de 1945 à nos jours. *Histoire de l'éducation*, 57, 142–144.

between teaching and education (learning the practices and attitudes deemed necessary for the conservation and transmission of patrimony).

14.2. Introduction of patrimonial education in the Moroccan school system

Since the supra-national framework for patrimonial education was submitted by UNESCO in 1972, each state has been obligated to adapt the principles outlined in international conventions to the educational contexts of the country (Barthes and Blanc-Maximin 2017). If we go by published official texts, patrimonial education appeared in 1999 in Morocco and the term "patrimony" is used for the first time in the National Charter for Education and Training.

In Morocco, educational policy is described in the Charte nationale d'éducation et de formation (National Charter for Education and Training). This document is the result of an agreement between different political tendencies that were set out in the Commission spéciale de l'éducation et de la formation – COSEF – (Special Commission on Education and Training).

In order to identify the place of patrimonial education in the school system and in the absence of a specific curriculum for the introduction of patrimony in the school system, we will start with an analysis of the content of the Charter, interpreting each idea that refers to patrimonial education: word, sentence or paragraph.

From our reading of the texts, we deduce several categories of values embodied in the Charte nationale d'éducation et de formation. However, in this section, we will only state the values that we believe are related to patrimonial education.

14.2.1. *Learning languages*

In recent years, the teaching of the Amazigh language has been introduced in preschool and the first two years of primary school. This teaching aims to promote a Moroccan cultural patrimony, from which the population has begun to detach itself.

14.2.2. *Citizenship education*

According to Article 2 of the Charter, the school system aims to train citizens who are attached to their country, their identity and their culture, by introducing sacred and intangible values into the school curriculum. In the same sense, the Charter clearly indicates the rooting of the Moroccan cultural patrimony in the school system. In the same vein, Article 89 insists on teaching Moroccan historical and geographical values to Moroccans living abroad (MLA).

14.2.3. Self-directed learning

The first article of the Charter stipulates the obligation of extracurricular activities to foster a direct link with patrimony and to promote self-directed learning. Education by choice is stated to give the learner the freedom to choose what is important to them.

14.2.4. Environmental education

The Charter emphasizes the acquisition by learners of values in the field of the environment, mainly on the notion of protection of natural patrimony and ecology.

Our analysis of the official texts shows a very weak presence of the word "patrimony". We have therefore favored an analytical reading of the Charter, in order to appreciate the place dedicated to patrimonial education in the Moroccan school system. The Moroccan school curriculum promotes "the appropriation of religious, ethical, civic and human values essential to becoming citizens who are proud of their identity and their patrimony, aware of their history and socially integrated and active" (Charte nationale d'éducation et de formation 1999). It is therefore a question of using the school to build a sense of pride and belonging in the pupils, through the transmission of cultural knowledge of the country.

14.3. Poorly integrated patrimonial education

If we remain within the analysis of official texts, formal education in patrimony would be the ultimate means of ensuring a sustainable conservation of patrimony. But by integrating ourselves into the wheel of the Moroccan educational system, we note a certain destabilization of the school form. Leaving aside the various points of imbalance, we will focus on patrimonial education in the Moroccan school system.

Moroccan education has, for years, been criticized primarily for promoting knowledge that is deemed useless in everyday life. Intellectual education, as presented in the dictionary of pedagogy (Ferdinand Buisson 1911), is mainly oriented to prepare pupils for university education on the basis of academic knowledge in the form of several school disciplines. But this is considered insufficient to form a good citizen developing personal (such as hygiene) and collective (such as the protection of patrimony) behaviors. Education can therefore only be intellectual. A certain tension between academic knowledge and utilitarian knowledge[2], which very rarely appear[3] in the school disciplines, has manifested itself. Utilitarian education refers to knowledge of action (Barbier 1996), which does not require the same degree of formality as intellectual knowledge, directly inscribed in practical activities.

It should be remembered that, in the face of disciplines that express intellectual education, we have witnessed the birth of new educations, in the form of physical education, civic education, artistic education, etc., which have clearly had a behavioral goal (education in know-how and values). Beyond the timid introduction of "education for [...]" as a full-fledged school discipline, the question is to understand whether the way of teaching this type of knowledge achieves the objectives motivating its integration into the school system. Are these disciplines enough to make good citizens?

Before addressing these questions, it is necessary to indicate that the Moroccan school system advocates novelty in several forms. The first, and most frequent, is a change in the curriculum of the disciplines taught: the school content tends to be rectified several times to take into account new demands. For example, the curriculum change planned for the 2021–2022 school year took into consideration Jewish history and patrimony in Morocco. The second is the introduction of new subjects, such as physical education and civic education, with the consequence of reducing the time allocated to other subjects or increasing school hours. As for the third, it is a matter of considering "education for..." as trans-, pluri- or interdisciplinary subjects (Lenoir and Sauvé 1998; Audigier et al. 2006). This is the case for patrimonial education, which is integrated into the Moroccan curriculum as a transversal learning process involving several disciplines in the transmission of information. Patrimonial education is defined as a non-disciplinary subject, influenced by powerlessness in the face of an overloaded curriculum.

At this point, we can claim that the tension between intellectual education and utilitarian knowledge still finds a compromise, but at what level?

Regardless of the way in which the authorities integrate the objectives of patrimonial education, we conducted a diagnostic study in two Moroccan schools to measure the impact of formal patrimonial education on pupils. In order to build a sampling strategy that would allow us to analyze our research subject from different angles, we created a varied panel of participants by interviewing pupils from two

---

2 Knowledge that has social, personal and collective purposes.

3 Some utilitarian knowledge is integrated in a volatile way into academic disciplines.

different regions: 107 from Marrakech and 98 from the Arganeraie Biosphere Reserve (ABR). As our research field is only taught in the 6th grade, only 12–15 year olds were selected for the study.

The participants therefore all had the opportunity to be informed about the Arganeraie Biosphere Reserve in the school curriculum.

First, we developed a questionnaire to determine their knowledge of Morocco's patrimony.

14.3.1. Degree of patrimonial knowledge among pupils in Marrakech

The questionnaire includes four questions about the Arganeraie Biosphere Reserve and the Souss Massa National Park. It emerged that 90% of the pupils in Marrakech said they had never heard of the Arganeraie Biosphere Reserve and 86% had never had the opportunity to learn about the Souss Massa National Park. These results are significant when we consider that the Arganeraie Biosphere Reserve is included in the Moroccan school curriculum in the form of a chapter highlighting the history of the argan tree, the importance of its preservation and the risks it faces. However, the majority of pupils are unable to remember such a patrimony.

14.3.2. Degree of patrimonial knowledge among pupils in Agadir

The same questionnaire was submitted to secondary school pupils in Agadir, on the territory of the Arganeraie Biosphere Reserve, and the result was that 82% of the pupils stated that they had never heard of it. These adolescents, however, are originally from the region and live on the territory of the reserve. Similarly, 80% of them said they had never visited a patrimonial site, such as the Souss Massa National Park.

A survey was also conducted among teachers to clarify the formal education of patrimony at school. Our sample consisted of about 15 primary school teachers from private and public schools. The objective was to understand how teachers convey information about patrimony and their ability to educate through patrimony.

The interviews revealed that 92% of the teachers stated that they had never attended any training related to patrimonial education.

Patrimony is taught the same way as other subjects.

I follow the instructions in the master book, I find that patrimony is addressed in the same way as other chapters in the book.

I have been in the teaching field for a very long time, no training has been done for patrimonial education, at least to my knowledge.

My pupils are required to take a regional exam at the end of the year, a question about patrimony may come up; I focus on rote learning of the information.

Many teachers tend to focus on knowledge acquisition at the expense of the mission set for patrimonial education including the transmission of values.

We also interviewed them about their ability to teach through patrimony, that is, using patrimony as an open book. Thus, 78% of them consider themselves incapable of managing teaching outside the classroom.

The diagnosis made of the school system reveals a multitude of flaws, such as, for example, the insufficient mastery of Moroccan patrimony (considered important for the development of a sense of belonging to the country), the inadequacy of teaching methods to transmit such knowledge and the lack of training of teachers to educate in patrimony, etc.

Formal patrimonial education cannot be assimilated only by a minority of pupils, those who feel comfortable in the current school system, sidelining the majority of pupils in opposition to the school culture. It is high time to think of a new context that places the collective interest at the center, allowing the conservation of identity, history, patrimonial and cultural differentiation. The transversal learning of patrimonial education is no longer enough in the face of the world's mutations that lead us to a loss of culture in order to reach a single identity[4].

14.4. New school form to be tested

To further our reasoning, we tested a new form of patrimonial education, namely the introduction of informal patrimonial education into the school system. This change involves prioritizing participatory learning, and thus connecting the pupil to their patrimony and letting them judge for themself the usefulness of the information. We would be in an approach where the pupil, in other words we will use informal education in patrimony before reaching a certain level of formal patrimonial education.

---

4 The progressive loss of the traditional dress code tends to impose a single global code (jeans, sweater).

The field of investigation is the Arganeraie Biosphere Reserve (ABR), the first of its kind in Morocco. In collaboration with two Moroccan schools (one in Marrakech, the other in Agadir), we set up a project entitled *"Mon Maroc, Mon patrimoine* (My Morocco, My patrimony)", which consists of traveling throughout Morocco to be introduced to Moroccan patrimony. The first destination was the Arganeraie Biosphere Reserve. With the agreement of the parents, we went for two days to visit the existing patrimony on the ABR. The travel and accommodation expenses were entirely taken care of by the school in Marrakech.

During this excursion, we noted that the pupils expressed a great interest in learning from the Indigenous people who act as guides in front of the historical monuments of the Arganeraie Biosphere Reserve. It should be noted that there were no official guides on the site of the historical monuments, only the inhabitants of the region volunteered to inform the visitors.

After showing our pupils the patrimony of the Arganeraie Biosphere Reserve, we administered a second questionnaire to analyze the influence of such a project on the group, through questions specific to the sites visited (questions similar to the first questionnaire), the history of the patrimony and the cultural values during the excursion.

The pupils' knowledge of the country's riches increased. It turns out that all of them were able to name the Arganeraie Biosphere Reserve among the patrimony they know about; 38.5% of them cited "the know-how of the argan tree" in the list of known patrimony, compared to 0% in the post-project questionnaire. Thus, intangible patrimony is beginning to be part of the knowledge of the pupils participating in the project.

At the end of the questionnaire, we ask the pupils to write a short paragraph describing their impressions after this excursion, we quote below some examples.

> The argan tree is an indispensable treasure for us. Yes, because it only grows in Morocco, it is a fantastic treasure [...] A tree adapted to its ecosystem, so we must take care of this Maghrebian wonder.

> The characteristics of the argan tree make it the ideal tree to fight against erosion and desertification that threaten the Moroccan South very seriously, it is urgent to preserve it.

> The patrimony existing on the Arganeraie Biosphere Reserve is the happiness and pride of Morocco.

The cave you enter may contain the treasure you are looking for! It is necessary that everyone becomes aware of the richness of our patrimony, which will not be able to continue or develop without real awareness. Me, my Morocco is my patrimony, and I was able to discover a small part of this precious jewel that is dear to my heart and that made me want to discover more about my culture and my origin. And believe me, the beauty of it leaves indelible memories in you.

The argan tree, the iron tree or the tree of life [...] It is a precious tree that we must protect. We must take care of it.

The argan tree is not just a tree, but a precious stone that we must protect, this is what makes our country more special and different.

The argan tree is a treasure in our country that we must protect, because it is a distinctive grace.

Although this represents only a small sample of 205 middle school pupils, we note that the word "protect" was used consistently by the pupils, and feelings of pride and belonging also appeared in the majority of their writings. By confronting the pupils with their patrimony, they appropriate a certain identity, reinforce their attachment to the country and develop in them the will to preserve and protect a rich patrimony. At the request of the pupils, a brochure was produced to formalize their experience.

The school form applied in patrimonial education is considered inadequate to the conceptions of the young generations. As we have already mentioned, the "educations for [...]" were created to face the different demands and expectations of society. As a result, the school form is obliged to follow the rapid transformations of society. Over the last two centuries, our links to memory, identity, culture and others have changed. This will inevitably have an impact on the school system. The introduction of "educations for [...]" in the school system implies profound changes in the knowledge taught, calling into question the practices (Audigier and Tutiaux-Guillon 2008). Thus, school knowledge must be oriented towards the construction of attitudes and behaviors that contribute to preparing pupils for numerous life situations, for a collective future linked to present attitudes.

If this case study is based exclusively on the development of patrimonial knowledge in pupils, we have observed certain modifications in the characteristics of the school form.

14.4.1. *Experience at the heart of learning*

In our case study, the pupils were taken outside the walls of the school. Thus, the teacher was no longer the master of the information, but rather people outside the national education system intervened in the transmission process. The second point to note was to integrate the experience into the learning process, which allowed the pupils to discover the richness of their country and to have a sense of continuity with the past (Berryman 2007). This arrangement is reminiscent of Pruneau and Chouinard's (1997) model, which focuses on the importance of experience in building a sense of belonging.

Our case study therefore adopted an educational approach with strong experiential overtones; in other words, one that prefers direct contact between the learner (pupil in our case) and the patrimony (the Arganeraie Biosphere Reserve). Thus, each pupil develops know-how linked to the experience.

14.4.1.1. *Non-existent school curriculum*

Our case study partially sets aside formal patrimonial education, the school textbook is not present, the knowledge acquired is mainly related to the Indigenous people of the region who tell the story of a surrounding patrimony. The objective of the project was to make the pupils aware of their patrimony and thus to promote its conservation and transmission to future generations. In this method, patrimony is used as a means of education, it takes the role of the school textbook. Thanks to this, we note that the patrimony has a stronger influence on its visitors, it conveys identity values (Letonturier 2019) inciting the pupils to want to get involved in its conservation.

14.4.1.2. *Lack of evaluation of acquired knowledge*

At the end of the "*Mon Maroc, Mon patrimoine*" project, no evaluation of patrimonial knowledge was scheduled by the teachers. Only a questionnaire was submitted two months after the field trip to analyze the educational impact of such a project on the pupils. As a result, the pupils mentioned the "ABR" designation, awarded to the region by UNESCO, as well as the patrimony located in the area.

It should be emphasized that learning without pedagogy can call into question the school model imposed on pupils and unquestioned for decades. Patrimonial education seems to have to take a new form in order to achieve the required objectives.

In this system, the most important element of the school framework, namely the evaluation of pupils' knowledge, is absent.

14.4.1.3. *Lack of school formatting*

Apart from the leaflet, which the pupils expressed a desire to produce, no other school documents were included in their folders. This can be explained by the fact that the teachers only saw the leisure aspect of this excursion. In fact, interviews with teachers reveal that the majority of teachers did not see the educational aspect of the project, only emphasizing the importance of allowing pupils to engage in activities outside of the school to get away from the curriculum.

It should be noted that, despite the absence of any school form, formal patrimonial education was partially present through the leaflet for the benefit of other pupils in the school. It should be noted that the text of this leaflet was corrected and validated by their French teacher, who certainly does not have any patrimonial qualifications or the ability to produce a document dedicated to the formal education of pupils. Therefore, this may call into question the reliability of the leaflet produced by the pupils.

14.5. Discussion

Our case study shows, on the one hand, the weaknesses of formal patrimonial education in reaching its objectives; on the other hand, the importance of integrating informal patrimonial education into the school system.

Indeed, we were able to highlight the educational aspect of the project, as well as its capacity to transmit knowledge to visitors. However, the reliability of the information collected by the pupils during the field trip remains questionable, as it is only transmitted by the Indigenous people of the region whom we considered to be the holders of information.

Patrimonial education can find a place in the school system, but under certain conditions: the first is to change the form of teaching this type of knowledge; the possibility of having a direct link with the source of information is essential in patrimonial education, it is essential to take into consideration other educational situations in the school form. The second is to integrate teachers into this type of educational project, assigning them a role. It would therefore be necessary to train teachers to validate patrimonial texts written by their pupils as a formal document for other audiences.

The experiential model tested during our project proved to be useful in transmitting knowledge and developing a sense of pride and ownership among participants. However, during the field trip, we felt that there was a lack of training for teachers in patrimonial education. The competence of the teachers to validate the knowledge acquired by the Indigenous people seems therefore essential for the implementation of educational projects.

The school form has undergone a number of changes in patrimonial education, and the integration of Indigenous people in the process of patrimonial education is considered legitimate in this type of project. Grassroots actors play a key role in transmitting information and stories about the patrimony around them. Therefore, patrimony and Indigenous people can be defined as an educational support.

Through this case study, we can also note the empirical dimension of such an educational project in favor of patrimony. We can attest to an identity construction among the pupils, through the sense of belonging felt in their writings and their involvement in wanting to share patrimonial knowledge with others. This contributes, in a way, to the tourism promotion of the ABR site. Although the main objective of the project is purely educational, it has played an indirect role in supporting the economy of the region. A large number of pupils returned with their families to visit the Arganeraie Biosphere Reserve. Thus, an educational project can have an impact in several areas at once, giving patrimonial education a broader dimension.

14.6. References

Aboutayeb, H. (2014). La réserve de biosphère de l'arganeraie : un nouvel écoterritoire touristique au sud du Maroc. *PASOS Revista de turismo y patrimonio cultural*, 12(4), 915–922.

Audigier. F. and Tutiaux-Guillon, N. (eds) (2008). *Compétences et contenus. Les curriculums en questions*. De Boeck, Louvain-la-Neuve.

Audigier, F., Crahay, M., Dolz, J. (2006). *Curriculum, enseignement et pilotage*. De Boeck Supérieur, Louvain-la-Neuve.

Awais, N. (2014). L'éducation aux valeurs : quelles attitudes pour quel monde ? *Actes du colloque "Les éducations à ...", levier(s) de transformation du système éducatif ?* 36–49.

Barbier, J.-M. (1996). *Savoirs théoriques et savoirs d'action*. Presses universitaires de France, Paris.

Barthes, A. and Alpe, Y. (eds) (2014). L'éducation au patrimoine dans les aires territoriales protégées, une dimension de l'éducation au développement durable ? In *Éducation au développement durable*, Diemer, A. and Marquat, C. (eds). De Boeck Supérieur, Louvain-la-Neuve.

Barthes, A. and Alpe, Y. (eds) (2018). "Les éducations à", une remise en cause de la forme scolaire ? *Carrefours de l'éducation*, 45(1), 23–37.

Barthes, A. and Blanc-Maximin, S. (eds) (2017). Quelles évolutions de l'école française face à l'éducation au patrimoine ? *Revue des sciences de l'éducation*, 43(1), 85–115.

Berryman, T. (2007). L'autobiographie environnementale : la prise en compte des dimensions écologiques dans les histoires de vie. In *Recueil des communications – Colloque international : Le biographique, la réflexivité et les temporalités : articuler langues, cultures et formation*, Pineau, G. and Bachelart, G. (eds). L'Harmattan, Paris

Bonnéry, S., Crinon, J., Simons, G. (eds) (2016). Les élèves face aux outils pédagogiques : quels risques d'inégalités ? *Recherche en éducation*, 25, 3–11.

Bourdoncle. R. and Barbier, J. (eds) (1996). Savoirs théoriques et savoirs d'action. *Recherche et Formation*, 27, 155–157.

Brougère, G. and Bézille, H. (eds) (2007). De l'usage de la notion d'informel dans le champ de l'éducation. *Revue française de pédagogie*, 1(158), 117–160.

Bruxelle, Y. (2007). Le partenariat, entre réticences et fascination : quels questionnements éthiques pour l'institution scolaire ? *Éducation relative à l'environnement. Regards – Recherches – Réflexions*, 6 [Online]. Available at: https://doi.org/10.4000/ere.3962.

Buisson, F. (1911). *Nouveau dictionnaire de pédagogie*. Hachette et Cie, Paris.

Castagnet, V. (2013). *L'éducation au patrimoine*. Presses universitaires du Septentrion, Villeneuve d'Ascq.

Chapoulie, J. and Prost, A. (eds) (1992). Éducation, société et politiques : une histoire des enseignements en France de 1945 à nos jours. *Histoire de l'éducation*, 57, 142–144.

Charte nationale d'éducation et de formation (1999). Charte nationale d'éducation et de formation [Online]. Available at: https://www.axl.cefan.ulaval.ca/afrique/maroc-charte-educ.htm.

Durkheim, É. (1992). L'enseignement de la morale à l'école primaire. *Revue française de sociologie*, 33(4), 609–623 [Online]. Available at: https://doi.org/10.2307/3322228.

El Ansari, R.E. (2013). Patrimoine et développement régional au Maroc. Association de science régionale de langue française (ASRDLF) [Online]. Available at: http://www.asrdlf2013.org/img/pdf/c_-el_ansari__patrimoine_et_developpement_regional_au_maroc.pdf.

Houssaye, J. (1993). *La pédagogie : une encyclopédie pour aujourd'hui*. ESF, Paris [Online]. Available at: https://doi.org/10.4000/rfp.1664.

Lenoir, Y. and Sauvé, L. (eds) (1998). De l'interdisciplinarité scolaire à l'interdisciplinarité dans la formation à l'enseignement : un état de la question. *Revue française de pédagogie*, 124, 121–153.

Letonturier, E. (2019). Patrimoine, identités et cultures militaires. *Inflexions*, 1(40), 45–60.

Monjo, R. (1998). "La forme scolaire" dans l'épistémologie des sciences de l'éducation. *Revue française de pédagogie*, 125(1), 83–93 [Online]. Available at: https://doi.org/10.3406/rfp.1998.1109.

Moreau, L. and Joshua, S. (eds) (1990). L'école entre crise et refondation. *L'Homme et la société*, 136/137, 228–229.

OECD (2003). Background report. Report, Reviews of National Policies for Education: Tertiary Education in Switzerland, 16–125.

Pagoni, M. and Tutiaux-Guillon, N. (eds) (2012). Les éducations à… : nouvelles recherches, nouveaux questionnements ? *Spirale*, 50.

Perrenoud, P. (1993). Curriculum : le formel, le réel, le caché. In *La pédagogie, une encyclopédie pour aujourd'hui*, Houssaye, J. (ed.). ESF, Paris.

Pruneau, D., Breau, N., Chouinard, O. (1997). Un modèle d'éducation relative à l'environnement visant à modifier la représentation des écosystèmes biorégionaux. *Éducation et francophonie*, 25(1), 150–165 [Online]. Available at: https://doi.org/10.7202/1080654ar.

Tawil, S., Cerbelle, S., Alama, A. (eds) (2010). *Éducation au Maroc : analyse du secteur*. UNESCO, Paris.

Vincent, G. (2019). *L'Éducation prisonnière de la forme scolaire ? : Scolarisation et socialisation dans les sociétés industrielles*. Presses universitaires de Lyon, Lyon.

Conclusion

From the Emerging Concept of a Cultural Space of Training to the Design of a Label

Problems

The various studies presented in this book demonstrate the need to broaden the scope of education in order to carry out, among other things, the task of transmitting knowledge and values, and to enable the development of a level of individual autonomy that is indispensable in our hypermodern environments (Roelens 2020). Autonomy, defined as the ability to act (functional), to choose (moral) and to think (intellectual), is in fact weakened by the conditions of acceleration and liquefaction that characterize hypermodernity, that is, "the continuous flux and change in the various fields of collective life, as well as in individual existences" (Roelens 2020, p. 61). These fragilities affect all individuals, whatever their level of education, status or age. Thus, one of the major challenges is to provide individuals with the means, in a variety of situations, to maintain, update or reconstitute this autonomy, enabling them to continue to reflect on, control and direct their actions.

The questions we can then ask ourselves are: outside school, university, the world of work, even, what institutions and resources can we count on to continue the mediation required to build this autonomy? And second, how can we guarantee resources that are able to meet the criteria for the validity of knowledge and values?

Meunier and Roelens (Chapter 7) offer an enlightening answer to this question, with particular reference to the role of museums. The various studies in this book highlight, in one way or another, collaborations between schools, universities and libraries, museums, historical and environmental sites – in short, cultural spaces. So,

---

Conclusion written by Theodora BALMON and Bruno GARNIER.

digging deeper, it seems to us that the cultural space of training can indeed be one of the catalysts of "hypermodern mediations", as Anik Meunier and Camille Roelens (Chapter 7) put it, to contribute to the empowerment to act, choose and think.

In this conclusion, we begin by briefly recalling the genesis of the concept of the cultural space of training, which immediately raised the question of the relevance of the boundaries between institutions in the educational field and those in the cultural field. Second, we look at how the text in this book has addressed this issue. Finally, we look at the possible evolution of the concept of cultural space of training with regard to the criteria of cognitive and social change that Taylor et al. (2010) place at the heart of their studies, particularly empirical studies. We also examine them with the help of Habermas' critical theory, one of whose essential aims is to grasp the cognitive basis underpinning the rational process, notably by means of exchange and consensus-building.

Genesis of a concept

In 2006, Joëlle Le Marec, initiating the concept of the cultural space of training, also raises the question of boundaries, asking "what division should be made" (Le Marec 2006, p. 16). Thus, she notes that "[...] museums and libraries are often associated with the media to empirically constitute the so-called 'informal education' sector" (Le Marec 2006, p. 14) – hence, museums and libraries are, here, attached to the communication and information sciences. On the one hand, this informal sector constitutes "a set of properties defined by default" (Le Marec 2006, p. 14), particularly in relation to the fields of formal education and training within dedicated institutions. On the other hand, a tendency to think in binary or oppositional terms is derived from this definition: formal versus informal knowledge and learning, approaches focusing on the learner versus those highlighting social logics – the learner-oriented approach being sometimes deemed depoliticizing, due to certain "naturalizing" cognitivist tendencies. These "great divisions", which the author describes as pitfalls, are perhaps not entirely avoidable, or even to be avoided, insofar as they can also be structured for reflection. However, throughout this book, the text deals more with the border as a space of synergy rather than separation.

Borders as common spaces

Through these empirical and theoretical writings, we can think of the border as a space where entanglements and implications are woven, enabling the creation or reinforcement of convergences for the transmission of knowledge and values and, ultimately, for an inclusive dynamic. Such is the case with Sylvie Condette's (Chapter 1) observation of the effects of primary schools in priority education zones collaborating with institutions, such as a leisure center and a media library, to support families who are uncomfortable with, at a distance from, or rejected by the school. Mary Grace Flaherty's research (Chapter 2) makes similar observations about libraries working on health issues with vulnerable populations. Support ranges from information to assistance in filling in online forms, to care intervention through cooperation with other public institutions. Pierre Kahn (Chapter 3), for his part, points out that the school has changed a great deal in recent decades, instituting many links outside the school. He also invites us to question the concept of the school form, which is so heuristic, but whose relevance would undoubtedly be diminished in view of the varied, differentiated and open systems that the school has endeavored to implement to better transmit and work towards a more inclusive society. Thus, the goal of developing the educational community is more than tangible in research questions.

The educational community is naturally conceived in terms of autonomous civic identity and the critical thinking that goes with it. Research carried out in museums places particular emphasis on these points. As Marion Trannoy Voisin explains (Chapter 5), the case of the citadelle de Corte, itself a project showing history in the making on the territorial scale of Corsica, conveys this ambition, even though the means of this citizen interaction have yet to be matured. Moreover, this goal of an autonomous civic identity is perhaps being called into question more and more, both by those who know and those who learn – and, indeed, by everyone – in our "hypermodern" world, where knowledge, and science itself, seem to be wavering. This is all the more reason for "hypermodern mediations", both as a concept of intelligibility of reality and as a means of acting in the face of that reality, as cultural institutions do, as Anik Meunier and Camille Roelens point out (Chapter 7). Faced with the need for "hypermodern mediations", it seems essential for teachers to be aware of the issues and their complexity, to acquire a "metadiscourse", therefore, and be trained to develop their critical thinking skills (Robert and Garnier 2018). Nahanaël Wadbled's analyses (Chapter 6), meanwhile, alert us to the possible failings of mediations and their implications. In the case under study, Wadbled shows, on the one hand, that museum guides can "propose an alternative discourse to history [but] one that presents itself as equally legitimate"; on the other, that some teachers tend to see the museum visit as an illustration of their lessons and less as an opportunity to develop their pupils' knowledge and reflections. At the crossroads of adult interactions, pupils do what is expected of them, demonstrating "polite inattention: facing the guides in an attitude of attention, they are actually attentive to what they see around the guides and not to what they say" (Chapter 6). In any case, the result is clearly at odds with historical critical thinking (Denos et al. 2013). Corinne Baujard also notes the value of museums in transmitting knowledge and ethical, aesthetic and cultural values, "essential aspects in the development of students' personality and citizenship" (Chapter 8). However, she also points out the precautions that need to be taken to ensure that technological and playful innovations do not become an end in themselves. For example, teachers need to be trained to take the measure of hypermodern mediations, as well as to be able to be a force of proposition in cultural spaces. One of the aims of teacher training is to enable candidates to know "how to strike a balance between technology and content in order to transmit knowledge. The museum is a place for training, as well as a place for exchanging knowledge" (Chapter 8). Géraldine Barron's research (Chapter 4) highlights the role played by the Conservatoire des Arts et Métiers museum in the 19th century in designing places of study to disseminate technical and scientific knowledge to children and adults alike – in other words, "a lifelong learning offer before its time" (Chapter 4). For both the Conservatoire des Arts et Métiers and the Musée de Marine, we see the elite's preoccupation with emphasizing "the complementarity between theory and application", and the "values of encyclopedism and universalism", inherited from the Enlightenment and the Revolution (Chapter 4).

The collaborative research carried out by Nathalie Bertrand (Chapter 9) in the field of literacy is also situated in this perspective of critical thinking, recognizing the hypermodern constraints of our environment, and the mediations they impose on the teachers themselves. Cultural institutions become partners in helping to reinforce or even build the capacities that trainee schoolteachers (elementary school or nursery schoolteachers in initial training) must possess in the face of the universe of the written sign, in particular (Chapter 9). Pascale Gossin and Isabelle Lebrat's work (Chapter 10) does not cite the term "literacy", but rather Roland Barthes, a promotor, if ever there was one, of semiology. Here again, trainee teachers (elementary school or nursery schoolteachers in initial training) will be able to discover resources outside the school, and within themselves, that they did not suspect, to improve their language teaching practice (Chapter 10).

Finally, the last section highlights the process of hybridization of teaching and learning modalities, which seems to have become a key to tracing paths towards knowledge. Through collaborative research, Rana Challah and Geneviève Lameul (Chapter 12) explain the contribution of boundary objects to the dynamic distribution of missions, between partners of different status – teacher-researchers, statisticians, design and research engineers and from different university components – in the convergence of a pedagogical project for student success. The work of Régis Malet and Martine Derivry-Plard (Chapter 13), dedicated to the design of university training courses according to the emerging, plurilingual, and pluricultural paradigm, in this globalized and hypermodern context, also reflects the need to rethink and overcome borders, notably through "telecollaborative spaces" setting up hybrid devices. The hybridization of modalities and devices is also perceptible in Theodora Balmon's presentation (Chapter 11), which proposes a reading grid for observing the types of learning, especially informal learning, that can result in knowledge, especially formal knowledge, in a public library context. Finally, Salma Itsmaïl's study (Chapter 14) opens up further perspectives by addressing the hybridization of learning in the context of "education for", in this case, patrimony and the environment, with the cooperation of a World Heritage site.

This review of work already provides material to support the concept of a cultural space of training, by promoting the convergence of efforts by an educational community for a more inclusive society, for the adaptation of forms of mediation in the service of the development of autonomy and critical thinking, for the diversification of literacy modalities according to audiences and objectives, for the combination of learning and teaching methods facilitating multidisciplinarity. Other contributions, however, make it possible to continue in this direction and to project an effective definition of the concept.

Portrait of cultural spaces of training

Thus, in 2010, researchers in the field of adult education are taking an interest in cultural institutions, but focusing more on the epistemic axis that underpins them, in terms of resources, organization and mechanisms (McKinley Parrish 2010; Taylor 2010). Le Marec (2006), moreover, also emphasizes this close link between cultural institutions and knowledge. Thus, for these adult education researchers, cultural institutions – museums, libraries, archives, historical and environmental sites, botanical gardens, wildlife parks – are first and foremost the architects of an ensemble comprising elements of know-how and evidence of knowledge, such as manuscripts, artifacts, documents, animals, plants, places of memory, monuments and landscapes. Although diverse, the common mission of these institutions is to select, preserve, organize and present this knowledge. They must guarantee access to a set of data according to the validated rules, at a given moment, of a community's scientific, academic and social history (Carr 1985, 1992, 2000; McKinley Parrish 2010; Taylor 2010).

These researchers also propose to complete the picture of the learning characteristics that these institutions foster. Rather than the informal–formal categories, they suggest considering the criteria of potential for cognitive and social transformation. These shifts in register, from the point of view of research fields to that of learning processes and outcomes, allow us to approach a positive definition – and no longer a hollow one – of cultural institutions with regard to knowledge, and thus of the cultural space of training.

On these points of cognitive and social transformation, Habermas' theory of rationality seems particularly useful for understanding the mechanisms and hoped-for results.

Definition of the term "training"

Before going any further, we need to define what we mean by "training."

In France, this term has taken on a restrictive note, aimed at specialization in response to economic constraints:

> If the roots of the 1970s idea of lifelong education can be found in themes of personal, economic, and social development   (popular education, social promotion, UNESCO's message, industrial expansion, etc.), the concepts of training born during the 1990s will have been marked by the rise of themes of economic and social prevention (Carré and Caspar 2017, p. 34).

Carré and Caspar (2017) recall Dumazedier's definition of continuing education:

> Compulsory or voluntary, formal or informal education of the entire population, at all ages of life, with a view to fostering personality development and social participation in a society undergoing permanent change.

But Carré and Caspar conclude that recent years have seen "the triumph of the notions of competence, flexibility, and employability and the unfortunately widespread use of their complement, exclusion" (2017, p. 34).

However, researchers Taylor et al. (2010) take up the question of cultural institutions by positioning themselves in the field of adult and continuing education, embracing the various domains of existence.

We also therefore propose to follow their example and not reduce the term "training" to its professional connotation. In this way, the concept of a cultural space of training can be expressed to a greater extent, as the work in this book already illustrates.

Following this clarification of the extended perimeter of training, we can continue our examination of the cultural space of training with regard to the notions of cognitive and social transformation supported by Taylor and McKinley Parrish.

Habermas' theory, focusing on cognitive determination at the roots of rationality and consensus formation, completes the examination.

Finally, we present some more operational elements relating to the learning context of cultural spaces of training.

Epistemic core and cognitive transformation

The works presented in this book underline the preoccupation of teachers and students alike with critical thinking. Critical thinking can be undermined, as in the case of the museum described by Nathanaël Wadbled (Chapter 6), or submerged by the playful, as Corinne Baujard points out (Chapter 8). Indeed, this is one of the perspectives that the plurilingual, pluricultural training paradigm promoted by Martine Derivry-Plard and Régis Malet intends to deploy, "multiplying intercultural situations to support open-mindedness and critical thinking" (Chapter 13). Faced with this imperative, cultural spaces of training have to guarantee access to legitimate knowledge and devices.

In 2010, Taylor and colleagues conducted empirical and statistical research to explore the factors of cognitive acquisition and transformation within cultural spaces. Three characteristics emerge.

First, these spaces are conducive to co-construction and generate moments of discovery. This can be seen, for example, in the work of Sylvie Condette (Chapter 1), Nathalie Bertrand (Chapter 9), Pascale Gossin and Isabelle Lebrat (Chapter 10) and Salma Itsmaïl (Chapter 14).

This can lead to spurts of interest, prompting the individual to question, experience and discover new concepts:

> This process is encouraged by the opportunities available to participate creatively and collaboratively in spaces that are free from normative social structures. Role-play, risk-taking, and experimentation are expected, with no overtly directed set of learning outcomes. (McKinley Parish 2010, p. 88)

Second, referring to the "cultural arbitrariness", according to Passeron and Bourdieu's theory, these researchers see cultural institutions as bases for questioning legitimate cultural narratives:

> One would refrain from viewing museums as repositories of neutral knowledge. Instead, museum objects are viewed as vehicles enabling visitors to understand how museum experiences are "produced,

legitimated, and organized" (McLaren, 1997, p. 21). (Borg and Mayo 2010, p. 35)

Participating in these narratives, renewing them, bringing out others that have been forgotten and doing so in greater interaction with the community is indeed the path taken by the projects at the Musée de la Corse (Chapter 5) and the Argarneraie Biosphere Reserve (Chapter 14).

Finally, cultural institutions can help build bridges between literacies, those of communities and those of academic fields and research, inviting not only the "knowers" but also pupils to change their posture towards knowledge (McKinley Parish 2010). Here, too, the experiences of Nathalie Bertrand (Chapter 9), Pascale Gossin and Isabelle Lebras (Chapter 10) and Géraldine Baron (Chapter 4) at the Conservatoire des Arts et Métiers and the Musée de Marine are instructive in this regard.

We are only citing a few empirical studies here, and more are yet to come. However, to ground the cognitive and cognitive transformation, we could undoubtedly benefit from Habermas' critical theory, particularly on the subject of the cognitive core.

Indeed, Habermas proposes considering the adjustment of the rational justification process according to situations, either those dealing with facts or those dealing with values. In the first case, Habermas speaks of the attainment of truth; in the second, of the search for universality. With these justification processes, the cognitive guarantee can be founded. It is not a question, however, of reviving a verticality, from the elites to the common people, nor of attempting to impose truths or social orders. Rather, it is a question of laying the foundations for co-construction, as in constructivist theory, on condition that it is not stripped of all epistemic substratum (Habermas 2014). Cultural spaces of training are a priori conducive to this constructivist elaboration, if we consider their resources and all the actions already cited, those aimed at an educational community for a more inclusive society, by means of collaboration, those of "hyper-modern mediations" in the service of the development of autonomy and critical thinking, the diversification of literacy modalities according to audiences and objectives, or those of the combination of learning and teaching methods facilitating multidisciplinarity.

Finally, Habermas' precepts, briefly outlined, can provide a framework for establishing the cognitive relevance of cultural spaces of training. This seems all the more necessary "in the age of globalization, post-truth, and alternative facts" (Chapter 13). The value of Habermas' theory lies in the fact that it provides tools for going beyond the perimeter of facts and thinking about biased and destructive social narratives, such as those of the "reinfosphere", those groups that form, particularly on social networks, driven by an emotional impulse, which they do their utmost to maintain at the expense of all impartiality, and most often to the detriment of groups or individuals who are already discriminated against (Rezende Ribeiro 2020).

Communication processes and social transformation

Cognitive rationality is essential, but not an end in itself in our social framework. For Habermas, it must be the driving force behind thinking in favor of social change. Moreover, this reflection should take the form of an exchange between individuals, and here again, cultural spaces of training could have a role to play. Indeed, according to Habermas (2014), places for political exchange and deliberation are still too rare, whether in the liberal conception, embodied by the United States, or the republican one, exemplified by France (Habermas 2014). In the first conception, we rely on the transcendence of a divine will, or that of the market as the authority that issues laws that are binding on subjects. This authority safeguards the interests of individuals, with the State seen essentially as the instrument for implementing laws. The other is rooted in a desire for self-determination of one's destiny by the people, a people whom the state is supposed to represent, but from whom, outside the ritual and institutional moments of elections in particular, it becomes autonomous. Habermas considers the first concept insufficiently normative, the second too normative; both, in the end, lack instances of opinion-forming in connection with the lived world:

> From this point of view, the conception of democracy based on discussion theory joins the distanced point of view of the social sciences, for which the political system is neither the summit, nor the center, nor, a fortiori, the structuring model of society, but a system of action among others (Habermas 2014).

Thus, after defining the cognitive principle, Habermas sets out to specify the public space and communicative process at the heart of rational opinion formation. This idea implies the availability of resources within the social fabric, accessible to the various components of society, capable of organizing debates in one form or another, and authorizing the expression of each and every one:

> Precisely these political communications, which pass through the filter of deliberation, depend on the resources of the lived world, that is, on a political culture founded on freedom and on politically emancipated socialization, including the initiatives of associations that contribute to opinion formation (Habermas 2014).

Certainly, cultural spaces of training can lay claim to this title of resources of the lived world. The work presented in this book provides numerous examples of this, from the links that have been forged between "disadvantaged" families and school thanks to leisure centers and media libraries (Chapter 1), to the health initiatives implemented as close to citizens as possible by American libraries (Chapter 2), to the visit to the Arganeraie Biosphere Reserve in Morocco by teachers as amazed as their pupils discovering their patrimony (Chapter 14).

Pragmatically speaking, however, certain precautions need to be taken if we are to achieve effective democratization of the spoken word. Indeed, the public arena is an ideal place for the exercise of symbolic violence by dominant groups – i.e., those who have had the means to legitimize their framings – on dominated groups, that is, those who have not had the means to defend their point of view (Bourdieu 1996). It follows that dominated groups may be censored, more or less tacitly, or even adopt attitudes of censorship and self-censorship through mimicry and integration. This is how inequalities can persist, and how a certain "naturalization" of them can take place. However, this deterministic mechanism is not insurmountable. Moments of social, economic and political crisis are conducive to change. Outside these periods of rupture or in parallel, Nancy Fraser's (1992) theory of counterpublics and competitive spaces offers a perspective on what can be put in place to accompany democratization. From this point of view, people who share the same difficulties come together to exchange ideas and make their voices heard. Fraser cites the particular situation of feminists. However, the philosopher warns against naivety:

> To avoid any misunderstanding, I make it clear that my purpose is not to imply that subaltern counterpublics are always and obligatorily virtuous (Fraser 1992, p. 139).

We can, in fact, observe that counterpublics resulting from democratic enlargement, in particular via social networks, do not necessarily, however, promote democratic dynamics. Reinfosphere spaces on social networks bear witness to this, using freedom of expression to exploit the emotional and create a hostile climate towards certain, generally vulnerable, groups or individuals (Rezende Ribeiro 2020).

In this context, the cultural spaces of training provide an endorsement for the communicative project that is rooted in their focus and evolutionary work on the epistemic core, the elements of knowledge and evidence we have already mentioned above. This communicative project is in itself the first link in the chain of social change. It is, moreover, an extension of the goal of encouraging teachers and trainers as "intellectuals in action" capable of "creating the conditions necessary for deliberative democracy to flourish in their classrooms, in the hope that this will extend to the societies in which they act" (Chapter 13).

Operating elements

After these brief forays into theory, it seems important to establish a few practical guidelines.

Cognitive and critical thinking

First of all, let us recall that the range of cultural spaces of training is vast: museums, libraries, archives, historical and environmental sites, botanical gardens, animal parks. The cognitive character of their missions, however, is specific, such as the selection and provision of resources and artifacts, and the design of devices to promote progress across epistemological fields (Carr 1992, 1995, 2000; McKinley Parrish 2010; Taylor 2010). At the same time, in an information context that is inflationary, segmented and de-hierarchical, they reorganize data, create articulations, elaborate new syntheses and propose metacognitive perspectives (Latour 2011).

Pragmatically, the transversal methods of critical thinking, in the various disciplines, should help to design projects that enable the practice of learning. For example, we can cite the following objectives for the historical discipline (Denos et al. 2013), but they are perfectly adaptable to multiple themes:

– grasp the reality of facts and ideas;

– see contradictory points of view;

– understand the context;

– being able to argue;

– making the link between past and present, here and elsewhere.

However, this cognitive and critical work also concerns the institutions themselves, which must examine the selection and design criteria (and biases) that govern them (Kemp and McKinley Parrish 2010) and reconstitute, as it were, their own normative foundation, by discerning the epistemic core as conceived by Habermas.

Participatory axis and boundary objects

The variety of pathways is a real challenge if we are to meet the needs and aspirations of an inclusive society. The level of collaborative research between different institutions, different services and people of different status, presented in the book, seems particularly significant in this respect. This may be indicative of a new way of thinking, if not of working.

The model of boundary objects, developed by Rana Challah and Geneviève Lameul (Chapter 12), could be a resource for training and transformation, depending on the context, as could the "telecollaborative" spaces outlined by Martine Derivry-Plard and Régis Malet (Chapter 13).

Reading grid for learning mechanisms

The draft diagram of the learning continuum and the characteristics of informality (Chapter 11), to be completed, can shed light on the main dimensions along which to position existing actions and those to be envisaged with regard to learning: action-reflection, intentionality-opportunity, degree of support by an educator-mediator. To this schema can be added, for example, the cumulative and/or transformative types of learning that can result from these arrangements, as distinguished by Schugurensky (2007), for the informal, in particular.

Building autonomy together

As mentioned above, in a hypermodern environment, the horizontal multiplication of mediations can go hand in hand with a weakening of people's autonomy. This autonomy must therefore be constantly reconquered, whatever our situation, status or age. Content and systems deployed – horizontally, vertically and reticularly – are among the hypermodern mediations that help consolidate and update this autonomy, whether in terms of aesthetics, ethics or, more broadly, critical thinking.

This supportive autonomy is also crucial in sensitive areas such as health and well-being, for example, as we saw with Mary Grace Flaherty's study (Chapter 2).

Literacy

The concept of "literacy" (Barré-de Miniac 2002) has taken precedence over the term "reading" itself, as evidenced by the change of name of the International Reading Association to the International Literacy Association, marking a less linear vision of the comprehension of literacy research over the decades.

Informational literacy and health literacy seem inescapable in the knowledge age, where, undoubtedly, the digital divide, but more broadly the cognitive divide, should be seen as structural, and not just conjunctural (Derville 2017; Garnier and Balcou-Debussche 2021). Vulnerable populations are the first to be affected. However, it turns out that, like autonomy, fragility is a reality that each and every one of us can face, as the hypermodern environment creates more solicitations and hazards.

Multimodal media literacy (Lacelle et al. 2015, 2019) specifies the particularities of access to knowledge, comprehension, analysis, as well as expression and production by means of multimodal content (textual, iconic, kinetic, sound, gestural modes), on traditional media vectors (print, radio, television, painting, sculpture, etc.), digital (digital text, sound and image, social networking, interface, support, cloud computing, twiteracy, etc.), seems particularly well suited to implementing modular programs, adapted to the audiences identified and their needs.

Competitive public space

Finally, exhibitions, conferences, debates, workshops, reading clubs and meetings are all occasions where discussion forums are formed, supported by preparatory study, realization and production work on specific subjects. Within this epistemic framework, it would be interesting to look at aspects of audience participation, so as to encourage expression, and to think of a formalization of exchange that can be shared and be perceptible, like a signal – not aggressive, but persistent – in an overloaded and noisy media landscape. Cultural spaces of training, whose networks are highly developed, could thus become a kind of competitive public space, first and foremost with those of the reinfospheres (Rezende-Ribeiro 2020) and the fake news of this post-truth era (Troude-Chastenet 2018).

Perspectives and labeling

The work described in this book opens up new avenues of research, providing an insight into the work that needs to be done to structure the concept of cultural spaces of training. The contribution and impact of cultural spaces of training have been seen at several educational levels, in a variety of disciplines, at all ages, and with a variety of actors in the fields of education and culture.

We have seen the potential of inter-institutional collaboration for an inclusive educational community, of mediatization designed to build and regenerate individual autonomy (the ability to act, choose and think) (Roelens 2020), of literacies in tune with the changing needs of the public and of hybridized forms of learning to address complexity and pluridisciplinarity.

These contributions and impacts seem all the more relevant in our destabilizing contexts of hypermodernity and reinfosphere. This is true for everyone, and even more so for the most vulnerable populations. Moreover, Habermas' critical theory supports our reading of these phenomena of destabilization, irrationality and inequality, as much as it enables us to model solutions.

In light of these observations and openings, the creation of a label for a cultural space of training could be both judicious and appropriate. In the first instance, this label could focus on the following criteria:

– strengthening the democratization of access to knowledge (e.g. through inter-institutional collaboration);

– guaranteeing access to cognitive resources and devices, such as those for literacies, in various fields, including the all-important one of health;

– adapting resources and devices to a variety of audiences, such as multimodal media literacies that emphasize the oral and visual, as well as the gestural;

– developing mediation to build autonomy (exhibitions, workshops, clubs, etc.);

– the creation of forums for exchange and support for this exchange practice (conferences, face-to-face and online discussion groups, etc.).

This combination of criteria for labeling the cultural space of training could enable the many and varied cultural institutions to strengthen connections and benchmarks at the local, national and international level, and to play a full part in the cultural, educational and democratic work we need to confront the trends that tend to destabilize knowledge and critical thinking.

References

Barré-de Miniac, C. (2002). La notion de littéracie et les principaux courants de recherche. *La Lettre de l'AIRDF*, 30(1), 27–33. https://doi.org/10.3406/airdf.2002.1519.

Borg, C. and Mayo, P. (2010). Museums: Adult education as cultural politics. *New Directions for Adult and Continuing Education*, 127, 35–44. https://doi.org/10.1002/ace.379.

Bourdieu, P. (1996). *Sur la télévision*. Raisons d'agir, Paris.

Bourdieu, P. and Passeron, J.-C. (2018). *La Reproduction : éléments pour une théorie du système d'enseignement*. Éditions de Minuit, Paris.

Carr, D. (1985a). Mediation as a helping presence in cultural institutions. *New Directions for Adult and Continuing Education*, 26, 87–96. https://doi.org/10.1002/ace.36719852610.

Carr, D. (1985b). Self-directed learning in cultural institutions. *New Directions for Adult and Continuing Education*, 25, 51–62. https://doi.org/10.1002/ace.36719852507.

Carr, D. (1992). Cultural institutions as structures for cognitive change. *New Directions for Adult and Continuing Education*, 53, 21–35.

Carr, D. (1995). The personal past in public space. *Journal of Museum Education*, 20(2), 3–5. https://doi.org/10.1080/10598650.1995.11510289.

Carr, D. (2000). In the contexts of the possible : Libraries and museums as incendiary cultural institutions. *RBM: A Journal of Rare Books, Manuscripts, and Cultural Heritage*, 1(2), 117–134. https://doi.org/10.5860/rbm.1.2.186.

Carré, P. and Caspar, P. (eds) (2017). *Traité des sciences et des techniques de la Formation*. Dunod, Paris.

Denos, M., Case, R., Lévesque, S. (2013). *Enseigner la pensée historique*. TC2 The Critical Thinking Consortium, Vancouver.

Derville, G. (2017). L'influence politique des médias au-delà de la propagande. In *Le pouvoir des médias*, volume 4, Derville, G. (ed.). Presses universitaires de Grenoble, Grenoble.

Fraser, N. (1992). Repenser la sphère publique : une contribution à la critique de la démocratie telle qu'elle existe réellement. *Hermes, La Revue*, 31(3), 125–156.

Garnier, B. and Balcou-Debussche, M. (eds) (2021). Parcours différenciés en éducation thérapeutique et littératie en santé. *Revue Education, Santé, Sociétés*, 8(1). doi: https://doi.org/10.17184/eac.9782813004383.

Habermas, J. (1978). *L'espace public : archéologie de la publicité comme dimension constitutive de la societé bourgeoise*. Payot, Paris.

Habermas, J. (1987a). *Théorie de l'agir communicationnel*, volume 1. Fayard, Paris.

Habermas, J. (1987b). *Théorie de l'agir communicationnel*, volume 2. Fayard, Paris.

Habermas, J. (2014a). Citoyenneté et identité nationale. In *L'intégration républicaine*, Habermas, J. (ed.). Fayard, Paris.

Habermas, J. (2014b). Le contenu cognitif de la morale, une approche généalogique. In *L'intégration républicaine*, Habermas, J. (ed.). Fayard, Paris.

Habermas, J. (2014c). Trois modèles normatifs de la démocratie. In *L'intégration républicaine*, Habermas, J. (ed.). Fayard, Paris.

Kemp, A. and McKinley Parrish, M. (2010). (Re)membering: Excavating and performing uncommon narratives found in archives and historical societies. *New Directions for Adult and Continuing Education*, 127, 45–56. https://doi.org/10.1002/ace.380.

Lacelle, N., Lebrun, M., Boutin, J.-F., Richard, M., Martel, V. (2015). Les compétences en littératie médiatique multimodale au primaire et au secondaire. In *Littératie : vers une maîtrise des compétences dans divers environnements*, Pharand, J. and Lafontaine, L. (eds). Presses de l'Université du Québec, Quebec.

Lacelle, N., Richard, M., Martel V., Lalonde, M. (2019). Design de cocréation interinstitutionnelle favorisant la littératie en contexte numérique. *Revue de recherches en littératie médiatique multimodale*, 9. https://doi.org/10.7202/1062034ar.

Latour, B. (2011). Plus elles se répandent, plus les bibliothèques deviennent centrales. *Bulletin des bibliothèques de France*, 1(56), 34–36.

Le Marec, J. (2006). Les musées et bibliothèques comme espaces culturels de formation. *Savoirs*, 11(2), 9–38.

McKinley Parrish, M. (2010). Reflections on adult learning in cultural institutions. *New Directions for Adult and Continuing Education*, 127, 87–95. https://doi.org/10.1002/ace.384.

Pharand, J. and Lafontaine, L. (2015). Introduction. In *Littératie : vers une maîtrise des compétences dans divers environnements*, Pharand, J. and Lafontaine, L. (eds). Presses de l'Université du Québec, Quebec.

Rezende Ribeiro, R. (2020). La réinfosphère brésilienne : fake news et intolérance dans la vie quotidienne numérique. *Sociétés*, 1(147), 43–52. https://doi.org/10.3917/soc.147.0043.

Robert, A.D. and Garnier, B. (eds) (2018). *La pensée critique des enseignants : éléments d'histoire et de théorisation*. Presses universitaires de Rouen et du Havre, Mont-Saint-Aignan.

Robichaud, A. (2018). *Habermas et la question de l'éducation*. Presses de l'Université Laval, Quebec.

Roelens, C. (2019). Bienveillance. *Le Telemaque*, 55(1), 21–34.

Roelens, C. (2020). Couler, surfer ou naviguer dans un monde liquide et accéléré ? *Revue francaise d'éthique appliquée*, 9(1), 59–73.

Ruel, J., Moreau, A.C., Alarie, L. (2015). Les usages sociaux de la littératie et les compétences à développer en vue d'environnements plus inclusifs. In *Littératie : vers une maîtrise des compétences dans divers environnements*, Pharand, J. and Lafontaine, L. (eds). Presses de l'Université du Québec, Quebec.

Schugurensky, D. (2007). Vingt mille lieues sous les mers : les quatre défis de l'apprentissage informel. *Revue française de pédagogie. Recherches en éducation*, 160, 13–27. https://doi.org/10.4000/rfp.583.

Taylor, E.W. (2010). Cultural institutions and adult education. *New Directions for Adult and Continuing Education*, 127, 5–14.

Troude-Chastenet, P. (2018). Fake news et post-vérité. De l'extension de la propagande au Royaume-Uni, aux États-Unis et en France. *Quaderni, communication, technologies, pouvoir*, 96, 87–101. https://doi.org/10.4000/quaderni.1180.

Appendix

Counterpoint "Hungry for Expeditions"

Having worked closely with Seymour Papert (Papert and Jaillet 2003), what was most prominent in his analysis of the pedagogical era was the school form. According to him, a pupil who fell asleep on their desk at the end of the 19th century and suddenly woke up at the beginning of the 20th would not have been disoriented (Papert 2003). He often followed Ivan Illich's lead on the idea that a society without schools was possible (Illich 1971), whose presentation by Joffre Dumazedier (1972) highlights the questions of form related to this work. According to Illich, a society that is not built on a school form of transmission and industrial construction of knowledge is possible. This Rousseauist vision of discovering knowledge in a way other than through the didactic structuring that had invaded the entire educational arena was one of the principles Pestalozzi sought to put into practice (Soëtard 1994, pp. 37–50). It was undoubtedly Töpffer, though a political conservative in his own right, or perhaps for this reason, who set up this experiment in discovery through his zigzag journeys (Töpffer 1859). The new pedagogies (Houssaye 1994) of the early 20th century, of which Freinet's pedagogy is a precursor in the radical transformation of the school form, did not, however, turn the tables. How can we consider the dimension of informal education? As can be seen from the contributions to the book, there are two approaches. Either we consider that meaning can be built by leaving school, because its walls are too formal, with all the positive and more measured effects we hope for; or we consider that meaning can be built by modifying the school form within the existing walls. The question of how knowledge is built and passed on has an anthropological dimension. Hall, whom Winkin (1981, pp. 86–91) includes in the invisible college of the new communication, can put it in a much broader perspective, based on structural approaches to the functioning of societies.

Appendix written by Alain JAILLET.

Formal and informal education are understood differently depending on where you are on the planet. In Africa, informal education refers to unofficial schooling. In other words, when the failing State can't provide for all needs, parents create a *tontine*[1] and finance what is known as a *"maître de(s) parents*[2]*"*.The expression exists in the singular or plural. Classes are held wherever possible, in a makeshift shack, under a tree, in an available room. The form of teaching at work is the ultimate crystallization of the classic school form. Children huddled together, a teacher one of the parents in front, trying to evoke a few notions on a hypothetical blackboard, talking a lot. The speaker doesn't need to be authoritative; with attention riveted on everything they say. A few days in Africa, but perhaps it's the same in other parts of the world, would enable everyone to re-scale the cursor of their malaise in the light of the inequality of human beings in relation to their rights or, more simply, their horizons. A surprise visit of a few minutes in this informal school would perhaps enable everyone to perceive the greed for knowledge that children born in some places are deprived of, stretching their necks to the point of impossibility to increase their field of vision and seek to gather a few projections of the knowledge they are made to glimpse. In other parts of the world, the school model is characterized by its school form, which Guy Vincent (1980) has defined and positioned in most of the chapters of this book. The school form is one of the key concepts that become institutionalized and heuristic. The school form is thus called upon to determine what is formal and what is informal. Whether it was the industrialization of the mutual school (Gauthier 1996, pp. 131-156) or the domination of the Jesuit's *L'Ecole des frères*, history records that it was the latter form that structured the 19th century. But this is to overlook the fact that, even if this was perhaps more a media posture than a major fundamental movement, this pivotal century also experimented with other forms. Inspired by Rousseau, many pedagogues excelled at demonstrating that other paths were possible, only to fail. After all, what remains of Pestalozzi, Töpffer, and Jean Macé (Ducomte 2015), apart from references (Houssaye 1994)? When it comes to alternatives to the classical school form, Töpffer occupies a singular place. Best known as the precursor of the comic strip (Caradec 1975), he left posterity two works, among many others (Töpffer 1859, 1853) of travel literature with his pupils that illustrate the Rousseauist vision of discovering the world in a way other than through scholastic "encaparaçonement" or encapsulation. Töpffer, son of a famous caricaturist of the time, enjoyed writing. An early eye disease dissuaded him from a career as an artist, which he nevertheless built up with his drawings, to become a teacher with Pastor Heyer in Geneva. The dowry of his wife, who was deeply involved in his adventures (this is an opportunity to mention a not-so-obscure actress, Anne Françoise Moulinié), enabled him to open his own boarding school, mainly for foreign pupils. He regularly organized voyages of discovery. But it seems that this was not so

---

1 Financial arrangement to contribute to something.

2 Community school run by parents.

unusual in 19th-century Swiss boarding schools. The preface to the book tells us so (Töpffer 1859, p. 2). Moreover, the process is intended to be a discovery of the world, with the emphasis on singularity and without the didactic cloak or obligation of the subject.

> While everyone is raving about the spectacle offered by Mont Blanc, the traveler Bryan lifts the rocks, searches the bushes, and sticks the *parpaillons* [butterflies], without giving the colossus a glance: "This," he says, "is just a hill covered with snow!" With this answer, he stands up to all the ecstatic ones, who get tangled up in an impossible argument, as happens when you want to prove beauty to someone who denies it, or who amuses himself by denying it. (Töpffer 1859, p. 20)

In his *Premiers voyages en zigzag* (1859), followed by *Nouveaux voyages en zigzag* (Töpffer 1853), he did not deny the Latin grammar classes, of which he was a fervent advocate, and which formed the basis of his boarding school, but he opened up a different path.

> In any boarding school trip, the day of departure is preceded by several days of waiting and preparations, which are disastrous for study and good Latinity. This is because, while the travelers are still keeping to their homes, going down to the classroom and performing all the usual school functions, the mind has been away for many days, heading for the mountains, where it climbs, breathes, takes a breath [*prendre un bol d'air* - take a bowl of air] for faraway cities, where it visits museums, theaters, public monuments, where they go into the inn and above all refrain from going into class. (Töpffer 1853, p. 1)

The institution he implements, because that's what it is, is not a didactic pursuit of illustration, problematization, or exemplification; it's confidence in the prospect of collective discovery whose only compass is the exasperation of the senses. Töpffer's voyages of discovery are therefore not a counterproposal of informality in reference to the formalism of the Latin classroom, but another formalization, adjoining another. Töpffer's vision of the school trip is clearly adidactic. It's a pedagogy of discovery. If we take Töpffer as a starting point for questioning this informal dimension, isn't the central question rather that of didaxia?

Sainte-Beuve, the 19th-century literary critic, adopted an approach to understanding authors based on intentionalism and biographism (Sainte-Beuve 1853). In other words, he liked to describe authors and their styles in terms of what made them who they were. In the preface to the author's posthumous *Nouveaux voyages en zigzag* (1853), he exegetes Töpffer, explaining how his literature, his drawings, and thus even his *Voyages en zigzag* are a shared artistic expression of the Romanticism of the time. As he could no longer paint because of his eyes, he took his pupils to contemplate the paintings of the world. Like Switzerland's Laferrière, who was deaf, a number of other pedagogues had to deal with a physical handicap for other educational purposes, "necessity makes law." For example, Freinet, for whom war left him with 70% fewer lungs, invented his own techniques (Audet 1996, pp. 177–190), because he couldn't do otherwise. As soon as the word "technique" is used, we are undoubtedly on the side of the form given to the teacher's approach by their techniques. However, many of these practices originate outside the classroom, and could be interpreted as informal practices. They are not. History records that Freinet discovered school walks during a trip to Heinrich Siemss' Altona school in Hamburg (Saint-Fuscien 2017, p. 219). The result was the practice of the "walking classroom." The activities of discovering nature, exploring fields, investing in places, visiting curiosities, are all structuring forms, not so far from those that Töpffer wanted children to experience a century earlier, but not only that. Can we not consider, on the one hand, that the encounter with landscapes and woods, the practice of books, the exploration of any unknown organized as a museum, or chaotic or policed in any other place, form the place of the sensitive, and on the other hand, that writing down one's experience should enable an "auto-rationalization" of knowledge? In other words, we're shifting form to the side of sensibility, but there's nothing informal about it. Whatever the context, Freinet's question was one of method, and therefore of form. Writing and rationalizing, organizing, what one has felt and what one has understood is the didactic motor of the school form, which he brought back into the enclosed space. Driven by the existing school form, the formalism of his techniques would grow. It's another form of didactics, but it's one that will become increasingly structured and organized.

The Freinet couple was undoubtedly one of the first figures of the ecologist educator, concerned with possible actions for body and mind, in the context of tuberculosis and the search for natural solutions up to and including naturism (Riondet 2013, pp. 133–148). Nature, and even the domestication of nature, was very much in evidence. Gardening was almost an injunction, and the ICEM website (Institut coopératif de l'école moderne: pédagogie Freinet[3]) abounds. In the midst of the 21st century's climatic protocrisis, this *quid pro quo* of informal education as a way out of the conventional enclosed space is invested in the garden. The practice of the school garden, one of Freinet's institutional techniques, has in the space of a few years become the media, commercial, and educational focus of the figure of an informal dimension of the school. The key word is "out of school" and "into ecology." Garden pedagogy, which we owe to a Canadian who seems to have renewed the school garden a century after Freinet, the gardening week in March,

---

3 Institut de coopération de l'école moderne (pédagogie), ICEM (Cooperative institute of the modern school: Freinet pedagogy), https://www.icem-pedagogie-freinet.org/.

garden school networks, a whole series of private foundation initiatives financed by industrial producers of tulip bulbs, horticultural federations, multinational seed companies, and community equipment vendors, all encourage teachers to take the plunge into gardening, and thus into the informal. There's no need to mention the names behind these initiatives, none of which could be criticized for malfeasance. No harm has been done to anyone, and all that remains is a whiff of incongruity when, in the climax, we identify a teacher-trainer (whom we won't name either) who, in parallel with her academic assignment, is setting up a private company to train teachers in practices that are presented as informal, because they are outside enclosed spaces.

This little journey, based on a few historical aspects, seeks to highlight the fact that what we understand as an informal approach is rather to be understood as being outside the classical closed walls, the site of a didactic approach to transmission born of centuries of practice and theorization.

In fact, the 1970s saw an attempt, in France at least, to transform the school form. In other words, a massive attempt to overturn the didactic practice of transmission, which is the dominant form of schooling, but not the only one. This episode is singular. Traces of it are almost impossible to find. However, every French pupil in the early 1970s can still recall an extraordinary experiment, in the sense that it was out of the ordinary—the 10%. On March 27, 1973, the Minister of National Education, Joseph Fontanet, issued circular No. 73-162 to the attention of rectors, inspectors of academies, and heads of secondary schools, which began like a thunderclap:

> I have decided to make 10% of the annual timetable available to secondary schools from the start of the 1973 academic year. A decree to be published will determine, in the disciplines and classes where they are necessary, the program reductions that will make it possible to devote this entire time quota to original activities related to teaching. (Fontanet 1973, p. 187)

The senators' commission, which looked into the matter, linked the operation with the creation of documentation centers in schools and approved the creation of 300 librarian positions (Chauvin 1973, p. 176). The Minister breaks down walls, breaks down timetables, breaks down frontal transmission. He encourages theater. He pushes for interdisciplinarity:

> The emphasis on the convergence of disciplines is intentional: it favors decompartmentalization. But, conversely, we would advise against adopting an overarching theme common to all disciplines. Given the current state of research, defining such a theme at the

graduate level in particular can only be highly artificial, and it is necessary to coordinate on a smaller scale, according to the points of intersection between the different programs. (Fontanet 1973, p. 188)

The PACTE (Projet artistique et culturel en territoire éducatif (Artistic and cultural projects in educational areas)) projects in 1979, then the PAE (Projet d'action éducative (Educational action project)) in 1981, are the heirs to this initiative (Crindal 2001, p. 18). But at the time, what were the effects of these 10%? No identified research or hoarding of experience is available. Of course, Meirieu (1985, pp. 54–59) uses Gianni to illustrate this moment of openness in the education system. He himself (p. 57) cites only one source (Rzewuski 1974) in an untraceable magazine. Fifty years later, apart from the general presentation (Condette 2020, p. 108), which makes it possible to avoid completely forgetting this phase of decompartmentalization, we have to look for the now distant testimonies of college students who are now close to retirement. Colleges had to provide 10% of schooling time, breaking down the usual school structure. This meant that there were no longer teachers of French, math, history, or physical education, but rather teachers who offered activities. These took the form of walks along the water's edge. How many reeds can there be? How do we find out? Who experiments with what? Systematic counting, sampling, sampling construction. Why are there only reeds? Teams, in which students from different levels could be mixed, worked on this incredible question. But then, why not estimate the number of insects in the meadow? But which insects? How to tell them apart? How to identify them? Other proposals involved a moped. Take it apart, put it back together. We dismantle the engine. But why? But why not? Combustion, explosion, mixing, proportions. Or we could explore the cellar of the former elementary school: inventory, structuring, traces, finding the meaning of traces, such as the map of France published under the Vichy regime, the portrait of Pétain, and making an inventory of the whole. The teachers' proposals were each more improbable than the last, insofar as they ended up recognizing nothing of the classic school form. Even more extraordinary was the fact that student representatives were to be consulted on the teachers' proposals, before they were presented to the school's board of directors.

This pedagogical upheaval only lasted a flight of swallows. The effects were undoubtedly inconclusive, not sufficiently structured, not sufficiently scholastic, no doubt. In other words, didactics that were not sufficiently predictive, measurable, or controllable. This is the point made by Meirieu (1985, pp. 57–58). PACTE projects, then PAE projects, were to follow, with more structures, school newspapers, clubs, and other initiatives that we no longer know whether to call formal or informal. From the compulsory generalization that was imposed on all disciplines, all teachers, all schools, voluntary work took over. And there have always been volunteer teachers, but does one swallow make a spring? Ambitions will be at a different level. The school walls will resume their role. And even if the school's structures have become a little more nomadic, they have remained. The principles of precaution, safety instructions – all of this posed the problem in a different way. But "discovery" classes, "nature" classes, "ski" classes, "sea" classes, "patrimony" classes, "history" classes, "ecology" classes, and so on, are a direct descendant of these pedagogical approaches, in which the school form intertwines classic transmissive didactics with the opportunity to discover others. This could be a tangible form of demarcation between the formal and the informal. The 1960s and 1970s also saw other attempts to open up the school environment. In the villages of France, far removed from urban centers and cultural activities, popular education movements provided the necessary support to country schools and colleges, in order to disseminate forms of culture that television could not yet transmit. Some of these activities were strictly linked to school hours. For example, the tours organized by CDM (Connaissances du Monde (Knowledge of the World))[4]. A flock of adventurers-backpackers-documentary makers, including the famous Mahuzier family (1981) and their nine children, took entire schools on a form of travel storytelling that instilled in schoolchildren the idea of a possible elsewhere. The films were screened in the presence of the authors, with in vivo commentary in the room, followed by discussions with these witnesses to other worlds. Country homes and village halls were mobilized for these sequences, which took place during school hours. There are virtually no records of these events. Other cultural approaches in the countryside, at the discretion of militant teachers, like that of the JMF (Jeunesses musicales de France (Musical Youth of France))[5], whose founder, René Nicoly, used music during the Second World War to combat the Vichy influence. After the Liberation of France, the JMFs began to spread music throughout the country. In towns, from the 1970s onwards, school concerts were organized, again during school hours. In the countryside, buses chartered by secondary schools, with the help of parents' associations, took children to evening performances in departmental capitals or major economic centers, as part of tours organized by this association. Thousands of children discovered classical and modern dance, symphony orchestras, and Lieder recitals during these nocturnal escapades. Strictly linked to the school to open up a sensitive experience of the world through testimonials, added to the school to introduce the expression of "noble" culture to children who had little chance of experiencing it, these moments were neither didactic nor prepared. They were in their singular expression attached to their subject. Formal or informal experiences? Their aim was to open up the world.

The famous American anthropologist Edward T. Hall (1984) has worked extensively on these ultimately cultural issues. He defined, through the comparative study of several very different cultures, that they all implemented an intersection of

---

4 https://www.connaissancedumonde.eu/notre-histoire.

5 https://www.jmfrance.org/notre-histoire.

what he termed "primary communications." This conceptualization is based on Sapir, Linton, and Kluckholn (Jaillet 2005, pp. 26–55), to whom he was more or less close. In his work, he highlights the fact that ten systems are in interaction, which enables us to understand how societies organize and function, by providing individuals with the keys to moving within them. Interaction, association, subsistence, distinction of gender functions, territoriality, temporality, knowledge, play, defense, and exploitation are the major categories of interaction structuring a culture. For our purposes, knowledge interacts with association to learn. In other words, no one is left alone in the process of appropriating knowledge. But this appropriation of knowledge in association is composed with the territory, but sometimes with exploitation (i.e. the mobilization of available resources) or play. Hall's work on time (Hall 1984) and space (Hall 1966), among others, shows that societies organize themselves according to a dual process. The first allows us to understand that all cultural phenomena can be understood in terms of notes, series, and patterns. The second, directly in line with the aim of this book, concerns the formalization of these processes. Drawing on the anthropologists already cited, he shows that we can understand the workings of a society in technical, formal, and informal terms (Jaillet 2005, pp. 39–50). Without going into too much detail, each of the ten primary communications systems interacting with the others does so in these three modes. According to these approaches, what characterizes societies is their formal functioning. In other words, what is commonly accepted and what each member of society, the bearer of the culture, can explain and describe, if asked. For example, when you enter a classroom, you line up in pairs. This is a very common practice and is undoubtedly the first form of schooling. It's formal in the sense that everyone knows that it exists and what its effects are. Hall shows that when necessary, i.e. to define what is accepted by society, what is considered formal can become technical. In other words, practice becomes a rule.

In its industrial project, the mutual school had pushed to the extreme the rules that governed every moment, minute by minute, of the classroom exercise (Gauthier 1996, pp. 135–141). The instructors' ballet was, it seems, a choreography with little room for improvisation. But a sufficiently integrated technical rule can tip the balance back to the formal side. In this way, everyone is able to describe the reasons for the operation, not necessarily to state the rule. A quick search, which anyone can reproduce with a search engine, shows that this technical rule of rank for pupils is always present in school by-laws, and especially in Catholic denominational schools (but that's another issue, not unrelated to what Hannah Arendt (1989) posits about the triptych religion-authority-tradition). For a formal dimension, there are not necessarily technical rules attached to it, but the reverse is not true. In other words, a technical rule always has a formal dimension. Hall makes it clear that human functioning is above all formal, in the sense in which he has defined it. Formal and informal, we should immediately add. Because whenever there is a formal way of functioning, there is always an informal counterpart. The latter is not as well mastered by the culture-bearers that are human beings. But it's just as strong. What makes it informal is that they can't easily describe it. There is no technical rule, for example, that forbids a professor of the history of education from wearing shorts to a lecture in front of their students. There's no formal impossibility either, shorts aren't so exotic a garment that humans can't accept them. However, at the Sorbonne, it would be astonishing if the fact went unnoticed and unquestioned. Because, informally, everyone comes wearing the outfit they feel suits the situation, without even having made a particular effort to decide. Before leaving, it's the suit, rather than the shorts, that's going to be the decision, without even having to make a choice. It's the informal dimension that can be just as prescriptive as the formal or technical ones. It should be noted that these distinctions are highly variable and cultural. On an Australian or Californian campus, it's not uncommon to meet university teachers wearing shorts. It's probably the opposite, a teacher in a suit, which would constitute an informal dissonance.

This detour via Hall's theories brings us back to what is implicit in, or even assumed by, many of the chapters in this book, the schooling form espoused by Guy Vincent. The article he co-authored with Bernard Lahire and Daniel Thin (Vincent et al. 1994) in the book that says it all about the question addressed here, "*L'éducation prisonnière de la forme scolaire?* [Is education a prisoner of the school form?]," illustrates throughout its development the difficulty of integrating the definition of the school form, without the instrumentation proposed by Hall. Thus, we could quote paragraph by paragraph what the authors are forced to deal with to make it clear that the question of knowledge transmission is not exempt from other concerns. In Hall's terminology, we would propose to refer to the primary communication systems of a society, from which no one can decide to withdraw. They are constitutive of societies. In their argument, the detour via "primitive" oral societies constitutes a kind of paroxysm, insofar as they construct an opposition between oral societies, with their informal principles, and scriptural societies, with their technical and formal principles. But whatever the society, all three registers exist. Just because a rule isn't written down doesn't mean it doesn't exist. Conversely, just because a rule is written, and therefore explicitly technical, doesn't mean it's not informal. This is the difficulty of understanding the workings of educational institutions when we fail to distinguish between these three levels. For example, Minister Fontanet's circular is essentially technical. It imposes a strictly different, open-ended form, specifying its contours very technically (dates, what not to do that would amount to reschooling the proposal, etc.). Formally, initiatives very similar to those present in or related to each of the chapters in this book were implemented. Informally, the resulting discrediting of new practices led to the transformation of the rule (PACTE, PAE), which directly and inexorably modified its form, and therefore its effect. Once again, let's take the example of informal schools in Africa. Formal operation, i.e. the performance of children and teachers in the improbable space provided for them, is not structured around any technical aspect. These schools don't exist, even though they do. They have no rules, no curriculum, no evaluation. If there is a technical dimension, it's the payment by the parents' tontine of a teacher who agrees to play this role. Very often, it's a young adult who went to high school in ninth grade, rarely more, because high schools are in cities, and all cities are centrifugal. Their legitimacy will reside in the informal because they will reproduce what they have learned from the attitude of teachers: they speak and they profess; and from what they have, their simple knowledge, without support, without artifact. It's the informal expectations of students and parents that will be the foundation of their ministry.

Hall (1979, pp. 185–208), again, proposes to identify the "fundamental cultural bases of education." In addition to reiterating the concepts already mentioned, he urges us to link them to the way the brain works, as human beings have no choice but to work with it. Without falling into positivist "neuroscientism," on the contrary, he invites us to pay attention to this double tension: what our brains can do and what our cultures want to do. If ideology is involved, when a culture imposes a model, through its technical rules, formal acts, and informal motivations, the answers are not basically monosemic. He is referring to the technical, formal, and informal forms of our Western societies, which are not as "Francocentric" as the history of the Republic would have us believe. Changing forms is not an immediate revolutionary undertaking. It takes centuries for cultures to stabilize themselves on lines of force. It takes centuries and often exceptional circumstances for them to destabilize, without ever being sure that the new balance will be very different from the old one. Whether it is appreciated or not, the dominant school form, in its three technical, formal, and informal aspects, has imposed itself through its history, its practices and, why not say it too, its efficiency. No doubt Vincent et al. (1994) are merely making an observation, noting the formidable efficiency in the sense of supremacy of the ossified form of what we propose to call classical didactics. It breaks down the material to be taught and makes the teacher responsible for disseminating the instructions for acquisition, taking into account, as best they can, how the pupils receive it. It is predictive in its curriculum rhythm, which can make it boring. Are there several possible approaches? Undoubtedly, the one that is uniformly applied is systematic. It has an essential advantage, serving two primary communication systems: subsistence and defense. In other words, it organizes the survival and life of society by preserving what already exists. Trivially speaking, it is not only, but principally at the service of the selection necessary for society to direct itself and preserve its structures. It legitimizes, according to an objectivation that is difficult to challenge, the orientation of those who will go on to preparatory classes for the Grandes Écoles and end up leading everyone. In these elite preparatory classes, the scholastic form is not a stroll in the park, but the ultratheorization of the world, by an authority recognized for the power of knowledge. The path to this level is gradual, but it runs right through the educational system. Why should we be surprised? Dimensions linked to citizenship issues are not absent, but ultimately secondary. In France, Parcoursup has at least served this purpose: the end of hypocrisy and the rationalization of destinies according to traditional academic performance. How can you blame cultures?

> This spring, the sky was so fresh, the greenery so inviting, that, contrary to our custom, we took a little extra excursion around our lake. Parents of families beware of making extra excursions, and rather, continue to turn invariably in the wisely ordered circle of acquired habits. Instead of feeling satiated by this excursion, we came back hungry for bigger, more distant and more memorable expeditions [...] (Töpffer 1841, p. 2)

References

Arendt, H. (1989). *La crise de la culture*. Gallimard, Paris.

Audet, M. (1996). La pédagogie Freinet. In *La pédagogie. Théories et pratiques de l'Antiquité à nos jours*, Gauthier, C. and Tardif, M. (eds). Gaëtan Morain, Paris.

Caradec, F. (1975). La littérature en estampes. In *Töpffer*, Horay, P. (ed.). Pierre Horray, Paris.

Chauvin, A. (1973). Avis, tome VII. Gouvernement de France, Paris [Online]. Available at: https://www.senat.fr/rap/1973-1974/i1973_1974_0040_07.pdf [Accessed 20 January 2022].

Condette, S. (2020). Les lycéens et leur participation à la vie de l'établissement en France (1968–2018). In *Histoire des élèves en France*, volume 2, Kropp, J. and Lambré, S. (eds). Septentrion, Lille. doi:10.4000/books.septentrion.97202.

Crindal, A. (2001). Enquête sur les figures de la démarche de projet en technologie. PhD Thesis, École Normale Supérieure, Cachan [Online]. Available at: https://tel.archives-ouvertes.fr/tel-00136619.

Ducomte, J.-M. (2015). *Jean Macé militant de l'éducation populaire*. Privat, Toulouse.

Dumazedier, J. (1972). Compte-rendu "Une société sans école d'Ivan Illich". *Revue française de pédagogie*, 21, 88–92.

Gauthier, C. (1996). De la pédagogie traditionnelle à la pédagogie nouvelle. In *La pédagogie. Théories et pratiques de l'Antiquité à nos jours*, Gauthier, C. and Tardif, M. (eds). Gaëtan Morain, Paris.

Hall, E.T. (1966). *La dimension cachée*. Le Seuil, Paris.

Hall, E.T. (1979). *Au-delà de la culture*. Le Seuil, Paris.

Hall, E.T. (1984). *Le langage silencieux*. Le Seuil, Paris.

Houssaye, J. (1994). *Quinze pédagogues. Leur influence aujourd'hui*. Armand Colin, Paris.

Illich, I. (1971). *Une société sans école*. Le Seuil, Paris.

Jaillet, A. (2005). *Manuels scolaires et films pédagogiques*. L'Harmattan, Paris.

Mahuzier, A. (1981). *Le Livre d'or des Mahuzier*. Presses de la Cité, Paris.

Meirieu, P. (1985). *L'école mode d'emploi, des "méthodes actives à la pédagogie différenciée"*. ESF, Paris.

Papert, S. (2003). *Conférence invitée EIAH*. CanalC2, Strasbourg [Online]. Available at: http://www.canalc2.tv/video/1868 [Accessed 20 January 2022].

Papert, S. and Jaillet, A. (2003). Vingt-cinq années d'EIAH. Entretien avec Seymour Papert, conférencier invité, mené par Alain Jaillet. In *Actes de la conférence EIAH*, Desmoulins, C., Marquet, P., Bouhineau, D. (eds). Institut National de la Recherche Pédagogique, Paris.

Riondet, X. (2013). Elise Freinet : de l'expérience naturiste aux pratiques de l'École Freinet. *Recherches & éducations*, 133–148 [Online]. Available at: https://doi.org/10.4000/rechercheseducations.1569 [Accessed 20 January 2022].

Rzewuski, J. (1974). 10 % de liberté, qu'en avons-nous fait ? *Entre Nous*, 42, March.

Sainte Beuve, C.A. (1853). Notice sur Töpffer, considéré comme paysagiste. In *Nouveaux voyages en zigzag à la grande chartreuse, autour du Mont Blanc*, Töpffer, R. (ed.). Victor Lecoux, Paris [Online]. Available at: https://gallica.bnf.fr/ark:/12148/bpt6k102663s/f18.item.r=nouveaux%20voyages%20en%20zigzag# [Accessed 20 January 2022].

Saint-Fuscien, E. (2017). *Célestin Freinet, un pédagogue en guerre 1914–1945*. Perrin, Paris.

Soëtard, M. (1994). Johan Henrich Pestalozzi. In *Quinze pédagogues. Leur influence aujourd'hui*, Houssaye, J. (ed.). Armand Colin, Paris.

Töpffer, R. (1841). *Voyage à Venise*. Schmid, Geneva [Online]. Available at: https://gallica.bnf.fr/ark:/12148/bpt6k1057720w [Accessed 20 January 2022].

Töpffer, R. (1853). *Nouveaux voyages en zigzag à la grande chartreuse, autour du Mont Blanc*. Victor Lecoux, Paris [Online]. Available at: https://gallica.bnf.fr/ark:/12148/bpt6k102663s/f18.item.r=nouveaux%20voyages%20en%20zigzag# [Accessed 20 January 2022].

Töpffer, R. (1859). *Premiers voyages en zigzag ou excursions d'un pensionnat en vacances dans les cantons suisses et sur le revers italien des Alpes*, 5th edition. Garnier Frères, Paris [Online]. Available at: https://gallica.bnf.fr/ark:/12148/bpt6k6580635w/f18.item [Accessed 20 January 2022].

Vincent, G. (1980). *L'École primaire française. Étude sociologique*. Presses universitaires de Lyon/Éditions de la Maison des Sciences de l'Homme, Lyon/Paris. doi:10.4000/books.pul.30073.

Vincent, G. (ed.) (1994). *L'Éducation prisonnière de la forme scolaire?* Presses universitaires de Lyon, Lyon.

Vincent, G., Lahire, B., Thin, D. (1994). Sur l'histoire et la théorie de la forme scolaire. In *L'Éducation prisonnière de la forme scolaire?*, Vincent, G. (ed.). Presses universitaires de Lyon, Lyon.

Winkin, Y. (1981). *La nouvelle communication*. Le Seuil, Paris.

Postface

The originality of this book lies in the fact that it examines a phenomenon that is rarely taken into account in the countless works, past and present, in the social sciences on schools, teachers, and students: the existence of cultural spaces of education and training outside the school institution. These spaces, which are of interest to children and adults alike, are not necessarily opposed to school, nor do they claim to replace it. They do, however, offer ways of accessing cultures and knowledge that are different from school education, with its formal knowledge and consecrated culture.

Without claiming to exhaust them, the various chapters of this book explore several of these spaces: the city, local educational communities, museums, public libraries, families, visits to historic sites, readingworkshops, media libraries, and so on. Despite their diversity, what these learning spaces have in common is that they offer forms of learning other than strictly school-based learning, while opening up access to other cultures too often ignored by schools: technical culture, neighborhood culture, family culture, the culture of places of memory, informal culture, artistic culture through direct contact with works and artists, the culture of the pleasure of reading, the culture of discovery, etc. Of course, many other areas of training and education could have been covered (cinemas, Internet discussion groups, social media, digital encyclopedias, popular universities or, for senior citizens, more or less scholarly conferences offered to the general public, etc.), but this would have led to a much too voluminous work. In that sense, this book should be taken for what it is: a first exploration of a vast field that is still fairly undeveloped.

Postface written by Maurice Tardif†.

From the outset, we'd like to make it clear that we're by no means specialize in these outside-of-school spaces. Most of our work focuses on compulsory schooling and school staff, particularly teachers. We are therefore part of the approach that the authors of the introduction to this book refer to as "scolarocentric," i.e. an approach that tends to equate school training with legitimate education alone, neglecting other real or potential educational spaces located on the margins of the school or outside it altogether. These same authors explain the dominance of the "scolarocentric" approach in the French social sciences by the hold exerted by the theory of the "school form" on work in the history and sociology of education: "The notion of the school form has thus greatly contributed to reinforcing the tropism exerted by the school on educational issues" (introduction to the book).

Indeed, according to the work of the school form theorists cited in this book, the school form is a kind of invariant configuration that makes it possible to think about and analyze the school's historical variations. Thus, between the school of the Frères des écoles chrétiennes (Brothers of the Christian Schools) at the end of the 17th century and the school of the 21st century, we could, thanks to this theory, identify the renewal of the same organizational, political, and cultural set-up, i.e. "the whole and the configuration of the constituent elements of what we call the school" (Vincent 1980, p. 10). The same would apply to school culture, which has been the normative model for education and training in legitimate culture and knowledge since the school's origins in the 17th century.

It's easy to see why one of the main aims of this book is to critically interrogate the historical enclosure that the school form and culture have imposed between their formal knowledge and legitimate culture (the only legitimate one, in fact), and knowledge and cultures outside the school, which have been largely devalued or simply ignored by the school institution. This critical questioning ties in with various currents of ideas and action that are today striving to open up schools to something other than themselves, notably by taking into account the multiplicity of sources of knowledge and forms of learning (experiential, informal, digital, community-based, etc.) offered by our highly complex and differentiated societies. What these currents of ideas and action have in common is that they seek or explore ways of providing cultural education and training outside the school environment.

However, as Pierre Kahn points out (Chapter 3), it is far from clear that the theory of the school form can account for the evolution of the contemporary school.

In truth, it would be very difficult to recognize in today's school the disciplinary universe specific to the school form. Its openness to the outside world means less the general schooling of social relations than what we might call the "de-schooling" of its own mode of socialization. It is no longer the school that informs the social, but the social of contemporary democratic individualism, which, with parents, cell phones, "youth culture," the recognition of the child "behind" the pupil and the submission of the disciplinary regime of establishments to the ordinary rules of law, penetrates the school and contributes to its deinstitutionalization.

In our view, this observation is in line with François Dubet's (2002) thesis on the decline of the "institutional program" that underpins some of today's major social institutions, which are characterized by their work with others. Even if they persist, these major institutions no longer manage, according to Dubet, to socialize individuals, i.e., to impose their norms and modalities or regimes of socialization. In today's schools, the actors including, above all, students and teachers, are as it were, torn between plural logics that the school can no longer unify or totalize within its traditional institutional program. Far from imposing its instituted school form, the school is now a space where players negotiate and tinker with the school order on the basis of subjective commitments and often improvised knowledge. Perrenoud (1993) and Schön (1994) have made extensive use of these ideas of bricolage and improvisation to describe teachers' pedagogical practices.

In any case, if we take Kahn and Dubet's point of view, we would have a potentially contradictory double reading of the contemporary school: a relatively stable school form, i.e., a form of socialization that remains invariant despite all its historical variations; an institutional form in a phase of disintegration, increasingly porous to external social influences, and which school actors must somehow patch up as best they can through their daily interactions and negotiations.

It seems obvious to us that this double reading necessarily calls for a series of questions about the cultural spaces of education and training, depending on whether we consider them in relation to a school form that is globally closed in on itself (which seems to us to be the case with the main thesis defended in the introduction) or, on the contrary, in relation to a declining institution whose margins are increasingly fragile and open to multiple social influences, including cultural, intellectual, educational, and formative.

In fact, the contemporary school – the Western school that has become globalized – seems to be caught up in opposing trends. On the one hand, it seems to be becoming more and more hegemonic, extending its influence on all societies and most forms of education and learning, including outside school and university institutions. However, this hegemony is historically very recent, and does not seem to me to stem from the school form that characterized the 17th-century school. It is directly linked to the nationalization of education and the modernization of societies, which required educated citizens and workers. In fact, from the 19th century onwards, the gradual proliferation of compulsory school attendance laws in all

Western countries meant that all children had to attend school, which became an integral part of state institutions. In the 20th century, this process became even more pronounced, with the extension of schooling downwards (pre-school) and upwards (the rise of compulsory secondary education), and its democratization to all strata of society. In Europe and North America today, the average child spends 200,000 hours at school. Furthermore, since the Second World War, the school system has become the most powerful social mechanism for qualifying individuals, preparing them to enter the job market, and occupies a socio-technical function. In post-industrial societies, schooling is seen as one of the main sources of human capital, and therefore of economic growth.

In short, these days, a cultured person is necessarily a well-educated person; conversely, an individual who had never attended school would not only be regarded as completely uneducated, but also as a serious social handicap and an economic burden for the community. So it's hard to believe that schools are losing their centrality in the social and cultural process of training and educating – and thus socializing – new generations of citizens and workers. In this sense, the scolarocentric perspective does not seem to us to derive from the theory of the school form, but quite simply from the inescapable character of the school in our societies. Whether we like it or not, school remains a central institution in our societies.

On the other hand, it's true that political, economic, social, and educational authorities, as well as parents and cultural and community actors and groups, are now demanding that schools open up to the world, to local communities, to families, to businesses, to cultural diversity, to digital technology, etc., while making room for knowledge and learning that have very little to do with formal knowledge and traditional school disciplines. For example, in North American schools, the ones with which we are most familiar, sexuality education, intercultural education, gender theory, critical race theory, Indigenous education, health education, feminist perspectives, computer programming, ecology, etc. are all taught, not without tension and conflict. In short, we're a long way from a school that transmits an eternal culture and sacred values.

In addition, as various chapters in this book remind us, schools in North America have long been open to local communities, not least because their governance has never been under the control of a central, centralizing State. In fact, decisions on school operations, curricula and textbooks, and the financing of education are taken by regional and local bodies (school districts and school boards), made up of citizens elected by local communities. Even at school level, principals enjoy a considerable degree of autonomy. Furthermore, since the 1980s, with the advent of decentralization policies, parents have become increasingly involved in school governance, including with regard to curricula and textbooks. Finally, the existence of close links between schools and external cultural spaces of training and education seems to us to be quite old on this side of the Atlantic. For a long time, American and Canadian schools have been offering their students extracurricular activities. American and Canadian schools have long been offering students out-of-class and out-of-school activities in cultural spaces such as those presented in this book. The reverse is also true: various actors (novelists, filmmakers, artists, scientists, etc.) are regularly invited to the schools, offering students access to educational and cultural modalities other than those provided for in the school curriculum.

How then, can we situate the purpose of this book among the potentially contradictory developments in today's schools, which oscillate between hegemony and openness to the diversity of educations and cultures? What is the relationship between these developments? The authors of this book agree that "the researcher concerned with the cultural spaces of training cannot, however, evacuate the question of the relationship between education inside and outside the school" (introduction to the book). They therefore call for "a change of perspective in which the school is no longer systematically at the center of the educational dynamic" (introduction to the book), which would promote the inclusion and capacitation of all educational actors both in and out of school.

In our view, this shift in perspective raises a highly complex political problem in our democratic societies: what authority will draw a dividing line between all these actors in and out of school, between these various spaces of education, culture, and knowledge? Indeed, if we take this proposal seriously, systematically removing the school from the center of the educational dynamic in our societies means rethinking, redefining, and, in a way, shifting the boundaries of school, culture, and training.

But these boundaries are more than just intellectual ones, separating different cultural spaces and different types of formal and informal knowledge: they also correspond to socio-political boundaries, the establishment of which has depended, since the 19th century, on the power of States. In Europe and North America, States have gradually monopolized control of schools. They have thus appropriated the power to define and circumscribe its organization, content and teaching methods. Yet, if the limits of the school today are indeed the result of the logic of State power, it is because the school itself possesses great power: those who govern it largely control the training of new generations of citizens and workers.

In this sense, it may be correct to argue, as Dubet does, that the school's traditional institutional program is in decline. But, in truth, this decline doesn't change much about the school's power, insofar as there are no other institutions or social spaces in our societies likely to replace it in the foreseeable future. In this respect, the global SARS-CoV-2 pandemic has clearly shown that, with successive school closures, our societies cannot function for long without schools, while the various attempts to set up distance learning formulas to make up for them have proved, at best, expedient and of little consequence.

However, if it is still up to the State, at least in democratic societies, to set a demarcation line between school culture and other spaces of culture and education outside the school, this demarcation line seems to me to be increasingly confronted today with attempts to circumvent or pierce it. In other words, we feel it's important to recognize that there are various powers outside the school in our societies, some of which are striving to penetrate school culture and training and turn it to their own advantage. How, then, are we to distinguish them from the spaces studied in this book, and where do we draw the line?

We don't know European education systems well enough to speak intelligently about them, but in North America, particularly the United States, and in a majority of South American societies, these powers seem powerful, and increasingly so.

In most countries of the Americas, religious movements (churches, congregations, groups, associations, leagues of believers, etc.) have been constantly intervening for several decades to modify school culture, i.e. both its content and its teaching and learning methods: what should be taught to pupils, how it should be taught and by whom. Evangelical proselytizing in the USA and Christian proselytizing in Spanish- and Portuguese-speaking countries are undoubtedly spearheading the assault on secular public schools, which are in principle religiously neutral. These religious movements are no abstractions: they are made up of parents of students, teachers, and principals, elected representatives at various levels of the education system, academics, politicians, entertainment industry stars, community groups, good citizen circles, preachers and so on. These religious movements organize a huge number of educational and cultural activities for children and teenagers outside school, many of which are similar to those presented in this book. In addition, in the USA and Canada, they control virtually all private education networks. In Latin America, their control over school systems is far more extensive and powerful, from pre-school to university. Last but not least, they wield considerable influence at the highest political and governmental levels of States, including the power of the vote, as clearly demonstrated by the elections of recent years in Brazil and the United States.

A second power that is particularly worrying for today's schools stems from the formidable expansion of digital technology, notably through the monopolies exercised by GAFAM (Google, Apple, Facebook, Amazon, and Microsoft), to which we must add the innumerable social media. At a conference at South by Southwest in 2022, Microsoft founder Bill Gates declared that "schools are at a technological tipping point." According to Gates, "tablets, smartphones, e-readers, digital textbooks, and the accessibility of digital video, including YouTube, are playing a major role in changing the way students learn." During the Obama presidency, the Bill & Melinda Gates Foundation funded the Federal School Support Program for the widespread use of technology by teachers and students, both in and out of the classroom. This program has mainly benefited charter schools, which are run by private companies or groups of parents or citizens who want to free themselves from the public network. In the Americas, but also in Europe, compulsory schooling represents a juicy market for GAFAM. But this market is no longer limited to the sale of technology to schools (computers, tablets, etc.), it now includes the supply of digital learning content. But digital content is also cultural and intellectual content. In Latin America, the Covid-19 pandemic served as a springboard for GAFAM and other social media to offer schools, teachers, and students online educational services on a massive scale, in a context where States were unable to do so for lack of resources or political will. In recent years, however, it has become clear that social media are powerful vehicles for a variety of ideologies that undermine the foundations of democracy, and therefore of the public school as one of the main crucibles of education for citizenship. These media and, more generally, the expansion of the Internet, based on the immateriality of information and the non-locality of information sources, inevitably call for critical reflection on the nature of the boundaries that now separate (or not) the school and the world outside the school. They show that spaces of culture and education outside the school are not necessarily physical or material places where students actually interact with people. From this point of view, we must ask ourselves whether the school form, with its rigid boundaries, is not becoming liquefied, in the sense that sociologist Zygmunt Bauman gives to this word: "A liquid modern society is one in which the conditions under which its members act change in less time than it takes for modes of action to congeal into habits and routines." (Bauman 2013, p. 32).

In presenting the growing hold exerted by these religious movements and GAFAM on schools in both the Americas, our aim is not to invalidate the educational and cultural interest of the out-of-school spaces explored in this book. What we are interested in is knowing on what basis to distinguish the latter from these powers outside the school, and above all from what line of demarcation. For us, the challenge posed by the school's current openness to other educational and cultural spaces cannot be reduced to educational and cultural questions: it clearly raises the problem of the sociopolitical limits of the contemporary school. And at the end of this book, this problem remains unresolved.

References

Bauman, Z. (2013). *La vie liquide*. Fayard/Pluriel, Paris.

Dubet, F. (2002). *Le Déclin de l'institution*. Le Seuil, Paris.

Perrenoud, P. (1993). Curriculum : le formel, le réel, le caché. In *La pédagogie, une encyclopédie pour aujourd'hui*, Houssaye, J. (ed.). ESF, Paris.

Schön, D.-A. (1994). *Le praticien réflexif*. Les Éditions Logiques, Montreal.

List of Authors

Theodora BALMON
LISA
Université de Corse Pasquale Paoli
Corsica
France
and
CRIFPÉ
Université du Québec à Montréal
Canada

Géraldine BARRON
ICT
Université de Paris Cité
France

Corinne BAUJARD
CIREL
Université de Lille
Villeneuve-d'Ascq
France

Nathalie BERTRAND
LISEC
Université de Strasbourg
France

Denise Gisele DE BRITTO DAMASCO
Pontifical Catholic University
São Paulo
Brazil

Rana CHALLAH
CREAD
Université de Rennes 2
France

Sylvie CONDETTE
CIREL
Université de Lille
Villeneuve-d'Ascq
and
LACES
Université de Bordeaux
France

Martine DERIVRY-PLARD
ECOr-LACES
Université de Bordeaux
France

Mary Grace FLAHERTY
University of North Carolina
Chapel Hill
United States of America

Bruno GARNIER
LISA
Université de Corse Pasquale Paoli
Corsica
France
and
CRIFPÉ
Université de Montréal
Canada

Pascale GOSSIN
LISEC
Université de Strasbourg
France

Salma ITSMAÏL
LIMPACT
Université Cadi Ayyad
Marrakech
Morocco

Alain JAILLET
BONHEURS
Université de Cergy-Pontoise
France

Pierre KAHN
CIRNEF
Université de Caen
France

Geneviève LAMEUL
CREAD
Université de Rennes 2
France

Isabelle LEBRAT
LISEC
Université de Strasbourg
France

Régis MALET
LACES
Université de Bordeaux
and
IUF
Paris
France

Anik MEUNIER
GREM
Université du Québec à Montréal
Canada

Camille ROELENS
CIRE
Université de Lausanne
Switzerland
and
CIREL
Université de Lille
Villeneuve-d'Ascq
France

Maurice TARDIF†
CRIFPÉ
Université de Montréal
Canada

Marion TRANNOY VOISIN
Musée de la Corse
Collectivité de Corse
Corsica
France

Nathanaël WADBLED
CREM
Université de Lorraine
Nancy
France

Index

Other titles from

in

Innovations in Learning Sciences

2023

BRIDOUX Stéphanie, GRENIER-BOLEY Nicolas, LEININGER-FRÉZAL Caroline
Research in University Pedagogy: Towards a Discipline-based Approach?

GUILLE-BIEL WINDER Claire, ASSUDE Teresa
Articulations between Tangible Space, Graphical Space and Geometrical Space: Resources, Practices and Training
(Education Set – Volume 14)

2022

BISAULT Joël, LE BOURGEOIS Roselyne, THÉMINES Jean-François, LE MENTEC Mickaël, CHAUVET-CHANOINE Céline
Objects to Learn About and Objects for Learning 1: Which Teaching Practices for Which Issues?
(Education Set – Volume 10)
Objects to Learn About and Objects for Learning 2: Which Teaching Practices for Which Issues?
(Education Set – Volume 11)

DAVERNE-BAILLY Carole, WITTORSKI Richard
Research Methodology in Education and Training: Postures, Practices and Forms
(Education Set – Volume 12)

HAGÈGE Hélène
Secular Mediation-Based Ethics of Responsibility (MBER) Program:
Wise Intentions, Consciousness and Reflexivities
(Education Set – Volume 13)

2021

BUZNIC-BOURGEACQ Pablo
Devolution and Autonomy in Education
(Education Set – Volume 9)

SLIMANI Melki
Towards a Political Education Through Environmental Issues
(Education Set – Volume 8)

2020

BOUISSOU-BÉNAVAIL Christine
Educational Studies in the Light of the Feminine: Empowerment
and Transformation
(Education Set – Volume 6)

CHAMPOLLION Pierre
Territorialization of Education: Trend or Necessity
(Education Set – Volume 5)

PÉLISSIER Chrysta
Support in Education

2019

BRIANÇON Muriel
The Meaning of Otherness in Education: Stakes, Forms, Process,
Thoughts and Transfers
(Education Set – Volume 3)

HAGÈGE Hélène
Education for Responsibility
(Education Set – Volume 4)